I0795671

Studies in Christianity and Judaism / Études sur le christianisme et le judaïsme : 6

Studies in Christianity and Judaism / Études sur le christianisme et le judaïsme

Studies in Christianity and Judaism / Études sur le christianisme et le judaïsme publishes monographs on Christianity and Judaism in the last two centuries before the common era and the first six centuries of the common era, with a special interest in studies of their interrelationship or the cultural and social context in which they developed.

STUDIES IN CHRISTIANITY
AND JUDAISM

Number 6

THE RHETORIC OF THE BABYLONIAN TALMUD, ITS SOCIAL MEANING AND CONTEXT

Jack N. Lightstone

Published for the Canadian Corporation for Studies in Religion / Corporation Canadienne des Sciences Religieuses
by Wilfrid Laurier University Press

1994

Canadian Cataloguing in Publication Data

Lightstone, Jack N.
The rhetoric of the Babylonian Talmud : its social meaning and context

(Studies in Christianity and Judaism = Études sur le christianisme et le judaisme ESCJ ; 6)
Includes bibliographical references and index.
ISBN 0-88920-238-9

1. Talmud – Criticism, interpretation, etc.
I. Canadian Corporation for Studies in Religion.
II. Title. III. Series: Studies in Christianity and Judaism ; 6.

BM501.L55 1994 296.1′2506 C94-930983-4

∞

Cover design by Jose Martucci, Design Communications

The Rhetoric of the Babylonian Talmud, Its Social Meaning and Context has been produced from a manuscript supplied in camera-ready form by the author.

Order from:

Wilfrid Laurier University Press
Wilfrid Laurier University
Waterloo, Ontario, Canada N2L 3C5

Printed in Canada

Dedicated to the memory of my mother,
Ethyl Nedivah Lightstone
זכרונה לברכה

Contents

Charts

Appendix

Preface

This book examines the character, use and social meaning of the formalized rhetoric which pervades the Babylonian Talmud. Indeed, so integral is that stock rhetorical vocabulary to the Bavli that were such language to be removed from the Talmud, little would be left that we would recognize as talmudic in character. For in so far as Bavli has a definite style, character and agenda, these are in large measure constituted by its stock language, which is the principal object of analysis in this volume.

Virtually from the era of its redaction, about the sixth century, the Babylonian Talmud became the rabbinic document par excellence. Through its lens almost all previous canonical rabbinic tradition was refracted. And although it lies beyond the ken of this book, during the medieval period all situations calling for a rabbinic response, in particular those calling for legal decisions, were retroactively passed through the Babylonian Talmud's filter. The initial criticism of the work of such codifiers as Maimonides (*Mishneh Torah*) in the twelfth century and Yosef Karo (*Shulkan Aruk*) in the sixteenth century had much to do with the perceived danger of encouraging the removal of the Talmud and its study from this recursive loop.

This era of the Talmud's initial ascendancy coincides, I shall argue, with the rise of the Babylonian rabbinic academies (the *yeshiva*) as the central institution of the rabbinic movement, with the Bavli as the centrepiece of the academy's curriculum. Within this institution, study of the Talmud in particular (even if not exclusively) defined what it meant to be a rabbinic sage or a disciple of the sages. Thus Maimonides, writing half a millennium after the redaction of the Talmud, states that the stature and authority of the early medieval sages and heads of the academies (*geonim*) rested upon the fact that "all of these heads of the academies [and sages] who functioned in the Land of Israel, and in the Land of Shinar [i.e., Babylonian], and in Iberia and in France studied the ways of the Talmud, and elucidated its secrets and explained its content, because its ways are deep [and lead] to enlightenment" [Maimonides' introduction to *Mishneh Torah*, trans. and interpolations are my own].

The Talmud, then, defined the role of the rabbinic elite. The text was the paradigm for the "way" one went about studying to become, and later exercised the power and authority of a rabbi. Thus the "way" of the Talmud, that is, its way of going about things as much as its content, became intertwined with social definitions, relationships and forms of organization. In short, the agenda of the Talmud, constituted in large measure via its stock rhetorical formularies, is replete with social meaning.

In moving from analysis of the character and use of rhetoric in the Talmud, on the one hand, to exploration, on the other, of the social meaning implicit in the Bavli's use of language, this book moves freely across the concerns and perspectives of literary and rhetorical analysis, anthropology and the history of religions. I have come to this particular mélange both indebted and in reaction to three scholarly traditions of the second half of this century: biblical and particularly New Testament studies; the appropriation and adaptation of the former to the literary-historical analysis of early rabbinic texts, especially by J. Neusner and others influenced by his work; and social anthropology and the sociology of knowledge. I learned much from biblical scholarship but ultimately found wanting the methods or assumptions of form-history and form-criticism, redaction criticism and structural analysis. In adapting these methods to the study of early rabbinic texts much of what was problematic was discarded in the process, yet scholars had to discard as well many of the concerns about the social context and meaning of ancient religious texts. Deeply influenced by social anthropology and the sociology of knowledge, I have reintroduced these concerns in my focus on the study of these documents' rhetoric. It is my hope that students of all of these fields, from senior undergraduates to scholars, will find in this volume something interesting and edifying. Many interdisciplinary endeavours evoke highly affective reactions from some scholars. Boundary-crossers or, even worse, boundary-effacers, in many social spheres, including the academy, are suspect. I hope that the fruits of my particular disciplinary mélange will add enough to the reader's understanding of the Babylonian Talmud that I may be permitted my mongrel approach.

There is a great deal of analysis of rabbinic texts in this volume. It could not have been otherwise, in my view. But I have presented those texts in English translation in an effort to make the volume accessible to the non-specialist interested in rabbinic literature. Indeed, it is my hope that, as an added benefit, the non-specialist will come away from this volume with a sense of the character not only of the Babylonian Talmud, but also of other seminal early rabbinic literature as well, notably the Mishnah, the Tosefta, halakic midrash and the Palestinian Talmud. The specialist will, I hope, find enough stimulation in the reading of this work to forgive the presentation of the texts in translation.

This leads me to the translations themselves. With very few (and noted) exceptions, they are all my own. My need to present the rhetorical and formulaic aspects of Bavli's language made other, more idiomatic but no less accurate and valuable, translations unsuitable for my purposes. Translations of biblical passages are cited from the *Revised Standard Version* printed in the *Oxford Anotated Bible*, Oxford University Press, although at many junctures I have had to use my own idiomatic translation of biblical passages in order to make intelligible the manner in which these passages are interpreted by rabbinic documents.

There are many people whose support and work are my ground and inspiration. My wife, Dorothy Markiewicz, and my children, Jennifer and Etan, stand foremost among them. A number of my students have contributed, through their own work as much as in commenting upon mine, to the methodological and theoretical perspectives which underpin this study. They include, Dr. Simcha Fishbane, Ms. Sandra Walker-Ramisch, Ms. Madeleine Mcbrearty, Ms. Louise Meyer and Dr. Ruth Vale. My research student, Mr. Joshua Joseph, along with Ms. Mcbrearty, worked on sections of the Babylonian Talmud not explicitly presented or analyzed here. Their work provided me with necessary inter-subjective validation of my method and with corroborating results. My colleagues in Concordia University's Department of Religion—Fred Bird, Charles Davis, Michel Despland, Rosemary Hale, Howard Joseph, Norma Joseph, Sheila McDonough, David Miller, Michael Oppenheim, Leslie Orr, Ira Robinson, John Rossner and Shrivinas Tilak—provide what I consider at one and the same time a uniquely stimulating, challenging and supportive intellectual environment. In our regular departmental colloquia, we have for almost two decades presented to one another preliminary drafts of our research work and have endeavoured in that context to render one another the most sincere compliment which one colleague can offer another, a careful sympathetic reading along with an insightful critique. I thank them all. A number of scholars graciously consented to read and comment upon the penultimate version of the manuscript. I thank Alan J. Avery-Peck, David Blumenthal, Michael Broyde and Vernon K. Robbins for their time and the expertise they brought to critiquing this work. If at times I have chosen not to heed their advice, the fault and the fallout are mine.

Much of this research has been presented over the last four years to members of the Canadian Society for Biblical Studies at their annual meetings, held in conjunction with the meetings of the Learned Societies of Canada. For almost a decade now, members of the CSBS have been a sounding board and often a stimulus for my research activities. More recently, a number of scholars coming together annually under the rubric of the Canada-Israel Conference on Social Scientific Approaches to the Study of Judaism and Jewish Society have also provided me with supportive, constructive criticism. Both groups are, to my mind, models of what scholarly associations ought to be.

Ms. Sandra Walker-Ramisch proofread and copy-edited the penultimate version of this work. I am grateful for her efforts. Peter Richardson, the series editor, and the staff at Wilfrid Laurier University Press copy-edited the final version. Their contribution to the work is immeasurable. Born perhaps as much from occasional frustration as from his wonderful sense of humour, Dr. Richardson commented that my tendency to use qualifying modifiers in complex sentences proves one of this book's hypotheses: the rhetoric of the Talmud provides an authoritative model of speech and reasoning for those schooled in the document.

The research for this book, which commenced a number of years ago, could not have been pursued without the support of Concordia University and the Social Sciences and Humanities Research Council of Canada. Both have provided me with generous research grants. The completion of the writing of this volume was greatly facilitated by the administrative leave graciously granted to me by Concordia for the period of 1 June 1992 through 30 November 1992.

My mother, to whose memory this volume is dedicated, died on 21 July 1991, in that year the day of the Fast of the 9th of Av which commemorates the destruction of the Temple in 70 CE and the cessation of its cult. It is that event which gave rise to Rabbinism, of which the Babylonian Talmud is the classical statement. It is only with the death of my mother that I have come to realize just how much of her is in myself. Would that I impart to my children what she has given me. In that vein, during the writing of this book, much of which overlapped with the saying of Kaddish for my mother, I have contemplated the wealth of meanings evoked by the biblical phrase, "one generation goes, and another generation comes" (Qohelet 1:4). For as I complete this work, I anticipate the Bar Mitzvah of our youngest child, Etan Elisha.

Jack N. Lightstone
Concordia University
Montreal, Quebec, Canada
20 November, 1992
ערב שבת חיי שרה, תשנ״ג, שבה יעלה
בננו איתן אלישע לתורה כבר מצוה.

Abbreviations and Editions

AZ	Avodah Zarah
b.	Babylonian Talmud, Vilna Edition, with attention to the following: Diqduqei Sofrim, Rabbinovicz, *Variae Lectiones in Mischnam et Talmud Babylonicum* (reprinted: New York, 1960); Florence ms., *Babylonian Talmud: Codex Florence, Florence National Library I-II 7-9* (Jerusalem, 1972); Munich ms., *Babylonian Talmud Codex Munich 95* (reprinted: Jerusalem, 1971); Vatican mss., *Manuscripts of the Babylonian Talmud from the Vatican Library*, Series A (Jerusalem, 1972), Series B (Jerusalem, 1974).
Bek.	Bekorot
Deut.	Deuteronomy
Ex.	Exodus
Ezek.	Ezekiel
Jer.	Jeremiah
Lev.	Leviticus
m.	Mishnah, H. Albeck, ed. ששה סדרי משנה (reprinted: Tel Aviv, 1967), with attention to the following: Kaufmann ms., G. Beer, *Faksimile-Ausgabe des Mischnacodex Kaufmann A 50* (reprinted: Jerusalem, 1968); Loewe ed., H. Loewe, *The Mishnah of the Palestinian Talmud* (reprinted: Jerusalem, 1967); Naples ed., משנה עם פירוש הרמבם, דפוס ראשון נפולי 1492 (reprinted: Jerusalem, 1970); Parma ms., כתב יד פארמא דרוסי 138 (Jerusalem, 1970); Parma ms. B, *Mishnah Codex Parma "B" deRossi 984* (Jerusalem, 1971).
Mek. deR. Ish.	H.S. Horovitz and I. Rabin, eds., *Mekhilta deRabbi Ishmael* (reprinted: Jerusalem, 1970).

Mek. deR. Sim.	Y.N. Epstein and E.Z. Melamed, eds., *Mekhilta deRabbi Simeon bar Yohai* (Jerusalem, 1955).
Num.	Numbers
SifD.	Sifre on Deuteronomy, L. Finkelstein, ed., *Sifre on Deuteronomy* (New York, 1956).
SifN.	Sifre on Numbers, H.S. Horovitz, ed., *Sifre on Numbers and Sifre Zutta* (reprinted: Jerusalem, 1966).
Sifra	I.H. Weiss, ed., *Sifra deBe Rav or Sefer Torat Kohanim* (reprinted: New York, 1963).
Sifre Zutta	H.S. Horovitz, ed., *Sifre on Numbers and Sifre Zutta* (reprinted: Jerusalem, 1966).
t.	Tosefta, M.S. Zuckermandel, ed., *The Tosefta: Based on the Erfurt and Vienna Codices* (reprinted: Jerusalem, 1963), with attention to the following: S. Lieberman, ed., *The Tosefta* (New York, 1955-73); S. Lieberman, תוספתא כפשוטה (New York, 1955-73); S. Lieberman, תוספת ראשונים (Jerusalem, 1939).
y.	Palestinian Talmud, Vilna Edition, with attention to the following: Leiden ms., *The Palestinian Talmud: Leiden M.S. Cod. Scal. 3: A Facsimile of the Original Manuscript* (Jerusalem, 1970); Rattner, B. Rattner, ספר אהבת ציון וירושלים (Vilna, 1901); Venice ed., *The Palestinian Talmud According to the Venice Text*, n.d.
Zev.	Zevahim

1

Introduction

This book explores the formalized use of language in an ancient religious document, the Babylonian Talmud—*talmud bavli*. Soon after its redaction in about the sixth century of our era, the Bavli displaced virtually all other rabbinic literary oeuvres at the top of the pyramid of authoritative and sacred texts revered and studied within rabbinic circles. To be sure, the Pentateuch and the remainder of the rabbinic canon of the Hebrew Bible, and the Mishnah, the first magnum opus of the rabbinic movement (*ca.* 200 CE), remained for the rabbis the highest formal authorities. "The Talmud"—named as if the fifth-century Palestinian Talmud (*talmud yerushalmi*) did not exist—provided the window upon all earlier holy texts. During the fifth to tenth centuries, study and mastery of "the Talmud" became the most important act and achievement which marked one as a rabbi, a "master."

In reading the Talmud, any ancient disciple of the rabbinic sages aspiring to the title rabbi, like the modern rabbinical student, would have faced the challenge of mastering a pervasive, consistent and highly laconic code of formalized linguistic terms by means of which the (renowned) dialectical analyses of the Talmud proceed. These recurrent, patterned formulae, therefore, not only constitute the Talmud's distinctive *style* of rhetoric, but they are the key to deciphering the very *meaning* of the Talmud's statements and passages. They are constitutive of the very rhetoric of the Talmud. To read the Talmud one must become at home in its stock recurrent rhetorical formularies. Gaining and imparting to others an intimate familiarity of such a laconic code of formularies implies a social context in which such rhetoric is common coin. To control that rhetoric would have marked one as a member of a group (Gumperz, 1985). Hence, just as the rhetorical formularies of the Talmud are constitutive of the text, so too is that rhetorical linguistic code, sanctified by the revered text, constitutive of social organization and identity—here of a decidedly elitist venue.

Certainly, any other rarified elitist code would have helped effect or perpetuate such a group and its organizational provenance. But we are faced with the fact that it was the Babylonian Talmud's language which did so. Why this should have been the case is difficult, particularly at the outset of this study, to specify. This development could have been fortuitous (which I doubt). Or (as I suspect) the state of affairs had to do with a confluence of political and social circumstances on the one hand, and on the other, some appropriate "fit" between those circumstances and a set of meanings and values implicit in the rhetorical language and formularies of Bavli. In either case, I maintain that such a stylized rhetorical code, which determines what matters are worthy of discussion and how they ought to be talked about, is itself replete with (implicit) meaning and values. The social institutions created or reinforced, in part by the perpetuation of this particular mode of discourse, are grounded in, and promulgate, these implicitly communicated meanings and values into which its members are socialized. By laying bare the nature and use of stock rhetorical linguistic formularies which characterize the Bavli and by venturing an interpretation of that rhetoric's social meaning and institutional ramifications, this book will, I hope, fill a lacuna in the study of the Babylonian Talmud and of late antique Rabbinism in the Mesopotamian-Babylonian area.

Before proceeding, there is much in my statement of purpose which would benefit from explication. In the remainder of this chapter I will therefore undertake a number of preliminary tasks. They are: (1) to introduce briefly the general theoretical framework that has informed my agenda in the following chapters; (2) to discuss some of the methodological and conceptual problems inherent in using rabbinic, and particularly talmudic, evidence to address such questions; (3) to give an account of the methodological and theoretical perspectives which may help in overcoming these problems and to outline how we shall proceed; (4) to situate this enterprise against the backdrop of the main contemporary trends in the study of the Babylonian Talmud; (5) to preview some of the findings in an effort to give readers a sense of direction as they work through an extended argument which begins in chapter 2 and ends in chapter 6.

The broad framework and overall agenda

This book emerges from a broader research agenda driven by an interest in the relationship between the editing of the sacred, canonical texts of early rabbinic Judaism and correlative (although not necessarily concurrent) social transformations within the communities which produced, and which imbued with authority, those texts. Previously published inquiry (Lightstone, 1994b) within this larger programme dealt with the production and promulgation of Mishnah among early third-century Palestinian rabbis. That work considered Mishnah in relation to the overhaul of institutionalized forms of Palestinian Rabbinism at the turn of the third century. This book considers the editing and promotion in the sixth century of the Babylonian Talmud, constituted with the aid of its distinctive rhetoric, in relation to changes in the type of religious virtuosity and authority claimed by the rabbis and in connection with the emergence and ascendancy of the *yeshiva* (the academy) and its presidency (at some point designated by the title "Excellency," גאון), as the principal institutions of the rabbinic movement in late Persian (and subsequently Muslim) Babylonia of the sixth and early seventh centuries.

In the ancient world the production of a text was overwhelmingly a social act of political significance and communicative of shared meaning of a normative, or would-be-normative, nature. The redaction and promulgation of documents, especially those promoted as authoritative, therefore constituted political behaviour which, in conjunction with other activities, helped to reflect and bolster existing or emergent social arrangements or facilitate political and institutional transformations (Goody, 1986). It is with these propositions as a point of departure that I explore the relationship between the redaction of the Babylonian Talmud and institutional transformations which revamped the organizational structure and locus of authority of sixth- and seventh-century Babylonian Rabbinism.

My analysis builds as well upon a particular set of methodological and theoretical perspectives regarding the manner in which highly redacted texts such as the Babylonian Talmud communicate meaning. Again, in previously published research I have argued that perceptions or meanings conveyed by such documents are to be sought not merely in what is communicated in its constituent passages, but largely in the pervasive, recurrent, rhetorical patterns or formal structures which the editors have used to create the final, unified product (Lightstone, 1983; 1988; 1994b). Such communication remains of course implicit only, and the perceptions thereby conveyed are non-discursive in nature. But such communication is no less cogent. When, moreover, these recurrent linguistic patterns replicate such other patterns as organizational structure, the implicit meanings communicated in each highly patterned domain reinforce those conveyed elsewhere. The overall effect lends an air of self-evidence, of "truth," to the resulting "system" of meanings (Douglas, 1975a; 1975b; 1978).

In light of these concerns and broad theoretical and methodological perspectives the chapters that follow undertake a number of distinct tasks. First, the book attempts (in chaps. 2 and 4) to provide some account of recurrent rhetorical patterns and formulaic linguistic usages which we may with some confidence take as characteristic of the Babylonian Talmud. That is, we seek that recurrent use of language which serves, in part, to make of the Bavli a whole and complete oeuvre. Second, this study tries (in chaps. 3 and 5) to elucidate the Bavli's use of language as revealed specifically by its recurrent rhetorical formularies through a comparison of the Babylonian Talmud's rhetorical features and comparable data provided by other, generally earlier rabbinic documents, namely Mishnah, Tosefta, Sifre on Numbers and the Palestinian Talmud. For behaviour, including behaviour of a literary kind, conveys meaning not only because we perceive in it recurrent patterns—that is, it is not random—but also because we recognize at some level that a recurrent pattern is one way and not another. To some extent meaning in language, as in patterned behaviour, is founded upon comparison. Third, the work will venture (in chap. 6) an account of the social meaning implicit in the Bavli's use of its recurrent rhetoric. Fourth, and finally, I shall explore (again in chap. 6) the relationship of that set of meanings and the social and organizational context of Rabbinism at the close of the Persian era and the dawn of Islamic rule in Babylonia.

Before proceeding, however, with the agenda just outlined, I will place my subsequent analyses first, against a backdrop of conceptual, methodological and theoretical concerns and perspectives, and second, of major trends in the modern academic study of the Babylonian Talmud.

Methodological and conceptual problems: From historical and literary analysis to social science

The larger programme of inquiry of which this book forms a part stems not only from an interest in the relationship between canonical text and society, but also from a basic methodological problem: how may one best use the textual evidence of ancient Judaism, in particular of early Rabbinism, to shed light upon the character and development of the early rabbinic movement, first in Roman Palestine, and second, in Parthian and Sasanian Babylonia? The methods and perspectives of historical criticism, form-criticism, redaction criticism and canonical criticism as developed by biblical scholars and as adapted by some students of rabbinic literature (e.g., Neusner, 1971; 1773; 1977; 1981) have all been useful in this regard. But these techniques seem to bring one no closer to reconstructing the nature and development of early rabbinic movements than to uncovering the development of earliest Christianity. If anything, these methods make impossible a retreat to a simple historicist's positivism and widen the gap between the text and the reconstruction of the social context about which the document purports to speak. With respect to the early rabbinic movement and its documents, let me rehearse some of the specific problems posed by the evidence.

The primary methodological problem which has haunted the modern study of ancient Judaism is that providing a history of a text and an account of its sources does not itself provide a social history. Only with the greatest difficulty, if at all, do these sources so analyzed offer data for the reconstruction of social contexts, or a history of Judaism.

The impasse in reconstructing historical descriptions of ancient Judaic communities' lives together and of their religion results not only from the limits of form, literary and redaction analysis and the remaining gulf between a history of a text and a history of a group. Serious problems stem also from the nature of the documents themselves. None of the extant documents left by ancient Judaic communities, including Rabbinism, are mimetic, to use W.S. Green's term (Green, 1983). They do not mimic the social worlds which produced them; they are tendentious, party documents whose purpose is to inculcate certain perceptions of reality rather than to mirror reality.

What a sociological or anthropological analysis, or even a social history of early rabbinic Judaism may entail is therefore limited by the nature of our sources. Only in the most minimal or general ways can one analyze, from a sociological perspective, the social structures, perceptions and norms of these groups and communities, for the texts permit only the most minimal or general social descriptions. This limitation may appear so obvious as not to justify the time devoted to making it. But I would maintain that the recognition of these limitations in scholarship is still more honoured in the breach.[1] Indeed, the enthusiasm, where it exists, to embrace questions of social description or sociological analysis has itself been an impetus to read rabbinic texts as mimetic of social realities.

Notwithstanding the difficulties in moving from textual evidence to a description of the document's immediate social milieu, a persistent

1. Over the last two decades, the most widely read social histories and social descriptions of early rabbinism have consistently treated mishnaic law, for example, as mimetic of social norms and praxis and rabbinic sayings as having a simple one-to-one correspondence to social and political conditions. One need only look at the first, historical chapter of Part II.2 of the *Compendium Rerum Iudaicarum ad Novum Testamentum: The Literature of the Sages*, published by Fortress Press, or at the "new Schuerer" (Schuerer, 1973-87).

item on the agenda of the modern study of both early Christianity and rabbinic Judaism has been the transition within these communities from the oral transmission of traditions to their collection and redaction in (relatively) fixed texts—in itself a false dichotomy—which ultimately attain authoritative status. The enterprises of literary, form- and redaction criticism all have attempted to shed light on different aspects of this social transformation. Canonical criticism has concentrated on the later aspects of this historical process. These scholars seek to uncover the function of the final authoritative document in the life of the community, endeavouring to find reflected in its official scriptures the perceptions and social norms of the group. They wish to lay bare the social and intellectual history of the community after a scripture's ascension within the community to authoritative status. The practitioners of literary and form-criticism are motivated by the desire to uncover the prehistory of the text, expecting thereby to reveal something of the history of the community prior to the document's redaction.

My research deals with the social meaning and more immediate effects of the turning point in this process—the very production and promulgation within a community of a relatively fixed text. This turning point, viewed as a social dynamic rather than as the act of an individual editor or editorial group, precedes the process of interpretation and its history, which comprise the data of the canonical critic. My research's focus does not belong to redaction criticism either, which tends to concentrate on the *Tendenzen* of redactors' uses of antecedent oral or written sources. I concentrate on the meaning and significance of the newly edited whole for the community in which it appears as a social fact. How may one responsibly carry out such an agenda and still fully account for the fact that early rabbinic texts, while reflecting a particular social context, cannot be taken as slavishly mimicking that social milieu or as offering a history of its development? The methodological and theoretical framework that I presently shall spell out allows me to bypass the limitations enunciated above, both of the standard historical and literary-critical methods and of the rabbinic evidence.

Methodological and theoretical underpinnings

Methodology and the descriptive task

In light of the difficulties referred to, my research first limits inquiry to canonical collections or documents, because these may be associated with a distinct Judaic community or circle. What is more, for any one such canon I examine principally that which appears pervasively characteristic of the document at its most general and redactional level. My aim is to determine what perceptions of "the world" are communicated, explicitly or implicitly, by these documents' most general and enduring literary traits and structures—this apart from statements made in the constituent literary units compiled by these documents' editors about "how things are" or "how things ought to be." That means that in order to achieve the necessary methodological control, I opt for bracketing explicit data about shared perceptions in favour of attending to those perceptions of the world implicitly communicated in the document's pervasive rhetorical and literary structures (see Lightstone, 1988). How these structures and patterns are communicative and by what means one may decode them I shall turn to presently.

That basic, repeated patterns can function as means of communication within a particular socio-cultural context has been convincingly established by anthropologists as far back as E. Durkheim. What anthropologists maintain about structured patterns of behaviour may also be said of highly formalized literary behaviour (see Lightstone, 1983; 1988; 1990; 1994b; 1994c), of which much of our evidence is the product. Much of early rabbinic literature is characterized by rendering the vast variety of what is said in relatively few structured ways of saying things. Idiomatic modes of speech or the formal traits of particular groups of tradents have been assimilated to one of several variations of a limited number of rhetorical patterns. In other words, these structures speak, first, for the redactors of these compilations (see Neusner, 1977; 1981; 1983b; 1986b; Green, 1979) and, second, for those for whom these compilations are normative expressions.

These pervasive rhetorical patterns convey meaning because of the lawlike, albeit implicit, rules governing (1) the elements of the structure, (2) the relations among those elements and (3) the range of permissible content of any one element. Such implicit meanings remain distinct from the particular content at any one instance of the structure (see Crossan, 1975; Polzin, 1977). One experiences these lawlike relations as the "way things really are," as part of one's knowledge of the world. It is this attention to pervasive patterns of language in the Judaic evidence and to the meanings therein implicitly communicated that governs much of this study.

By limiting inquiry to canonical documents or collections, I do not intend to present an image of a monolithic, always normative, yet developing "Judaism." Rather I expect to take account of, and methodologically to control for, the rich diversity of Judaic forms and views by attempting to tie distinct formulations in texts to discrete communities. That a text or collection is canonical for some community allows one to make that link. A canon has a function and authority within a group (see Sanders, 1972:xvii). I am particularly interested in identifying that group or community within which a text or collection initially came to play that role and enjoy that authority in order to discern what the redactors' formulations meant in context.

Theory and the 'explanatory' task

The second of my tasks derives from the first. That certain ideas and perceptions of reality are available to a community in no way helps us understand how some of these perceptions attain an air of undeniable truth while others do not. With reference to what dynamics, social or psychological, may one account for the plausibility of a certain set of widely shared beliefs and perceptions in evidence among members of a particular group?

In attempting to formulate a theoretical account of the self-evidence of shared perceptions within a given community, I begin with a premise which I believe to be empirically well founded: few beliefs professed about the meaning of human activity or of history by any one human community appear to be intrinsically more plausible than those maintained by any other group. To be sure, some ideas and beliefs may be empirically better founded than others. But the empirical status of perceptions does not take the social scientist very far in accounting for the cogency of shared perceptions within a given cultural setting (see Douglas, 1975a; 1975b).

As intimated earlier, the theoretical basis for our study's hypotheses and methodological approach is that shared perceptions of "how the world is" are rendered self-evidently appropriate for the group by means of the homological relationship which exists across the various structured realms of the community's shared universe.[2] Among these structured realms, the pattern of social relationships is particularly important, even if not entirely determinative. Implicit in these structures is "knowledge" of the world. Encountering the same implicitly com-

2. Based primarily upon Douglas (1973; 1975a; 1975b; 1978) and Geertz (1966), I have spelled out at greater length elsewhere a theory, particularly well suited to our type of highly patterned literary evidence, of the plausibility of shared perceptions (see Lightstone, 1988:1-8).

municated perceptions in arena after arena within a single cultural context provides these perceptions with a quality of self-evidence for members of the group.

The structured, rhetorical patterns of a community's paradigmatic texts, such as the Mishnah for the late second- and early third-century Palestinian rabbinic community, or the Bavli for the rabbinic movement at the end of the Persian period in Babylonia, is one such structured realm which may be looked to for implicitly communicated perceptions of reality.

This is not to say that the social structure determines outright the community's shared perceptions of the world and the cosmos. Other structured realms, especially social organization, bias a group's perceptions (Douglas, 1975a: 207; see also 1975b; 1978) as implicitly expressed in highly patterned texts. Such biassing takes place against a backdrop of antecedent sentiments, perceptions and social patterns (Durkheim, 1982:108-10, 125). That is to say, the group's experience of social and other patterned relationships effectively limits the range of what is plausible, given what is historically available to the group in question. There is a history to social facts, and any bias is exerted in one direction or another along a continuum of what is historically available to the group under study. This insistence on a sensitivity to a diachronic dimension in addition to the synchronic is particularly important to the study of religion, in which the idea of the authority of tradition or the social entrenchment of authoritative (canonical) texts often is a significant cultural datum. This, as we shall see, will prove particularly germane to my analysis of the social meaning and significance of the Bavli's rhetorical traits.

Having said, however, that other structured realms, and chief among them the social realm, may bias what is plausible against a backdrop of what is historically available to group, it follows too that the structured patterns of a text, having been accepted as authoritative, become just such a social fact. The text's structured patterns may not only reflect and reinforce a social order, but also aid in its further crystallization and development along lines present embryonically at the time of the text's production, acceptance and promulgation. The relationship between structured realms in the social and perceptual universe of some group is neither unidirectional nor oriented entirely towards stasis. Rather, as the evidence in the following chapters will suggest, that relationship is dynamic and complex.

The theoretical propositions outlined above concerning the cogency of implicitly communicated knowledge provide a basis for only some of the issues and problems related to my inquiry as defined earlier. The sociology of literacy offers some useful insights in considering the social dynamics which accompany the production and promulgation of a public, authoritative text. What social impetuses incline a community to engage in such a literary enterprise, and what tend to be the social effects of the very production, promulgation and acceptance of such public texts?

Addressing these types of questions with respect to Mishnah or the Babylonian Talmud forces me to rehearse previously mentioned difficulties. While Mishnah and Talmud reflect their social milieux, neither text portrays or mimics its social context. There exist, furthermore, precious few independent witnesses to the development of early rabbinic institutions and organization. Any historical or social scenarios of early rabbinic institutions must remain significantly qualified. Still, a body of theoretical and ethnographic literature exists on the social implications of literacy, which, if allowed to illuminate the admittedly problematic rabbinic evidence, does produce some compelling hypotheses. That the latter may not be given to conclusive testing does not negate the heuristic value of the exercise.

With respect to early rabbinic documents in general and the Talmud in particular, a useful set of theoretical propositions emerges from Gumperz's notion of "the speech community" (Gumperz, 1985). As an extension of his discussion, I would hypothesize that a community's authoritative texts, particularly those exhibiting a pronounced rhetorical style, provide within a given social setting an authoritative model for speech. First, speaking in a style reminiscent of the text may attest to the interpreter's learning, representing years of study of the canonical documents. Second, such a correspondence between literary style and human speech conveys the authority of the canon to the speaker. Third, the existence of a shared pattern of discourse, mimicking that of the canonical literature, among a group of those learned in the texts may serve to define and set apart these people as a distinctive class of religious virtuosi within the larger social unit.[3] The highly patterned and distinc-

3. The preceding three points follow from remarks of Gumperz (1985) concerning the socio-linguistic study of minority or occupational groups. He states: "Other scholars dealt with the languages of occupationally specialized minority groups, craft jargons, secret argots and the like. In some cases such as in the Romany of the gypsies and the Yiddish of the Jews, these parlances derive from foreign importations, which survive as linguistic islands surrounded by other tongues. Their speakers tend to be bilinguals, using their own idiom for in-group communications and the majority language for interaction with outsiders .... Despite their similarities, the classical administrative and liturgical languages—such as the Latin of medieval Europe, the Sanskrit of south Asia and the Arabic of the

tive nature of Late Antique rabbinic literature lends itself well to such a social dynamic. The exploration of such a dynamic, within the limits imposed by our evidence, may therefore shed further light on the social location of Mishnah or the Babylonian Talmud as canonical texts within their respective contexts.

A final set of general propositions which informs this research concerns the social requisites and effects of the very production of a text touted as authoritative. In this regard, the work of J.R. Goody remains instructive. In Goody's view, the production of written authoritative texts produces organizational transformations in the community in question (Goody, 1986). Beginning with observations akin to those we have distilled from Gumperz's notion of speech community, Goody argues that the promulgation of a written canon contributes to the increasing emergence and differentiation of religion as a distinctive entity within culture and society. Because of this differentiation and as a more direct result of the production of sacred documents, institutions of learning emerge dedicated to the preservation of the documents and the production of those schooled in them. In other words, the production of canonical texts is closely tied to the institutionalization of schools as well as to the imparting to its students and teachers of specialized roles and elevated status. Goody remarks, in addition, that these developments "are often associated with restrictions on the uses and extent of literacy" (Goody, 1986:17). The rabbinic interdiction against committing oral tradition to writing (obviously not always honoured) and the promulgation of official written texts in oral form, as is supposed to have been the case for Mishnah, suggests the value to our discussion of the link, proposed by Goody, between the redaction of sacred texts on the one hand,

Near East—are not ordinarily grouped with special parlances because of the prestige of the cultural traditions associated with them. They are quite distinct from ... popular speech, and ... their use can be learned only through many years of special training .... Knowledge of these languages in the traditional societies where they are used is limited to a relatively small elite, who tend to maintain control of their linguistic skills in somewhat the same way that craft guilds strive for exclusive control of their craft skills" (Gumperz, 1985:221-22). Gumperz's remarks about minority and elitist groups' use of idiomatic language or jargon as a self-defining characteristic is suggestive indeed with regard to the possible social repercussions of the centrality of the study of the Babylonian Talmud among early medieval rabbis and their disciples. As I have noted at the outset of this chapter, mastery of its idiomatic, laconic and formulaic vocabulary is essential to being able to read the Talmud at all. Such mastery would no doubt mark one as a member of the guild of rabbis or would-be rabbis.

and the emergence of both religious virtuosi and academies as recognized autonomous social groups and realms, on the other.

These then are the theoretical and methodological perspectives which inform both my broader research agenda and the analyses in this particular volume of the formalized rhetoric of the Babylonian Talmud. Before previewing what the reader will find in proceeding through the subsequent chapters of this book, however, let me briefly locate this inquiry against some of the main trends of the modern study of the Babylonian Talmud.

The context of modern scholarship on the Babylonian Talmud

The evolution of rabbinic Judaism and of the Talmud in nineteenth- and twentieth-century scholarship

The study of rabbinic texts, especially the Babylonian Talmud, was of paramount significance for rabbis from early medieval through modern times. Study of the Talmud was an end in itself, a meritorious activity endowing the student with sanctity and authority. In addition, rabbis used the Talmud as an authoritative source book for rabbinic thought and law. Already in the medieval period students of the Talmud sought to identify recurrent literary traits and consistencies in the Talmud's use of terminology. The "Introduction to the Talmud" attributed to R. Samuel HaNagid provides an early example. That document sparked several others from late medieval and Renaissance times attempting to comment and to expand upon the "Introduction." The eighteenth and nineteenth centuries saw the composition in traditional rabbinic circles of a number of works concerning general traits of the Talmud, among them: *Yad Malachi* by Malachi Cohen and *Pahad Yitzhaq* by Isaac ben Samuel Lampronti (in the first and second halves of the eighteenth century respectively); *Mavo leTalmud* by Zvi Chajes and *Sedei Hemed* by Hayyim Hezekiah Medini (in the middle and latter part of the nineteenth century respectively). Apart from the intrinsic importance of the Talmud to these authors, all of these works are overwhelmingly steered by their authors' need to derive authoritative normative law from the Talmud's contradictory legal opinions and inconclusive deliberations. These works attempt to see in many of the Talmud's literary formulae some indication of talmudic editors' disposition to favour one view over another. This preoccupation and its concrete effects sets these works apart from quite different studies, commencing in the nineteen century, of early rabbinic literature.[4]

Since the 1830s, the literary history of early rabbinic texts has been a principal subject of research on the part of scholars of Judaic origins. These texts, more than the Hebrew Bible, were seen as keys to understanding the history and development of Judaism as known at the end of the medieval period and the beginning of the modern era. Since the early modern students of rabbinic texts were, until after World War II, official or quasi-official proponents of one or another competing mode of Judaism, their very definition of the research problems, and the theoretical and methodological assumptions brought to their investigations, were influenced greatly by the types of apologies and theologies offered by their respective factions of modern Judaism. The theological or ideological challenge which informed their work, sometimes consciously but often not, was to justify change in Judaism in response to modernity, while allowing for the claim to authenticity despite that change (see Neusner, 1970; Lightstone, 1991).

This usually unstated, motivating agenda encouraged scholars to demonstrate continuous and contiguous development and evolution from post-biblical times to the end of the Persian period (see Lightstone, 1991). Since rabbinic texts constituted both their primary data as scholars and the authentic ground for whatever mode of modern Judaism with which they identified, most modern scholars argued that early rabbinic texts were themselves the product of literary accretion. Thus the Talmud, in their view, developed in stages, the work of each stage undertaken on the bedrock of the former. The evolution of post-biblical Judaism paralleled the evolution of what was considered the quintessential rabbinic text, the Babylonian Talmud.

The methodological and theoretical rails laid down by this 150-year-long scholarly tradition still steer many contemporary researchers.

4. I am grateful to Dr. Michael Broyde (Emory University) for his insistence that I consider the work done in medieval and early modern, traditional rabbinic circles on the Talmud's terminology and methodology. While I have benefited greatly from consulting the works mentioned, I insist that their overriding interest in using the Talmud's recurrent terminology as a means of divining the talmudic editors' leanings toward one view over another often leads to interpretations which veil rather than reveal the rhetoric of the Talmud and the significance of that rhetoric. Indeed, the need to see in such terminology an encoded message concerning which view is normative in the eyes of the editors highlights the fact that the Talmud, as constituted largely by its rhetoric, is often interested in quite other things and steered by an entirely different purpose. What that may be is the subject of the last chapter of this book.

Why this is the case I have discussed elsewhere (Lightstone, 1991). In the current context, it is more important to note that the research thereby generated is problematic from a number of perspectives. With respect to the Babylonian Talmud, the third major canon of rabbinic Judaism (after the canons of the Hebrew Bible and of the Mishnah), research concerning the role of the penultimate redactors and the meaning and (social) significance of the final document received little attention as a result of this methodological and theoretical baggage. By assuming, and then concluding, that the Talmud as we have it grew by a slow process of accretion, the role of the penultimate redactors is limited to "bringing the curtain down" on a centuries-long performance which commenced with the promulgation of the Mishnah *ca.* 200 CE. The final document communicates no meaning which was not in the main conveyed or anticipated before. Indeed the redactors are viewed as those who put to rest a process which was in its terminal degenerated phases, largely as a result of persecution and attendant cultural decline (see Tenenblatt, 1972).

In maintaining this view modern scholars have in essence reaffirmed the position stated by Sherira Gaon, whose Epistle of 988 CE was itself composed at the request of the sages of Kairouan in the face of the Karaites' challenge to the authenticity of rabbinic literature. For Sherira, the process of "talmudization," namely, that process of analysis characteristic of the Babylonian Talmud, and the collection and redaction of the results of the same, commenced with the death of Rabbi Judah the Prince at the beginning of the third century, as an attempt to understand the Mishnah. These processes of analysis, on the one hand, and of collection and editing, on the other, continued unabated until the latter decades of the fifth century (Sherira, ed. Levin, 1971:50-63). Sherira waffles on whether this accumulating tradition was transmitted orally or in a written form (see Sherira, ed. Levin, 1971:62-63; 71-72) before the work of the Saboraim in the sixth century. Consistent with this view, Sherira even offers "settings in life" for various linguistic patterns and formularies characteristic of the Babylonian Talmud's modes of analysis (see Sherira, ed. Levin, 1971:53,57). Sherira, then, in combination with the apologetic requisites of nineteenth- and twentieth-century modes of Judaism, has informed, even set, the agenda and the initial working hypotheses of much of modern scholarship on the Babylonian Talmud.

Recent scholarship on the Bavli by D. Weiss-Halivni, D. Kraemer and J. Neusner

Within the last decade a number of important monographs by Jacob Neusner (1986b; 1991a; 1991b), David Weiss-Halivni (1986) and David Kraemer (1990) have appeared. All three authors attempt to describe and analyze that which is most characteristic of the Babylonian Talmud as a final and complete oeuvre. All three have in addition attempted to account for these characteristics in terms of some explanatory framework, whether historical or theological.

In a number of respects, however, the works of Kraemer and Halivni continue to reflect the agenda which has characterized modern scholarship on the Babylonian Talmud since the latter half of the nineteenth century. A central problem remains the pre-history of the Babylonian Talmud and its constituent elements prior to its ultimate or penultimate redaction. To quite differing degrees, to be sure, the explicit assumptions remain in both works that the Talmud grew by continuous and contiguous accretion and that many of these strata are identifiable and recoverable. Both Kraemer and Halivni maintain that attributions in the text to rabbinic tradents are in some significant sense a reliable means of pulling apart the Talmud in order to identify and isolate its historical layers. And in both scholars' works the origins of the very language, style and structural patterns exhibited in the Talmud in its final form may also be assigned to one or another of these antecedent strata on the basis of attributions to named figures. In Kraemer's view, that literary forms and even rhetorical formulary language are pervasive in the Talmud in its final or penultimate form, and appear as well in sections bearing attributions to figures supposed to have flourished several generations before the period of the redactors of the whole, is to be explained by the extreme conservatism of later tradents and redactors. These latter, according to Kraemer, faithfully preserved and then replicated the literary style, structures and rhetorical formularies of their predecessors several generations earlier. A number of assumptions must be taken for granted in adopting this methodological approach. We must presume to know more about the social, historical, institutional and ideological contexts of third- to sixth-century Babylonian Rabbinism than we could ever hope to know. With so many questions begged, even in Kraemer's otherwise methodical book, much of the outcome of his investigation is virtually assured before it has begun.

Both works, however, exhibit traits which fundamentally set them apart from their predecessors; namely, a concern to characterize and to understand the significance of the whole as it emerged at the end of the Sassanid period in Babylonia. In this regard both, and Kraemer in particular, bear comparison with Neusner.

Neusner (1986b) wishes exclusively to divine the character of the whole. His "purchase" on the work of the final redactors and the significance of that work derives not from sorting out the prehistory of the Talmud or the talmudic tradition. Neusner attempts to describe the traits of the Babylonian Talmud as a whole and complete oeuvre, and seeks to gain entry into the set of meanings conveyed by the whole via comparison with the characteristics of other (earlier) rabbinic works, themselves taken as complete entities. Neusner's monograph, *Judaism: The Classical Statement* (1986b) uses several methodologies, for part of the study is founded upon analyses of previous monographs (*Pharisees before 70*, I, 1971; *Development of a Legend*, 1970), the approaches of which were designed to respond to quite different questions, among them how the Babylonian Talmud treats earlier materials.

In the later sections of the work, Neusner relies upon his more recent methodology, formulated expressly to permit the comparison of distinct documents, each taken as a final and complete entity, within a single taxonomic framework. As in his study of the Tosefta, carried out some 15 years ago, Neusner proceeds in this section of the monograph to classify component sections of the Bavli in terms of their topical relationship to other antecedent foundational documents. Thus a component unit of the Babylonian Talmud might comment upon, complement or supplement the Mishnah text at hand. Alternatively, a talmudic unit might take as its point of departure some passage of scripture or the alleged report of what a Talmudic sage did or said. By tabulating the proportion of the Babylonian Talmud accounted for by materials following within one or another topical category, and by comparing these summary statistics to those resulting from comparable analyses of other rabbinic documents, in particular the Palestinian Talmud, Neusner may say something of the redactional policy, and hence of the interests and theology evidenced by the Babylonian Talmud as a whole, over against different competing interests of other ancient rabbinic texts, such as the Palestinian Talmud. It does not matter whether the editors of the Bavli knew, and consciously shaped their work over against these other works; in some instances that may be the case. Of methodological importance is the appreciation of an encompassing agenda of the whole, an appreciation enhanced by systematic comparison with possible alternatives.

What *Judaism: The Classical Statement*, Neusner's first monograph on the Bavli, lacks is an appreciation of the modes of discourse and recurring rhetorical structures which cut across the sections of the Bavli, notwithstanding a section's topical class as commentary, complement or supplement of either Mishnah, scripture or the (alleged) words and deeds of a rabbinic sage. What is characteristic of the Bavli as a whole, and therefore of the work of its final or penultimate redactors, is not merely the distinctive statistical distribution or frequency of topical classes in which the various sections may be placed. The Bavli, as can be readily shown, is not simply the result of the compilation of sections with respect to implicit or explicit rules governing relative proportions in the whole of "types" of sections. Rather the editors also do something within and, indeed, across these constituent sections, and what they do is remarkably consistent. In several more recent monographs (Neusner, 1990c; 1991a,c,d,e; 1992) Neusner moves beyond the methodology of *Judaism: The Classical Statement* to consider that the Bavli's editors tend overwhelmingly to combine sections into coherent essay-composites. Neusner finds only a few instances in all of Bavli where the editors have created mere (albeit "massive") "miscellanies."

Beyond recent scholarship on Bavli

My work builds upon, and extends Neusner's, but takes matters in a quite different direction, one recalling Kraemer's interest in the Talmud's encompassing modes of argument. I will inquire about the ideological and social meaning of the pervasive use in Bavli of a consistent and formulaic rhetorical vocabulary and idiom in forging not only its elaborated composite essays, but also these composites' constituent passages, as well as a goodly number of the individual statements therein.

This focus of my overall research programme is born of the initial impression that most of the tractates of the Babylonian Talmud, and their constituent chapters, appear at first glance to do much the same things with the alleged antecedent traditions cited and do so with much the same stock language. The resulting literary patterns, structured with respect to this recurrent rhetorical vocabulary of logical operators, themselves pervade the whole. I seek in these recurrent structured patterns implicitly communicated sets of meanings, because such pervasive, recurrent patterns point to established normative relationships between classes of objects. These recurrent patterns resemble the grammar and syntax of language, on the one hand, and structured patterns of behaviour in the social realm, on the other. The cogency of that which is communicated implicitly in either social or literary "behaviour" lies, in my view, precisely in the effects upon the social actor/reader of encountering recurrent, homological and, therefore, mutually reinforcing patterns both in revered documents and in the structured pattern of social relationships of the community which produced or received these documents.

Why should these interests which govern this study have escaped more sustained attention by others? This is explained perhaps by some social facts about modern scholars of ancient rabbinic literature. Most scholars prior to the 1960s carried out their work within parochial Jewish institutions of higher learning. Even now, many currently working in university settings "grew up" from childhood with these texts, so they too are, as it were, part of the "guild of masters and disciples of talmud study." Those scholars are the elite insiders of which Gumperz (1985) speaks. The rhetorical code of the Talmud is their code. It is difficult for such an insider to see the Talmud's rhetorical code as anything other than natural within the social frame of the guild, and what is experienced or perceived as natural rarely is felt to require explanation. But there is nothing self-evidently appropriate or natural about the Talmud's use of language. This is so even for ancient rabbis, as our comparisons of talmudic language and the use of language in the Mishnah, the Tosefta, Sifre on Numbers and the Yerushalmi will starkly reveal. To be sensitive to the idiomatic character of the Talmud's rhetorical code means ironically both to master it, and as an outsider to see that rhetoric as something begging for inquiry and explanation and to attempt to uncover its meaning and significance for the insider. Such are the seemingly contradictory desiderata which have produced this study and its results, which I shall briefly preview.

Previewing the conclusions

This study falls into three parts: (1) analyses of aspects of the stylized rhetoric of the Babylonian Talmud (chaps. 2 and 4); (2) comparisons of the Talmud's rhetoric and the rhetorical formulaic language evident in other, earlier rabbinic documents (chaps. 3 and 5); (3) a discussion of the meaning and social significance of the rhetoric of the Bavli, as well as an account of the organizational transformations within late Persian Rabbinism which correlate with, and which perhaps are reflected in or nurtured by, Bavli's sustained rhetoric (chap. 6).

The reader will find in the first and second enterprises close analyses of the formulaic rhetorical language of representative or exemplary sections of the documents in question. In the case of the Bavli, those texts are b. Avodah Zarah 14b-16a, b. Bekorot 2a-3b and b. Bekorot 3b-5b. I do not undertake in this volume a comprehensive study of the Bavli, similar to Neusner's taxanomic studies documenting the relative frequency of broadly defined types of passages. My focus is upon more finely grained data, the stock linguistic formularies which in the Talmud bind words into statements, statements into analytic passages and passages into more elaborated composite essays. So I look at the bits and pieces of some sample of texts. Others may test my results on additional data.[5]

I am confident that the passages presented here are not atypical of the whole *in terms of their use of rhetoric*. Neusner has demonstrated the remarkable consistency of the Bavli on other grounds and criteria. The passages herein analyzed fall well within the norm, as he has defined it. My sense of the Bavli, resulting from selective, and wide-ranging, but often more casual, study, leads me to believe that in terms of their use of rhetoric, these passages are not eccentric and reflect the norm. That being said, further, similarly analyzed data stand behind this work than is presented in our analyses in chapters 2 and 4. The entirety of chapters 2 and 3 of b. Bekorot and the entirety of chapter 4 of b. Ta'anit have been subjected to the same detailed rhetorical analysis as performed before the reader in this volume.[6] The results throughout are consistent.[7] Let me, then, briefly summarize them here.

Analyses of passages of b. Avodah Zarah, b. Bekorot and elsewhere have led me to differentiate two classes—in reality, "ideal types"—of rhetorical formularies, both of which permeate the Talmud.[8]

5. I am, in this regard, sensitive too to the danger inherent in my analyzing ever more data with my current results serving as a built-in bias.

6. For the analyses of b. Bek., chapters 2 and 3, I am grateful for, and dependent upon, work by my research student, Mr. Joshua Joseph. The analyses of b. Ta'an. 4 were undertaken by a doctoral candidate, Madeleine Mcbrearty.

7. I have undertaken another exercise as an additional check that the rhetorical language of the passages analyzed in this book (and rhetorical traits of b. Bek. 2-3 and of b. Ta'an. 4) are not atypical or eccentric features of the Bavli. I have documented the frequency and distribution in b. Bek., b. Ta'an. and seven other tractates of the use of a number of linguistic formulae which in my analyses emerged as among the key items of Bavli's rhetorical vocabulary. The results of this exercise appear in Appendix A. I thank once more Dr. Michael Broyde, whose gadfly questions led me to conceive and to undertake this further check.

8. I must state emphatically that this differentiation is not a taxonomy; it is not a hard and fast classification of "things" with reference to entirely mutually exclusive defining characteristics. Rather my classes or categories are intended to be what Weberian scholars would call "ideal types," which actual data may more or less

One class constitutes a group of "logical operators" by means of which an "argument-statement" comprising an individual unit of discourse is created. Here is a simplified (contrived or ideal) form:

If circumstances, *since* operative principle,
then conclusion.

The preposition, "if," the conjunction, "since," and the adverb, "then," create, along with the substantive material which follows each, a small indivisible unit of argument. The Babylonian Talmud is replete with these units of argument formed by a rich but limited vocabulary that function as logical operators. Since these formulaic, logical operators are the building blocks of individual argumentational units of thought—producing an "argument-statement"—their removal from such sentences leaves behind virtually nothing intelligible as an organized thought or statement. These formularies are part and parcel, then, of the grammar and syntax of individual units of thought in the Talmud. I have dubbed them "dialectical formularies."

Dialectical formularies tend overwhelmingly to be in Aramaic. They appear in both attributed and unattributed argument/analytic-statements, which these formularies serve to constitute. As such, individual formulaic operators do not stand alone; one notes a decided tendency to structured sequences of such stock formularies, which are generally complex, in the formal grammatical sense.

Dialectical formularies may be distinguished from, but are not necessarily independent of, another broad type of recurrent rhetorical formula or formulary[9] which pervades the Babylonian Talmud. This sec-

closely resemble. Identifying data with respect to these two ideal types serves to facilitate examination of types of patterns of relationships in the document, patterns which stock rhetorical language help constitute. This understanding of what I mean by identifying two types of formularies is key to not misconstruing the significance of my placing a term in one broad class or another of rhetorical formularies. In principle and in practice, viewing a particular datum as resembling one "type," thereby revealing something significant about its character and function, does not preclude subsequently examining that same datum within the context of another type, which exercise may illuminate some other aspect of that datum's meaning and role. Treating typologies as taxonomies is a basic methodological flaw haunting many studies.

9. I use "formula" to refer to a single, standard rhetorical term: such as, "What is the reason?"—the example cited. "Formulary," by contrast, will refer to a stock structured sequence of "formulae" which when juxtaposed with items, phrases or sentences providing the idiomatic content, provide the structure or form of a literary unit. As I shall show, stock dialectical operators tend to appear within formularies. The same tendency is not a pronounced feature of the second type of rhetorical language which I shall presently describe. Since, when referring in general to this second class, it will prove cumbersome to speak always of

ond type of formulary, again overwhelmingly Aramaic, invites argument of a particular nature: for example,

What is the reasoning?

The Babylonian Talmud exhibits a rich but still relatively limited number of this second class of formularies. While inviting argument and/or answers of a particular type, these formularies are not grammatically integral to the argumentation which follows them. Nor are they part and parcel of any argument or statement which preceeded and (allegedly) engendered them. Those statements and arguments stand on their own, grammatically intelligible, quite apart from this second class of formularies. However, these formularies structure and order preceding and subsequent statements and arguments into a more extensive, broader analysis. They join individual parts and help to create a larger, literary composition, roughly corresponding to what traditional talmudic exegetes refer to by the Aramaic term *sugya*. They aid as well in linking a number of *sugyot* together to form larger superordinating composites, extended "essays." Because of their structuring function, I have called this second class of formularies "structural formularies" to distinguish them from "dialectical formularies."

These formularies, both structural and dialectical, so pervasive in the Bavli, stand out in stark relief from the use of language in Mishnah, the Tosefta and Sifre on Numbers analyzed in chapter 5. Even the sample passage from the Yerushalmi, that other "Talmud," falls far from the Bavli's mark.

What the Talmud undertakes with its argument-statements, elaborated composites (*sugyot*) and superordinating composites, constituted in large measure by these dialectical and structural formularies, is the open-ended analysis, seemingly for its own sake, of passages or even phrases of the Mishnah and excised pieces of other sacred sources and traditions. As I shall argue in my conclusions, the Talmud thereby deconstructs those sacred authoritative sources from which it draws its materials. Each of these documents, even the Mishnah, in some sense disappears as an objective, externally constraining and integral whole. Moreover, the process of critical analysis, pursued in large part as an end in itself, displaces these sources as the locus of that which is authoritative.

"formularies and formulae," when making general reference to this second class, I shall use the term "formulary," as I do with dialectical formularies. When I am not talking about types of rhetorical language in general, but refer to specific, recurrent rhetorical terms, I shall use "formulae" or "formulary" in a manner consistent with the definitions given in this note.

These rhetorical patterns, like the formularies which help create them, constitute a sustained and pervasive characteristic of the Babylonian Talmud. The open-ended "debates" which characterize the structure of the Talmud must, therefore, be seen as the products of the work of the penultimate redactors; by artifice they bring into open-ended, inconclusive deliberations any antecedent "parties" to the analysis of rabbinic tradition. Not only is this analysis often incomplete and without concrete results, but also (and perhaps, therefore) the Talmud's analyses are intended to be exemplary: they invite the continuation of a process of inquiry on the basis of the models provided in the text. On the one hand the text invites completion while, on the other hand—to its recipient—it appears to be a closed document brought to completion by redactors at a certain moment in time. We are faced with a tantalizing paradox; a text which invites completion, addition and extension of its analysis is experienced by the group that received and promulgated it as an autonomous, fixed and enduring "object in the world."

Precisely by representing this paradox, albeit implicitly, to members of the community, the Talmud provides an homology for those social and institutional transformations undergone by Babylonian Rabbinism over the Sassanid period. I argue that by modelling an open-ended, critical analysis of all antecedent, authoritative, rabbinic tradition, including the Mishnah, the Bavli reflects and legitimates a "type" of religious virtuosity and authority which differs considerably from that reflected in Mishnah's literary traits. The latter's rabbi was "master" because he claimed knowledge of the things of this world and the rules which applied to them, as portrayed in Mishnah's hierarchically organized lists (see Neusner, 1981). In this respect mishnaic rabbis claim the authority of the priests of the Jerusalem Temple (destroyed some one hundred and thirty years before the editing of Mishnah). The talmudic "master," by contrast, claims authority by virtue of critical and analytic acumen applied to all antecedent knowledge of "the way things are in the world," including knowledge of the world offered in Mishnah's lists. Reflected in the pervasive rhetoric of the Talmud is a "type" of religious virtuosity which I shall dub "scholastic."

In addition to reflecting changes in the type of religious virtuosity and authority claimed by the rabbis of Sassanid Babylonia, the Talmud's rhetoric models or helps legitimate transformations in the organization of Rabbinism at the end of the Sassanid era. I shall argue that toward the latter part of this period individual rabbinic circles comprising masters and disciples gave way to the emergence of autonomous, more complex and well-structured institutions of learning—the rabbinic academies, in which scholars and students engaged in the study of the Talmud. The Talmud became both the object of, and the model for, analysis. In this respect, it appears that that which is implicitly communicated in the Talmud was clearly heard. Just as the Talmud "emerged into the world" as an objective, autonomous realm of discourse deconstructing the objective texts and traditions which preceded it in order to incorporate and supplant them, so too the academy emerged as an autonomous institutution for talmudic discourse, as invited by the exemplary nature of the Talmud's passages.

Prior to the emergence of the academies, the rabbinic movement had assiduously avoided the establishment of such *yeshivot*, in spite of the fact that Judean-Galilean Rabbinism offered from the mid-third century a model in their "houses of study" (Lightstone, 1994b; Goodblatt, 1975). As J. Neusner has shown, Babylonian rabbis of this same period were visible in the public realm as officers of the various administrative entities which comprised the semi-autonomous Jewish government ruled by the Exilarch (Neusner, 1969-70), although in this public sphere, no autonomous, organized rabbinic institution existed. But Sassanid rulers systematically disempowered such autonomous forms of ethnic governance as the Exilarch's administration. In the reign of Noshirwan Jewish self-government all but disappeared. The Exilarch may have retained extensive prestige, but little more for the remainder of Sassanid rule. If Rabbinism had earlier "hitched its wagon" by design or by necessity to the Exilarch's administration, such a locus for the exercise of rabbinic power and authority no longer remained viable by the sixth century. From this period of turmoil emerged a document, the Talmud, and a new autonomous realm of rabbinic activity, the rabbinic academy. Both the text and the institution encompassed and superseded that which preceded them.

2

Bavli's Structural Formularies

This chapter and chapter 3 are concerned with identifying and analyzing those rhetorical formulae and formularies which help constitute the larger literary units of a "chapter" of the Talmud. In comparison with later sections of this book, I adopt a longer focal length in the current and the subsequent chapter; that is, I examine the rhetoric of the Bavli at a more "macro-level." My goal is multiple. First I isolate rhetorical language which knits together and structures small, individual, literary units into more encompassing analytic "essays." Second, this chapter and the one which follows attempt to shed light upon the creative use which the Bavli's editors make of their stock rhetorical formulae and formularies in "spinning out" these larger units. Their work is not merely to collect, preserve and compile in some intelligible order antecedent units of rabbinic tradition with linguistic formulae serving as joining language. Rather editors exhibit, and model for their intended readers, skill at creation and invention when using their stock rhetorical tools to extend ever further their analytic "essays," into which still more earlier rabbinic traditions may be integrated and become objects of inquiry. In a detailed examination in this chapter of b. Avodah Zarah 14-16a in its own right, as well as in a comprehensive comparison carried out in the next of this passage with its "cognate" in the Palestinian Talmud, y. Avodah Zarah 1:6, I highlight not only the rich array of rhetorical formulae and formularies serving to knit together Bavli's analytic essays but also the penchant of Bavli's editors creatively to use their rhetorical tools in spinning out extended, analytic composite "essays."

What I have called "structural formularies" in the main serve Bavli's editors in this enterprise. In chapter 1 I differentiated two types of rhetorical formulary that permeate the Talmud. One type, "logical operators," are the means by which the argumentation within a small unit of discourse develops. These formulaic logical operators provide the building blocks of individual argumentational units of thought—producing an argument-sentence. I dubbed them "dialectical formularies." I distinguished dialectical formularies from "structural" formularies, which invite argument of a particular type but tend not to be grammatically integral to the argumentation that follows them. Nor are they part and parcel of any argument or statement that preceded and (allegedly) engendered them. These formularies structure and order preceding and subsequent statements and arguments into more extensive, broad analyses. They join individual parts and provide direction in the creation of a larger, however contrived, literary composition. Such extended literary composites roughly correspond to what traditional talmudic exegetes refer to by the Aramaic term, *sugya*. They aid as well in linking together a number of *sugyot* to form larger encompassing composites or extended "essays."

In order better to analyze the character and role of structural formularies in the talmudic passage which follows, I have formatted the presentation of b. AZ 14b-16a to highlight its literary features. The placement of text in relation to the left margin represents visually the passage's formulaic rhetorical terms as either structural or dialectical in character: structural formularies are at the margin flush left; dialectical formularies are indented 2 centimetres from the left margin; everything else (the idiomatic substantive materials of argument-sentences or the outright citation of some authoritative source) is indented 4 centimetres from the left margin.[1] My contrived examples in chapter one would appear in our chart thus:

What is the reasoning?
        If
                circumstances,
        since
                operative principle,
        [then]
                conclusion.[2]

Hebrew is given in Roman typeface; Aramaic in italics; citations of Mishnah, whether from m. AZ 1:6 itself or from elsewhere, are in capitals. Enumeration of individual composites, whether entirely independent or themselves part of even larger encompassing composite "essays," are given in roman numerals; arabic numerals number units of argument within a composite.

1. Where a lengthier cited "source" displays language which may be similarly characterized as either structural or dialectical, I have charted the cited passage using the same protocols.
2. This visual representation of differentiated types of rhetorical language may appear to anticipate the primary observations upon which this book bases its conclusions. The reader will find, however, that such charting facilitates the discussions in the remainder of this chapter and in chapter four. Whether I have in fact prejudiced the analysis of the data will, in any event, be quickly discernible in the course of that discussion.

Babylonian Talmud, Avodah Zarah 14b-16a

Mishnah Avodah Zarah concerns itself with limiting the contact between Israelites and idolators. Of course, it is assumed that Israelites do not, or ought not to, practise idolatry. M. AZ, however, is concerned to stop any indirect contribution on the part of an Israelite to the idolator's practice of idolatry. No Jew may derive benefit, directly or indirectly, from the idolator's practice of his or her cult. In a related vein, m. AZ regulates contact between a Jew and the paraphernalia of idolatrous practices. Finally, m. AZ limits social contact between Israelites and idolators, first, because this may lead to other more serious participation and, second, because the moral standards of idolators are assumed to be so low as to represent a danger to others.

Babylonian Talmud, Avodah Zarah 14b-16a takes as its point of departure m. AZ 1:6, which reads:

Mishnah Avodah Zarah 1:6

A. [In] a locale [in] which they are accustomed to sell a small cattle [e.g., sheep or goats] to idolators
B. they [are permited to] sell
C. [In] a locale [in] which they are not accustomed to sell [small cattle] to them
D. they do not [permit one to] sell
E.1. And in any locale, they do not [permit one to] sell to them
2. large cattle [e.g., oxen]
3. calves
4. and foals [of asses or of horses]—
F. whether whole, or maimed.
G. R. Judah permits in the case of a maimed [animal],
H. and Ben-Batayra permits in the case of a horse.

Before turning to the Bavli's treatment of m. AZ 1:6, it is worth appreciating the literary character of this mishnaic passage in its own right. I call attention to the typical and skilful weaving together of the parts to form a rather elegant whole—literary and redactional work which in its means and overall effects distinguishes the Mishnah from both the Talmuds for which Mishnah formed the authoritative base. (Later, in chapter five, I shall examine more closely aspects of the Mishnah's use of language as one point of comparison in assessing the Bavli's rhetoric.) The Mishnah passage falls neatly into five sections. A-B and C-D are anonymous, identically structured and phrased rulings. E-F offers a third anonymous law; it commences with language replicating the two foregoing apodictic statements, but ends with a list at E.2-E.3.

The ruling attributed to Ben-Batayra (H) glosses and disputes E.4. H, however, does not reflect the terminology of E.4., as would be the case in most mishnaic disputes. The opinion attributed to R. Judah at G appears to dispute all of E. In fact, it is the gloss of E at F ("whether whole, or maimed") which has permitted the redactors' introduction of G. The operative verb "permits" at G and H appears nowhere in the preceding sections. Neither does its paired opposite, "forbids." Again the use of matched opposing pairs would be more typical of a classically formulated mishnaic dispute.

Let us now turn to the larger encompassing composite "essay" of the Babylonian Talmud which ostensibly comments upon the above-cited Mishnah passage.

Babylonian Talmud, Avodah Zarah 14b-16a

I

1. Is that to say (למימרה) *that*
there is no
prohibition
[and] there is
[i.e., it is a matter of] custom [only]?

2. *[No]*
where
it is the custom [to have] a prohibition, it is [so] accustomed;
where
it is the custom [to have] a dispensation, it is [so] accustomed.

3. And they rebuffed it (ורמינהו) [by citing the following from m. AZ 2:1]

4. ONE DOES NOT STABLE A CATTLE AT THE INNS OF IDOLATORS,
BECAUSE THEY ARE SUSPECT WITH RESPECT TO BESTIALITY.

5. Said
Rav:
IN A LOCALE WHERE they permitted TO SELL, they permitted to billet
[IN] A LOCALE WHERE they forbade to billet, they forbade TO SELL.

6. But
R. Eliezer
says:

Even IN A LOCALE WHERE they forbade to billet, it is permitted TO SELL.

7. *What is the reason* (מאי טעמא)?

8. An idolator worries that his [own] animal will become infertile.

9. *But even so [must]*

Rav

[have] reversed [his view].

10. *For*

Rav

said the opposite [as well].

11. *Said*

R. Shila b. Abimi

in the name of

Rav:

An idolator worries that his [own] animal will become infertile.

II

1. AND IN ANY LOCALE THEY DO [NOT PERMIT ONE TO] SELL TO THEM LARGE CATTLE, etc.

2. *What is the reason* (מאי טעמא)?

3. *Let it be [assumed]* (נהי) *that*
we do not fear BESTIALITY *[will take place];*

4. *[rather, now]*
we fear that [the idolator] does work *with it [on the Sabbath].*

5. *But*
let it [the animal] be worked [on the Sabbath]!

6. *Since* (כיוון) *[it is the case] that*
[the Israelite] sold it,
[the idolator] has acquired it [and the animal is no longer subject to the laws of the Sabbath].

7. [Rather],
[they instituted] a decree [against the sale of large cattle]
on account of

[cases of idolators] borrowing [the animal and working it on the Sabbath],

and on account of

[cases of idolators] leasing [the animal and working it on the Sabbath, in which two cases the animal is still owned by the Israelite.]

8. [But]

[also in the case of] borrowing *he acquires [possession of] it,*

[and so too in the case of] leasing he acquires [possession of] it.

9. Rather (אלא)

Said

Rami b. R. Yiva

On account of

[cases of selling animals on a] trial [basis];

since

at times when one sells it oneself close to the the setting of the sun on the onset of the Sabbath, and he himself said to him come try it, and he listens to him, and he goes on account of him.

10. But it is alright (וניחא)

that he goes, [is it not?]

11. But

he is driving his animal on the Sabbath.

12. And

he who drives his animal on the Sabbath is liable for a sin-offering [if the act was done in error] (see b. Shab 153b).

13. R. Shisha b. R. Idi

challenged it (מתקיף לה):

14. But

[in the case of] leasing,

who [holds that]

he acquired possession of it [in the first place]?

15. And so we have learned [in m. AZ 1:9]:

EVEN IN THE LOCALE WHERE THEY SAY [THAT IT IS PERMITTED] TO LEASE [A HOUSE TO AN IDOLATOR], THEY DID NOT SAY [THUS IF THE HOUSE WILL BE USED] AS A DWELLING, BECAUSE [THE IDOLATOR] WILL BRING INTO IT AN IDOL [AND THE ISRAELITE WILL THEREBY BE PARTICIPATING INDIRECTLY IN IDOLATRY].

16. And if it should occur to you (ואי סלקא דעתך)
[that in] leasing, [the lessee] *acquired [possession],*
[then in] this [case just cited]
whatever he wishes to bring into his house, let him bring in.

17. Idolatry
differs
in that
it is [a more] severe [case].

18. As it is written [in Deut. 7 and cited in m. AZ 1:9],
"YOU SHALL NOT BRING AN ABOMINATION [I.E., AN IDOL] INTO YOUR HOUSE."

19. R. Isaac b. R. Mesharsheya
challenged it (מתקיף לה):

20. But
[in the case of] leasing,
who [holds that]
he acquired possession of it [in the first place]?

21. And so we have learned [in m. Ter. 11:9]:
AN ISRAELITE WHO LEASED A COW FROM A PRIEST, MAY FEED IT BEANS THAT ARE HEAVE OFFERING;

BUT A PRIEST WHO LEASED A COW FROM AN ISRAELITE—EVEN THOUGH ITS FEEDING IS HIS OBLIGATION, HE MAY NOT FEED HER BEANS THAT ARE HEAVE OFFERING.

22. And if it should occur to you (ואי סלקא דעתך)
[that in] leasing, [the lessee] *acquired [possession],*
[then] why [in case just cited]
should he not feed her [heave offering], [since] the cow [presumably] is his?

23. Rather
learn from this (שמע מיניה)
[that in] leasing, [the lessee] *has not acquired [possession]*

24. And now
that you have said
[that in] leasing, [the lessee] *has not acquired [possession],*
25. [we conclude that]

25.1. [they instituted] a decree [against the sale of large cattle] on account of [cases of idolators] leasing [the animal and working it on the Sabbath],

25.2. [and they instituted] a decree [against the sale of large cattle] on account of [cases of idolators] borrowing [the animal and working it on the Sabbath],

25.3. [and they instituted] a decree [against the sale of large cattle] on account of [cases of idolators buying an animal on a] *trial* [basis and, with the complicity of the Israelite, working it on the Sabbath].

III

1. Rav Ada permitted the sale of an ass by the agency of a broker.

2. [Why could he have permitted it in this case?]

If

[as we have deduced above, they instituted a decree [against the sale of large cattle]

on account of

[cases of idolators buying an animal on a] *trial* [basis and, with the complicity of the Israelite, working it on the Sabbath],

[then] this one [i.e, the Israelite owner who uses the services of a broker]

does not [even] know [the buyer, such that he can] listen to him and go on account of him [and be complicit in driving the animal of the Sabbath].

3. And if

[as we also have deduced above,] they instituted a decree [against the sale of large cattle]

on account of

[cases of idolators] borrowing and leasing [an animal and working the Israelite's animal on the Sabbath],

since

[the animal] is not his [i.e., the broker's, to lend or lease], he does not lend or lease [the animal].

4. And furthermore

[we may conclude in this last case that the broker will neither lend nor lease the animal]

on account of

[the fact] that *he does not [wish to] reveal [to the prospective buyer] any blemish in it.*

IV

1. Rav Huna sold a certain cow to an idolator.

2. Said to him

Rav Hisda:

What is the reason (מאי טעמא)

the master did thus [in apparent violation of m. AZ 1:6]?

3. He [Huna] said to him:
Say [that]

[the idolator] bought it for slaughter.

4. *And whence* (מנא) *will you say that* (תימרא)
we have [so] said [i.e, taught] (דאמרינן)
as in this case (כי האי גוונא)?

5. As we have learned [in m. Shev. 5:8]:

THE HOUSE OF SHAMMAI

SAY:

ONE MAY NOT SELL TO HIM [A NON-JEW] A THRESHING COW ON THE SABBATICAL YEAR;

BUT

THE HOUSE OF HILLEL
PERMIT [SUCH A SALE],

BECAUSE HE [THE NON-JEW] MIGHT [INTEND TO] SLAUGHTER IT.

6. Said

Rabbah:

7. What is similar (מי דמי) *[about the cases]?*

8. There

[in the case just cited] a person is not commanded with respect to causing his animal to rest on the Sabbatical Year;

here

[in the case of Huna's sale of his animal] a person is commanded with respect to causing his animal to rest on the Sabbath.

9. Said to him

Abbaye:

And [is it the case that] everywhere that

a person is commanded [with respect to it] it is forbidden?

10. But, lo,

[consider the case of] a field—for a person is commanded with respect to its rest on the Sabbatical Year—

11. But we have learned (marginal note Vilna ed. emends: as it has been taught) [see t. Shev. 4:5]:

The House of Shammai

say:

A person may not sell a ploughed field [to a non-Jew] during the Sabbatical Year (t. missing: ploughed).

But

The House of Hillel
permit [such a sale],

because he may leave it fallow (t. missing: because … fallow).

12. R. Ashi

challenged it (מתקיף לה):

13. And [is it the case that] everywhere that

a person is not commanded [with respect to it], *it is permitted?*

14. But, lo, [consider]

[agricultural] tools—

for

a person is not commanded with respect to causing [agricultural] tools to rest on the Sabbatical Year.

15. And we have learned [in m. Shev. 5:6]:

THESE ARE THE TOOLS WHICH A PERSON (m. reads: AN ARTISAN) IS NOT PERMITTED TO SELL TO THEM [i.e., TO NON-JEWS] ON THE SABBATICAL YEAR: A PLOW AND ITS ACCOUTREMENTS; A HARNESS; A SEEDER; AND A HOE.

16. Rather

Said

R. Ashi:

Whenever it is possible

to posit (lit.: hang it on) [some extenuating circumstance], we [so] posit,

and [this] even though

one is commanded [explicitly with respect to the matter];

and whenever it is not possible
to [so] posit, we do not [so] posit.
even though
one is not commanded [explicitly with respect to the matter].

V

1. Rabbah sold a certain ass to an Israelite suspected of selling [large cattle] to idolators.

2. Said to him
Abbaye:
What is the reason
the master did thus [in apparent violation of m. AZ 1:6]?

3. He [Rabbah] said to him:
I sold it to an Israelite.

4. He [Abbaye] said to him:
But, lo,
He goes and sells it to an idolator.

5. [Rabbah responded: Does it make sense that]
to an idolator they sell [when one can posit extentuating circumstances],
[but]
to an Israelite they do not sell [lest he in turn sell it to an idolator]?

6. He [Abbaye] responded to him:
IN A LOCALE IN WHICH THEY ARE ACCUSTOMED TO SELL A SMALL CATTLE to Samaritans, THEY [ARE PERMITTED TO] SELL;

[where they are accustomed] NOT TO SELL, THEY DO NOT SELL.

7. *What is the reason* (מאי טעמא)*?*
8. If one says (אילימא)
it is on account of
their being suspect with respect to bestiality,
[then in the view of] whom (ומי)
are they suspect?

9. For (ו)*, lo, it is taught (see t. AZ 3:2 and 3:1, in that order):*
9.1. THEY DO NOT BILLET CATTLE AT THE STABLES OF IDOLATORS (m. AZ 2:1)—

9.2. [neither] male [cattle] with male [idolators],
9.3. and [not] female [cattle] with female [idolators],

9.4. and one need not mention [the obvious cases of]

9.5. female [cattle] with male [idolators],
9.6 and male [cattle] with female [idolators].

9.7. And they do not entrust cattle to their shepherds.

9.8. And they do not leave themselves alone with them

9.9. And they do not entrust a minor child with them so that he will instruct him in the study of books,

9.10 and to instruct him crafts.

9.11. But THEY DO BILLET CATTLE AT THE STABLES OF Samaritans (m. AZ 2:1)—

9.12. [whether] male [cattle] with female [Samaritans],
9.13. and female [cattle] with male [Samaritans],

9.14. and one need not mention [the obvious cases of]

9.15. male [cattle] with male [Samaritans],
9.16. and female [cattle] with female [Samaritans].

9.17. And they do entrust cattle to their shepherds.

9.18. And they do leave themselves alone with them

9.19. And they do entrust a minor child with them so that he will instruct him in the study of books,

9.20. and to instruct him [in] crafts.

10. Therefore (אלמא)

they [Samaritans] are not suspect.

11. But moreover (ועוד)
it is taught (תניא) *(see t. AZ 2:4):*

11.1. They sell to them
11.2. neither weapons,
11.3. nor the accoutrements of weapons,

11.4. And they sell to them
11.5. neither a block [for placing on prisoners' feet],
11.6. nor collars [for placing on prisoners' necks],
11.7. nor leg-irons,
11.8. nor iron chains;

11.9. the same [holds for] an idolator, as [for] a Samaritan.

12. *What is the reason* (מאי טעמא)*?*
13. If we say (אי נימא)
that
they are suspect with respect to shedding of [innocent] blood,
[then in the view of] whom (ומי)
are they suspect?

14. Lo, you have said [as cited above] (see again t. AZ 3:1):
And they do leave themselves alone with them [i.e., Samaritans].

15. Rather
[one does not sell them weapons, etc.]
on account of [the fact] that
[the Samaritan] will go and sell it to an idolator.

16. And if you say (וכי תימא)
[there is a distinction to be made between and Israelite and a Samaritan because] a Samaritan does not do repentance but an Israelite does do repentance,

17. then (ו)*, lo, said*
R. Nahman:
Said:
Rabbah b. Abuhah:
Just as
they said it is forbidden to sell to an idolator,
so too
it is forbidden to sell to an Israelite suspected of selling to an idolator.

18. He [Rabbah, upon learning of the just-cited tradition,] hurried after him [the Israelite to whom he had sold the ass] for a distance of three Persian miles—

19. and there are those who say [that it was]
one Persian mile in the badlands—

20. and he did not meet him.

VI

1. Said
R. Dimi b. Abba:
Just as
it is forbidden to sell [arms] to an idolator,
[so too]
it is forbidden to sell [arms] to bandits.

2. How are [the two cases] comparable (היכי דמי) [i.e., why do we need both]?

3. If
he [the bandit] is suspected of killing,
[then] it is self evident (פשיטא) *that*
these are [i.e., we are dealing with]
idolators [and the second part of the above-cited tradition is not required].

4. And if [it is the case] that
he does not kill [and he is an Israelite],
why
[should one] not sell arms to him [in which case the second part of the above-cited tradition is again not required]?

5. [Indeed, we must] always [assume in this case] (לעולם) *that*
he does not kill [and he is an Israelite],

6. and here [in this case] with what are we dealing (והכא במאי עסקינן)*?*
7. [It is] the case of (ב)
a hold-up, [during which] sometimes he acts to save himself [and may kill or injure his pursuers].

VII

1. Our Rabbis taught:
1.1. They do not sell them [i.e., idolators] shields;

1.2. and there are those who say:
They sell them shields.

2. *What is the reason* (מאי טעמא).
[that they forbid such a sale according to the former opinion]?

3. If [you were] to say (אילימא)
[that it is] on account of [the fact] that
they defend themselves,
4. [then] if so,
even
wheat and barley
also
[should] not [be sold to idolators, since they use them as well to sustain themselves].

5. Said
Rav (Rosh: R. Pappa):
Is it possible (אי אפשר)
[that] here too (הכי נמי)
one can say [the same with respect to]
shields?

6. [Rather] it is this [which is] (היינו)
the reason that (טעמא ד)
it is not [permitted to sell shields to them]—

7. when (דכי)
their weapons are complete[ly used up],
[then]
they kill with them [i.e., with their shields]

8. And there are those who say: They sell them shields—

9. [they hold that] when (דכי)
their weapons are complete[ly used up],
[then]
they surely flee.

10. Said
R. Nahman:
Said
Rabbah b. Avuha:
the law is in accordance with (הלכא כ)
[the view of] those who say [that they do sell shields to them].

VIII

1. Said
R. Adda b. Ahavah:

They do not sell them iron bars.

2. *What is the reason* (מאי טעמא)*?*

3. [It is] on account of [the fact] that
they forge from them weapons.

4. If so
even hoes and pick-axes
also
[should not be sold to them].

5. Said
R. Zavid:
[Indeed, even so] with regard to (ב)
Hindu tools.

6. Said
R. Ashi (n.b.: word order has been emended by myself):
But
In our times we sell to Persians,
7. since
they defend us.

IX

1. CALVES AND FOALS, [etc.] (= m. AZ 1:6, sections E.3-E.4)—

2. *It was taught* (תניא) *(see t. AZ 2:3):*
2.1. RABBI JUDAH PERMITS IN THE CASE OF A MAIMED [ANIMAL] (= m. 1:6, sec. G),
2.2. because it cannot be healed
2.3. and live (sec. 2.3. missing in T.).

2.4. They said to him:
But do they not
have her mounted [by a male], and she gives birth?

3. *And since*
they have her mounted, and she gives birth,
they [the rabbis] came to [opinion of]
delaying it[s transfer of ownership to the idolator].

4. He said to them:
If she [indeed] will give birth !?

5. *Why* (אלמא)
[does R. Judah believe she will not give birth]?

6. She [if maimed] will not receive a male [attempting to mount her].

X

1. BEN BETAYRA PERMITS IN THE CASE OF A HORSE—

2. *It was taught* (תניא) *(see t. AZ 2:3):*

2.1. BEN BETAYRA PERMITS IN THE CASE OF A HORSE,

2.2. with which he does work [on the Sabbath], for which one is not liable for a sin-offering.

2.3. And
Rabbi Judah [the Patriarch]
forbids
2.4. on account of
two things:
2.5. one,
on account of
the teaching regarding the accoutrements of weapons,
2.6. and
the other,
on account of
the teaching regarding large cattle.

3. *Well and good* (בשלמא) *[the reason stated, namely,]*

4. on account of
the teaching regarding the accoutrements of weapons,
5. *[as] there are those that* (איכא ד)
are killed by its kick.

6. *But* (אלא) *[with regard to the other reason stated, namely,]*
the teaching regarding large cattle,
7. *what is [the reasoning of R. Judah the Patriarch]* (מאי היא)*?*

8. *Said*
R. Yohanan:
When it grows old they [hitch it to a mill and] they grind with it [grain] in millstones on the Sabbath.

9. *Said*
R. Yohanan:

The law accords with [the view of] (הלכא כ)
Ben Betayra.

XI

1. *It was asked of them* (איבעיא להו):

2. [In the case] of a fattened ox,
3. *what is [the law regarding] it* (מהו)*?*

4. *Ask of* (תיבעי ל)
5. *R. Judah [and you would get one response].*

6. *Ask of* (תיבעי ל)
7. *Our Rabbis [and you would get another response].*

8. *Ask of* (תיבעי ל)
9. *R. Judah [and you would get one response].*

10. *Thus far* (עד כאן)
R. Judah permitted
11. *only in the case of*
a maimed [animal],
12. *which*
does not fall within the category of [the prohibition with respect to] work [on the Sabbath].

13. *But this one*
[the fattened ox]—
14. *since*
he leaves it [until] it looses sufficient weight to work, and] it does [eventually] fall within the category of [the prohibition with respect to] work [on the Sabbath],
15. it [would be] forbidden[, in R. Judah's view, to sell it to an idolator].

16. *Or perhaps* (או דילמא):
17. even
Our Rabbis *forbade*
18. *in that case*
[i.e., of a maimed animal]
only,
19. *whose*
normal course is other than for slaughter.
20. *But,*
21. *this one*
[i.e., the fattened ox],

22. *whose*

normal course is for slaughter—

23. even

Our Rabbis *[would have] permitted.*

24. *Come and hear* (תא שמע)

25. *that which said*

Rav Judah:

Said

Samuel:

26.1. Those of the House of Rabbi [Judah the Patriarch] used to sacrifice a fattened ox on [i.e., in honour of] their [the Roman's] festival day.

26.2. [Rabbi Judah] deducted [from his revenues] forty thousand [in coin as a bribe] so that they did not sacrifice it on the self-same day, but on the morrow.

26.3. [Later, Rabbi Judah] deducted [from his revenues an additional] forty thousand [in coin as a bribe] so that they did not sacrifice it [i.e., they did not hand it over] alive, but [already] slaughtered.

26.4. [Still later, Rabbi Judah] deducted [from his revenues an additional] forty thousand [in coin as a bribe] so that they did not sacrifice it at all.

27. *What is the reason* (מאי טעמא)

[for Rabbi Judah the Patriarch's actions]?

28. *Is is not on account of [concern that] perhaps*

he [the idolator] will leave it [until it looses sufficient weight to be used as a work-animal and be worked on the Sabbath]?

29. *But according to your reasoning* (ולטעמיך)

30. *[when it states explicitly:]*

so that they did not sacrifice it on the self-same day, but on the morrow—

31. *what is the reason* (מאי טעמא)

[for such a statement]!?

32. *Rather*

Rabbi [Judah the Patriarch] wished to do away with the thing [altogether], and he thought about how to do away [with it], and came [to the view that the best strategy was to have it done away with] little by little.

33. But is it [so] that

one leaves it [the fattened ox] to get strong and one does work [with it]?

34. Said

R. Ashi:

Said to me

Zavida:

[With respect to] a [fattened] ox—we leave leave it [to slim down] and one does the work of two [normal oxen].

The redactional plan and structural formularies of b. AZ 14b-16a

The editors of the Bavli have given us in this passage 11 extended composites or *sugyot*, which together form the semblance of a unified whole, an encompassing, extended composite. That sense of a larger whole appears to derive in part from one of two factors related to content. First, and most obvious, several of the extended composites take as their point of departure, and in turn treat issues deriving from, the subsections of the Mishnah passage *ad locum*. Thus: section I of the Bavli ostensibly comments upon sections A-D of the Mishnah; section II ostensibly comments upon E-F; section IX ostensibly comments upon (E.3-)G; section X takes as its point of departure H. The order and unity of the Mishnah, therefore, lends order and unity to the larger composite of the Bavli. The unity and coherence of the Bavli seem comparable to that exhibited by any more-or-less systematic commentary. Within the sphere of ancient rabbinic texts, the Bavli, in this one particular regard, resembles Tosefta.

But the Bavli is not commentary in any normally understood sense of the term. That is clearly indicated when one considers that only 4 of the 11 subcomposites directly take as their point of departure a section of the m. AZ 1:6. What of the other 7, sections III-VIII and section XI? In addition, each section is itself an extended composite, some as long as 34 units of discourse. Clearly the redactors' forging of a "whole" is only partially accounted for by the borrowed unit of Mishnah. That is to say, the fact that the Bavli is in part formulated as commentary explains only in part the endeavour of the penultimate redactors in creating a "final," "complete" and "unified" oeuvre. Let us first examine points of departure of composites III-VIII and XI in relation to one another and to composites I,II, IX and X (which commence directly with Mishnah). The opening units of the former are key; let me cite them, formatted as above.

Composite #	Opening Units		
III	1. Rav Ada permitted the sale of an ass by the agency of a broker?		
	2. [Why could he have permitted in this case?]		
IV	1. Rav Huna sold a certain cow to an idolator		
		2. Said to him	
			Rav Hisda:
	What is the reason		
			the master did thus?
V	1. Rabbah sold a certain ass to an Israelite suspected of selling to idolators.		
		2. Said to him	
			Abbaye:
	What is the reason		
			the master did thus?
VI	1. Said		
			R. Dimi b. Abba:
		Just as	
			it is forbidden to sell [arms] to an idolator,
		[so too]	
			it is forbidden to sell [arms] to bandits.
	2. How are [the two cases] comparable?		
VIII	1. Our Rabbis taught:		
			1.1. They do not sell them [i.e., idolators] shields
		1.2. and there are those that say:	
			They sell them shields.
	2. What is the reason?		
XI	1. It was asked of them,		
			2. [In the case of] a fattened ox,
	3. what is [the law regarding] it?		
	4. Ask of		
			5. R. Judah.

6. Ask of

7. Our Rabbis.

Sugya III opens in narrative form with a report that a certain authority permitted the sale of a large animal to an idolator by the agency of a go-between. The implied question which generates the remainder of the composite is, By what reasoning could he have done so, given that Mishnah has expressly forbidden the sale of large cattle to idolators? Or to put matters differently, Why might the involvement of a go-between make a difference? The opening of section III, therefore, continues with the theme of section II, namely, the prohibition at E. of Mishnah; III offers an authoritative, ostensibly differing opinion of the law. In addition, in response to the implied question regarding the possible reasoning behind III.1's permissiveness, III.2 and III.3 offer arguments directly refuting reasons posited in composite II for the Mishnah's proscription. In sum, III's "narrative" varies slightly the circumstances of Mishnah E, discussed in II, and in considering answers to the question, "by what reasoning?" considers and rejects two rationales first analyzed in II.

The literary traits which bind III to II redactionally are not, however, bonds of content only. If they were, section III would not have progressed further than III.1., the narrative recounting Ada's ruling. Rather the implied question at III.2. demanded an argument which could be framed in reaction to reasons posed earlier. It is then the *question* (even if implied) *in combination with the introduction of new allegedly authoritative source material* which permits (1) the generation of a new *sugya* (2) meaningfully linked to and contiguous with the preceding composite. Thus it is these essentially structural factors which permit the redactors to weave whatever antecedent materials they possessed into a "unified" whole—both within an individual *sugya* and across *sugyot* to form larger encompassing composites.

A similar analysis of the opening sections of IV and V serve to confirm our claim. IV.1. and V.1. offer "narratives" giving evidence of allegedly authoritative views of rabbis on the issue of selling large animals to idolators. Both "narratives" appear to contradict Mishnah E as discussed at II. Both IV.1. and V.1. are followed by the (formalized and formulaic) question, "What is the reason?" In both cases, the question (only thinly disguised as narrative) invites analyses and arguments. Equally important, within these elaborated *sugyot*, the question, "What is the reason?" and the immediate argument or response is followed by further contradictory or confirmatory sources introduced or followed by stock formularies which demand further analysis.

The *sugyot* at VI, VII and VIII are generated in much the same fashion and similarly linked to the preceding composites. VI-VIII, however, have left the issues of Mishnah E altogether. They are linked to, and contiguous with, III in turning to the cognate issue of selling weaponry to idolators, a matter raised in the "tannaitic" sources cited at III.11 (which parallels t. AZ 2:4). Indeed, the opening unit at VI, in addition, reflects the language and construction of a cognate unit V.17 (and may have even previously circulated with it).

Like the openings of III, IV and V, IX.1 also varies the case of Mishnah E. It does not, however, offer an allegedly authoritative source with a ruling contrary to Mishnah's. Rather IX.1-IX.7 asks how Judah or the anonymous "our Rabbis" would deal with these circumstances given what we know of their opinions as reported in Mishnah and/or in other tannaitic/toseftan traditions, some of which have been cited in the previous *sugya* at X. The structural formulaic, "ask of ... ask of," occasions a rather lengthy composite. Further structural formularies, such as "come and hear," allow the introduction of new sources; "or perhaps" and the now familiar "what is the reason" permit the introduction of new hypothetical rationales for the alleged protagonists.

To summarize our observations thus far, individual *sugyot* when not related to a common Mishnah systematically considered are linked to one another not only thematically but also by structural factors and rhetoric. This is achieved by the citation of an allegedly authoritative source, introduced or followed by a formulary demanding further analysis and, therefore, spawning a new *sugya*. The analysis invited by these structuring formularies also permits returning to arguments of earlier *sugyot* and their testing in the new context.

I might add at this point that, since these formularies are "stock" (they fulfill a similar function thoughout virtually the entirety of Bavli), a great many of the individual *sugyot* and their combination into larger composites represent the work of the penultimate or final redactors. These structural formularies are stock in yet another important sense. It is evident, even upon the limited basis of the passage cited, that they are *termini technici*, for their functional or rhetorical purpose and significance outstrip considerably their literal, discursive, lexical meanings. The structural formulary, "ask of ... ask of...," provides a vivid example. Unlike the question, "what is the reason?" the novice reader of the Babylonian Talmud would certainly have difficulty divining the redactors' intentions in the language "ask of ... ask of...," even if the literal meaning of the clauses poses no difficulty whatsoever. Only having seen the language used in instance after instance does its significance as an invitation to a further particular type of analysis, become apparent.

These interim conclusions concerning the Babylonian Talmud and the role of structural formularies in spawning and forging "the whole" stand out sharply when one compares the Bavli to the Palestinian Talmud, to which I now turn.

3

Bavli's Structural Formularies in Comparative Relief

The previous chapter commenced the analysis of the Babylonian Talmud's rhetoric at the "macro-level"; that chapter examined how the penultimate or final editors used the stock rhetorical formularies and formulae to integrate individual units of discourse or argument into composites (called *sugyot* by traditional students of the Talmud). I explored in particular the manner in which the Talmud's editors creatively used the elements of their rhetoric to "spin out" and to link together *sugyot* into larger encompassing composite essays. What I have called Bavli's "structural formularies" provide its editors with the tools enabling these literary enterprises. A detailed comparison of the Bavli passage examined in the previous chapter with a similarly analyzed section of Palestinian Talmud will, however, facilitate further discussion of character and function of stock structural rhetoric in the Babylonian Talmud. This exercise will serve to highlight the richness of the Bavli's stock of structural formulae and formularies and their role in Bavli's relatively pronounced penchant for spinning out new *sugyot* and larger encompassing composite essays.

To these ends, I turn to the composite in the Yerushalmi (y. AZ 1:6) that also takes m. AZ 1:6 as its point of departure. To permit comparison of the two Talmuds' use of stock rhetorical formularies, I shall endeavour to apply to the Yerushalmi passage the same differentiation of "types" of rhetorical language that I applied to the Bavli. The presentation of the Palestinian Talmud uses the same conventions as the translation of the Bavli: structural formularies appear flush left; dialectical formularies are indented 2 centimetres; the remainder appears 4 centimetres from the left. Hebrew is in Roman type, Aramaic in italics and Mishnah citations in capital letters.

Talmud Yerushalmi, Avodah Zarah 1:6

I

1. What?

And is one permitted to rear [small cattle]?

2. Said

R. Ba:

As is the case of

the Mahir, which is sixteen [Roman] miles by 16 [Roman] miles, [in which district one may rear small cattle].

II

1. They should have said:

2. *The one who said* it is permitted TO SELL [also maintains] it is permitted to billet (emended to: לייחד) [a cattle owed by an Israelite with an idolator]

3. And

the one who said it is forbidden TO SELL [also maintains] it is forbidden to billet.

4. [Said]

R. Yonah:

[Said]

R. Leazar

in the name of

Rav:

And even

in the case of the one who said it is permitted TO SELL,

it would be

[nevertheless] forbidden to billet.

5. And what distinguishes

[endeavoring] TO SELL

from

[endeavoring] to billet?

6. From the moment one sells it to him it is the cattle of the idolator.
7. From the moment he billets it with him, it is [still] the cattle of the Israelite,
8. and he [the idolator] is suspect with respect to it[s treatment].

III

1. [IN] A LOCALE [IN] WHICH THEY ARE NOT ACCUSTOMED TO SELL [SMALL CATTLE] TO THEM, THEY DO NOT [PERMIT ONE TO] SELL.

1. Why?

2. Because

one removes it from the purview [of the laws pertaining to] shearing.

3. Consider (הגע עצמך)

that it was a goat.

5. Because
one removes it from the purview of the laws of the firstling.

6. Consider
that it was a male.

7. Because
one removes it from the purview of the priestly gifts.

9. Henceforth [if this were the reason]
one should not sell him wheat,
10. because
one removes it from from [liabililty for] the dough offering.

11. One should not sell him wine and oil,
12. because
13. one removes them from [liability for] the blessing [said before partaking thereof].

IV

1. [IN] ANY LOCALE THEY DO NOT [PERMIT ONE TO] SELL TO THEM LARGE CATTLE.

2. Why?
3. [In the case of] a large cattle, there is with respect to it [the matter of] liability for a sin offering [as when one uses them to do labour on the Sabbath].
4. But
[in the case of] a small cattle, there is not with respect to it [the matter of] liability for a sin offering [since one does not do labour with small cattle].
5. But
will [the idolator] not milk and will he not shear [small cattle on the Sabbath, an act incurring a sin offering]?

6. *One [can] say:*
7. *there [in the former case],*
it [the animal, by its own labour] is liable.

8. Verily, here
he [by reason of an act which is his only] is liable.

9. Since [i.e., from the moment]
he has sold it to him

is it not

considered the non-Jew's animal [i.e., no longer subject to the laws of the Sabbath]?

10. Said

R. Ami the Babylonian

in the name of

Ravnin:

that there [in the former case, with respect to large cattle]

Sometimes one sells it on trial and he [the idolator] returns it after three days, and it happens that [on the Sabbath] he works an animal which is an Israelite's.

11. Henceforth [if this were the reason]

[selling] on trial [should be] forbidden, when not on trial, [selling should be] permitted.

12. This [,the latter, was forbidden] on account of [fear that the idolator might work the animal on the Sabbath in] that [,the former, case].

V

1. [If] one transgressed and sold [cattle to an idolator], they fine one.

2. Just as

they fine one for [cases in which] the law [forbids such a sale],

so [too]

they fine one for [cases in which] custom [forbids such a sale].

3. And whence (ומנ״ין) [do we learn]

that they fine one for [cases in which] custom [forbids such a sale]?

5. *A certain*

person sold his animal to a Roman.

6. The case

came before

Resh Laqish,

7. And

he fined him double [the value of the animal],

8. so that

[the Israelite] will [feel compelled to arrange that the idolator] return the camel to him.

9. Said

R. Yose b. R. Bun:

10. [he must have fined] the agent, [not the Israelite owner],

11. and

they accused him, this man [of being] the [Israelite] agent of the Romans.

12. [Said]

R. Simeon b. Laqish:

[the foregoing] accords with [the view of]

R. Judah,

13. as it has taught (דתני) (cf. t. Bek. 2:1)

in the name of

R. Judah:

15. He who buys an animal from a non-Jew and it gave birth [and the offspring was] a firstling —

16. they estimate with him its [the firstling's] worth,

17. and

they give half the value to the priest.

18. [If the Israelite] gave it to him in trust,

19. One estimates with him what its value is worth,

20. and

he gives [an amount equal to] all of the value to the priest.

21. And

sages

say:

22. Since

the hand of the non-Jew intervenes,

23. [then]

[the animal has ceased [to be subject to] the law of the firstling (cf. m. Bek. 1:1).

24. [Of] greater [legal weight] than

[the law according to] R. Simeon b. Laqish

is

[the law according to] R. Judah.

25. That which said

R. Judah

[was said] on account of

the laws of the firstling.

26. That which said
R. Simeon b. Laqish
was said] for
the laws of [the sale of] large cattle.

VI

1. R. JUDAH PERMITS IN THE CASE OF A MAIMED [ANIMAL].

2. R. Judah
stated [his view] only (2.1.- 2.3. parallels t. AZ 2:3)
2.1. IN THE CASE OF
A MAIMED [ANIMAL]
which
cannot be healed.

2.2. They said to him:
and is it not [the case] that
he [the non-Jew] brings over to her [the maimed animal] a male, and he mounts her and she gives birth?

3. He said to them:
moreover I stated [my view] only
in the case of a male horse
which
cannot be healed.

4. They said to him:
and is it not [the case] that
[the non-Jew] brings to him a female, and she is mounted by him, and she gives birth?

5. [Said]
R. Abin
in the name of
Ravanim
that there (דתמן)
it is stated that (זאת אומרת ש)
it is forbidden to sell to them [unborn] foeti.

6. *There* (תמן)
we have learned (תנינן) [in m. Bek. 1:1]:
7.1. HE WHO BUYS THE FOETUS OF AN ASS OF A NON-JEW,
7.2. AND HE WHO SELLS TO HIM [THE FOETUS OF AN ASS],
7.3. EVEN THOUGH IT IS NOT PERMITTED,

7.4. AND HE WHO FORMS A PARTNERSHIP WITH HIM [THE NON-JEW],
7.5. AND HE WHO RECEIVES FROM HIM [THE NON-JEW, SUCH A FOETUS IN TRUST],
7.6. AND HE WHO GIVES [SUCH A FOETUS] TO HIM [THE NON-JEW] IN TRUST
7.7. IS EXEMPT FROM THE LAW OF THE FIRSTLING.

8. R. Haggai
inquired before (בעא קומי)
R. Yose:
Does this not state that
it is forbidden to sell them [unborn] foeti?

9. He said to him:
R. Abin
[speaking] in the name of
Ravanin
has already anticipated you:
10. that there (דתמן)
it is stated that (זאת אומרת ש׳)
it is forbidden to sell to them [unborn] foeti.

VII

1. BEN BETAYRA PERMITS IN THE CASE OF A HORSE.

2. Ben Betayra
stated [his view] only
IN THE CASE OF a male HORSE,
3. which
kills its owner in battle.

4. And there are those who say:
which
pursues females.

5. And there are those who say:
which
stands and urinates.

6. What [cases account for] the differences among them?

7. A gelding.

8. [With respect to] the one who says:
which
pursues females —
9. [a gelding] does not pursue [females].

10. But [with respect to] the one who says:
it stands and urinates —
11. even so this one
[i.e., the gelding] stands and urinates.

12. R. Tanhun b. R. Hiyya
[said]:
when they [i.e., horses] do harm [to people] they [idolators] hitch it to millstones [and make the horse work on the Sabbath].

13. [Said]
R. Yose b. R. Bun
in the name of
R. Huna:
Ben Betayra and R. Nathan
have both said [essentially]
the same thing.

14. *As it has taught* (דתני) [in t. Shab. 8(9):34]:
14.1. [If on the Sabbath] one removed [from a private to a public domain] cattle, or (ו) wild beasts, or birds —
14.2. whether alive or dead —
14.3. one is liable [on account of transgressing the Sabbath].

14.4. R. Nathan
says:
[In the case of] dead [ones], one is liable;
14.5. [in the case of] live [ones], one is exempt.

15. And
Our Rabbis —
they are [of the view that]
one is liable for a sin-offering [in the latter case].

16. *But*
[would] they have responded to him [Ben Betayra] (ואינון מיתיבין ליה) *thusly?*

17. In accordance with his approach they responded to him —
18. In accordance with your approach,
19. when you [Ben Betayra] say:
because of
the law of the Sabbath rest [which is not at issue in the sale of a horse to idolators, since riding a horse on the Sabbath is not prohibited by biblical law],
20. then I [would] be [of the view that]

when they [horses] do harm they hitch it to millstones [and the horse is made to do work on the Sabbath in a fashion which is prohibited by biblical law].

21. Rabbi [Judah the Patriarch]
says (see t. AZ 2:3):
21.1. Say I
that it is forbidden
21.2. on account of
two things —
21.3. on account of
[the laws pertaining to the sale of] the accoutrements of weaponry [to idolators],
21.4. and on account of
[the laws pertaining to the sale of] large cattle [to idolators].

VIII

1. And it has taught (דתני) (see t. AZ 2:2):
so [too] is
a large wild beast
like
small cattle [with respect to the matter of selling to idolators].

2. Who taught it (מאן תניתה)?

Rabbi [Judah the Patriarch].

3. [However] the words of
the sages [are]
4.[as]
R. Bisnah
[said:]
R. Hannan b. Bar
[said] in the name of
Rav:
A large wild beast
is like
large cattle [with respect to the matter of selling to an idolator.

Even a cursory reading of this supposedly parallel treatment by the Palestinian Talmud of m. AZ 1:6 serves to reveal the stark differences between the Babylonian and Palestinian texts. First, there appears relatively little in the Palestinian passage which directly corresponds to the extended composite in the Babylonian Talmud. This impression is confirmed by Chart 1 which systematically documents the appearance of parallel units of discourse in b. AZ 14b-16a and y. AZ 1:6. The section numbers in the chart refer to those in the foregoing presentations of the full texts of the passage. In order not to dismiss even the most remote parallel I have highlighted not only passages in both documents which are virtually identical, but also other corresponding units. In the third column I have indicated whether a "parallel" corresponds as well to a passage in the Tosefta. Where a correspondence appears in all three columns we must consider whether the existence of the correspondence between Bavli and Yerushalmi derives from each's independent knowledge of some common repository of "tannaitic" source-passages.

CHART 1: Schematic synopsis of b. AZ 14b-16a and y. AZ 1:6

*	all parallels are noted with an *
bold	signifies virtual identity of parallels (none appear below)
italics	signifies close correspondence between parallels
underlined	signifies more remote correspondence between parallels
NC	signifies no corresponding passage in the other document
(X.1.)	signifies corresponding passage is to be found at location identified as section X.1.
t. AZ 2:3	where corresponding passages in Bavli and Yerushalmi are also paralleled in tosefta, the toseftan passage is noted in the third column

BAVLI	*YERUSHALMI*	*TOSEFTA*
NC	I.1.-I.2.	
I.1.-I.4.	NC	
**I.5.*	*II.1.-II.3.*	
**I.6.*	*II.4.*	
I.7.-I.11.	NC	
NC	II.5.-II.8.	
NC	III.1.-III.12.	
NC	IV.1.-IV.8.	
II.1.-II.5.	NC	
*II.6.	IV.9.	
*II.7.-II.9.(II.24.3.)	IV.10.-IV.12.	
II.10-II.24.2.	NC	
*II.24.3.	(IV.10.-IV.12.)	
NC	V.1.-V.26.	
III.1.-III.4	NC	
IV.1.-IV.16.	NC	
V.1.-V.20.	NC	
VI.1.-VI.7.	NC	
VII.1.-VII.10	NC	
VIII.1.-VIII.7.	NC	

BAVLI	*YERUSHALMI*	*TOSEFTA*
_*IX.1.-IX.2._	_VI.1.-VI.3._	_t. AZ 2:3_
IX.3.-IX.6.	NC	
NC	VI.4.-VI.21.	
*X.1.-X.2.2.	VII.1.-VII.2.	t. AZ 2:3
_*X.2.3.-X.2.6._	_(VII.21.)_	_t. AZ 2:3_
NC	VII.3.-VII.11.	
X.3.-X.7.	NC	
_*X.8._	_VII.12.(VII.20.)_	
NC	VII.13-VII.19.	
(X.8.)	VII.20.	
(X.2.3.-X.2.6.)	VII.21.	(t. AZ 2:3)
X.9.	NC	
NC	VIII.1.-VIII.4.(end)	
XI.1.-XI.34.(end)	NC	

One finds correspondence, whether close or remote, at only nine points. Three instances of the nine may be accounted for by an independent reliance upon a common tradition for which there is a corresponding pericope in Tosefta at t. AZ 2:3. Put differently, of the 151 discrete units making up the 11 *sugyot* of the Bavli passage only 17 have corresponding units of speech in the Yerushalmi. Moreover, 9 of these 17 also parallel Tosefta AZ 2:3. Thus, discounting those units for which one may refer to t. AZ 2:3, only 8 of 151 discrete units in Bavli, a mere 5 percent, have even remote correspondence in Yerushalmi.

If, then, the redactors of the Babylonian Talmud knew the Palestinian Talmud, edited some 100 to 150 years earlier than Bavli, the Babylonian editors have chosen to disregard in large part the work of their Palestinian predecessors.[1] Alternatively, at the other extreme, the Palestinian Talmud was unknown to the editors of the Bavli. Certainly the Bavli's redactional plan and strategies, and the significance and meaning therein implicitly communicated, either did not wholely derive from, or move far beyond those of the Palestinian Talmud.

This latter conclusion is substantiated by a comparison of the structure of *sugyot*, or extended composites, and the use of structural formularies in Bavli and Yerushalmi respectively. Chart 2 provides a structural synopsis of b. AZ 14b-16a and y. AZ 1:6. In both columns structural formularies appear at the left margin.

1. As A.J. Avery-Peck has remarked to me, Bavli parallels the Yerushalmi in terms of its relationship to Mishnah (see Jaffee, 1989). To Avery-Peck's statement I would add: at those junctures where Bavli engages in Mishnah "commentary." Bavli diverges in not being limited to Yerushalmi's more restricted agenda. See also Neusner, 1986b.

CHART 2: Synoptic chart of structure and use of structural formularies in b. AZ 14b-16a and y. AZ 1:6

b. AZ 14b-16a	**y. AZ 1:6**
	I.
	what?
	[question]
	[answer]
I.	II.
is that to say?	
[possible opinion]	
[no]	
[contrary opinion]	
and they rebuffed it	they should have said
[m. AZ 2:1]	
[opinion]	[opinion]
[contrary opinion]	[contrary opinion]
what is the reason?	
[answer]	
but x must have reversed	
[reformulation of x's opinion]	
	what distinguishes [two aforementioned cases]?
	[answer]
	III.
	[citation of m. *ad locum*]
	why?
	[reason]
	[hypothetical case]
	[revised reason]
	[hypothetical case]
	[reason]
	[*reductio ad absurdum*]
II.	IV.
[citation of m. *ad locum*]	[citation of m. *ad locum*]
	why?
	[reason]
	[counter to reason]
	[counter to counter]

what is the reason?	
[assume reason is not]	
[another reason]	
[counter-view]	
[reason for counter]	[new reason]
[new reason for m.]	
[counter to reason]	[counter to reason]
[new reason]	[new reason]

but is it alright?
[circumstances of afore-mentioned reason]
[objection]
[confirming legal view]

x challenged it
[posited circumstances]
[rhetorical question implying opposite view]

and so we have learned
[cites m. AZ 1:9]

and if it should occur to you
[hypothetical view]
[implying opposite view]

it [case at hand] differs
[reason]
[supporting scripture]

x challenged it
[posited circumstances]
[rhetorical question implying opposite view]

and so we have learned
[cites m. Ter. 11:9]

and if it should occur to you
[hypothetical view]
[implying opposite view]

rather
learn from this [i.e., m. just cited]
[probative view]

and now that you have said

[probative view just stated]
[reason for law with respect to case a]
[reason for law for case in m. *ad locum*]
[additional reason for law in m. *ad locum*]

V.
[statement of law complementing m. *ad locum*]
[extension of aforementioned law also complementing m. *ad locum*]

and whence
[the last-mentioned law]?
[story about x's ruling in seemingly similar circumstances]
[rationale appended to story]

[above accords with x]
as it has taught [in name of x]
[citation of parallel to t. Bek. 2:1]
[statement: y's ruling takes precedent over x's]
[statement: legal domain of x's view]
[statement: legal domain of y's view]

III.
[statement of x's view]
[implied surprise re: x's view]
[reason countering x]
[additional reason counter x]
[extension of additional reason also countering x]

IV.
[narrative re: what x did]
[narrative: y asks] what is reason?
[narrative: x gives reason]

and whence will you say that
we have said [thusly]?

as in this case

as we have learned
 [citation of m. Shev. 5:8]

[x:] what is similar
[re: cases]?
 [x's argument establishing difference]
 [y's rhetorical questioning of y's argument]
 [positing of new case, perhaps parallel to above]
but we have learned (emend:
as it has been taught)
 [citation of t. Shev. 4:5]

x challenged it
 [rhetorical questioning previous reason]
 [another comparable case]
 [reason in new case counters earlier case and reason]
and we have learned
 [citation of m. Shev. 5:6]

Rather
 [new reason posited by x]

V.
[narrative re: what x did]
[narrative: y asks] what is
reason?
 [narrative: x gives reason]
 [narrative: y counter-reason]
 [narrative: x offers rhetorical question as counter]
 [narrative: y counters with citation of m. *ad locum*]

what is the reason [for m. *ad locum*]?
 [hypothetical reason]
 [rhetorical question (implying opposite)]
for lo it is taught

[citation parallels
t. AZ 3:2 and 3:1]

therefore

[opposite view to
hypothetical reason]

but moreover it is taught

[citation parallels
t. AZ 2:4 (implies hypothetical reason)]

what is the reason [for last-cited t.]

[hypothetical reason]
[rhetorical question
(implying the opposite)]

Lo you have said

[citation of t. AZ 3:1
(implying opposite)]

Rather

[reason]

And if you say

[hypothetical difference between above
and case of narrative]

then

[a says b says: extrapolation from last-mentioned
reason to case of narrative]

[narrative: x tries to
undo his actions]

[alternative version
of latter]

VI.

Said [x]

[extrapolation from last-mentioned reason to new
case]

How are they comparable (*sic*)
(i.e., why do we need both)?

[hypothetical reason for
new case]
[statement that aforementioned reason superfluous]

[opposite hypothetical
reason for new case]
[rhetorical question implies

law for new case is wrong

always
[last-mentioned hypothetical
reason]
and here with what are we dealing?
the case of
[posits new circumstances]

VII.

Our rabbis taught
[tannaitic source: disputed
statement of law]

what is the reason [for
first-mentioned view]?
[hypothetical reason]
[*regressum ad absurdum*]

said [x]
[rhetorical questioning
of hypothetical reason]
rather
the reason that
[new reason]

[statement of disputants'
view as above]
[reason for latter view]

Said
[x said y: "law accords
with those who say:"
latter view]

VIII.

Said
[x: legal view further
extending views in
previous sections]

what is the reason?
[hypothetical reason]
[*regressum ad absurdum*]

said
[y; extrapolation of aforementioned view]

said
[a: but: opposite legal view]
[extenuating circumstances of present]

IX.	VI.
[citation of m. AZ 1:6, i.e., *ad locum*]	[citation of m. AZ 1:6, i.e., *ad locum*]
It was taught: [citation parallels t. AZ 2:3, citing and glossing m. *ad locum*; + they said to him: rhetorical question]	It was taught: [citation parallels t. AZ 2:3, citing and glossing m. *ad locum*; + they said to him: rhetorical question;]
[question rephrased as reason leading to opposite view, i.e., anonymous view of m.]	
[he said to them: rhetorical question (countering previous rhetorical question)]	[he said to them: revised opinion;]
	[they said to him: rephrased rhetorical question]
why [the last-mentioned opinion-question]? [reason]	
	[said x in name of y: there it is stated: restatement of law at m. Bek. 1:1]]
	There we have learned [citation m. Bek. 1:1]
	[a inquired before b:

	does it not state: restatement of law at m. Bek. 1:1?]
	[he said to him: x and y (above)...: restatement of law at m. Bek. 1:1]
X.	VII.
[citation of m. *ad locum*]	[citation of m. *ad locum*]
it was taught [citation parallels t. AZ 2:3; restates and glosses a named opinion in m.;	[distant parallel to t. AZ 2:3; restates a named opinion in m. *ad locum*]
x forbids, glossed by two reasons]	(See below item marked **)
	[glosses with reason]
	[alternative gloss]
	[alternative gloss]
	what is the difference among them? [statement of case] [statement that one gloss not relevant to case] [argument that another gloss is relevant to case]
well and good [restatement of one of aforementioned glosses]	
[reason]	
But [restatement of other aforementioned gloss]	
what is [the reasoning]?	
said [y: new reason for second view in t. AZ 2:3 cited above (= anonymous	[x: offers new reason for m.'s anonymous ruling] (See ## below)

view of m. *ad locum*)]

[a in the name of b: statement that c (=m's ruling, as cited above in t. AZ 2:3) and d have said the same thing]

as it has taught

[citation of t. Shab. 8(9): 34: anonymous law, d disputes]

[our rabbis are: reason for anonymous law at t. Shab. 8(9):34]

but they [i.e., the anonymous tradent of m. *ad locum*] have responded to him [i.e., the dispute in m., cited above in t. AZ 2:3] [how]?

In accordance with his approach they responded to him

[imputed reason of disputant]

##[counter-argument (= reason for anonymous ruling of m. *ad locum*)]

**[Rabbi says: say I — forbids, glossed by two reasons 9 (= t. AZ 2:3)]

Said

[y: law accords with — named disputant in m. *ad locum*, cited in t. AZ 2:3]

VIII.

And it has taught:

[citation of t. AZ 2:2]

Who taught it?

[name]

[view of sages: as
x said, y in the name of z:
disputing opinion]

XI.

It was asked of them:
 [case]
what [is the law]?

ask of
 [x]
ask of
 [y]

ask of
 [x]

 [statement of x's view
 in other case, as per
 m. *ad locum*]

 [reason]

 [application of reason to
 new case above (see $$
 below)]

 [hypothetical opposite
 attributed to x for new
 case]

Or perhaps

 [y's view in case as
 per m. *ad locum*]

 [hypothetical reason]

 [application of reasoning
 to case at hand]

 [hypothetical opposite
 view attributed to y for
 case at hand]

come and hear:

[that which said a, said b:
narrative: actions of
x (above) in case resembling
the one at hand]

what is the reason [for x's
actions in narrative]?

$$[hypothetical reason
as posited above]

But according to your reasoning—
[cites circumstance from
narrative above]—
what is the reason?

rather
[other, correct reason for
x's actions in narrative
above]

but is it [so] that

$$[hypothetical reason
as posited above]

[said a: autobiographical
narrative: b said to me:
$$ statement of fact
supporting hypothetical
reason as posited above]

The structural synopsis of chart 2 yields several visual impressions. First, with respect to both Bavli and Yerushalmi, the length of individual *sugyot* appears to be highly variable. An actual count confirms this and shows, in addition, that that variation takes place roughly in the same range for Bavli and Yerushalmi. Thus the number of discrete units in Yerushalmi's *sugyot* are in turn: 2, 8, 12, 12, 26, 10, 21, 4 (total 95, mean length of *sugya* 12 units). The 11 *sugyot* of Bavli comprise the following number of units: 11, 26, 4, 16, 20, 7, 11, 7, 6, 9, 34 (total 151, mean length of *sugya* 13 units). Chart 3 categorizes *sugyot* in both Bavli and Yerushalmi with respect to the number of constituent discrete units comprising the *sugya* and provides a count of the number of *sugyot* in each category.

CHART 3. Length of *sugyot* in b. AZ 14b-16a vs. y. AZ 1:6

# of discrete units in sugya	*# of sugyot in category*	
	b.	*y.*
1-5	1	2
6-10	4	2
11-15	2	2
16-20	2	0
21-25	0	1
26-30	1	1
31+	1	0

On the basis of these (albeit limited) data one would be hard pressed to maintain that Bavli tends to have longer *sugyot* than Yerushalmi, although there may be a slight tendency in that direction. In any case, we shall not demonstrate much in that regard with the evidence at hand.

Chart 2, more than chart 1, vividly represents the paucity of direct parallels in the two passages. Correspondence is minimal, at best, for Bavli's composites I, II, IX (which also parallels t. AZ 2:3) and X (which again parallels t. AZ 2:3). Morever, no correspondence whatsoever is evident for Bavli's *sugyot* III, IV, V, VI, VII, VIII, or XI. I take this latter observation to be significant, because these *sugyot* of the larger encompassing composite in Bavli are precisely those that do not take the Mishnah text at m. AZ 1:6 as their point of departure. As a preliminary hypothesis, I would maintain that one of the Bavli's pervasive traits, brought into relief by comparison with Yerushalmi, is the tendency to spin out composites/*sugyot* which distance themselves from the Mishnah text by one or several successive removes. Yerushalmi, by contrast, remains throughout much more closely tied to the particular Mishnah pericope at hand. Indeed, all of Yerushalmi's eight *sugyot* in the passage cited take aspects of m. AZ 1:6 as their point of departure.

Structural factors, especially Bavli's structural formularies and formulae, facilitate not only the creation of individual extended composites but also the spawning, and the binding together into a reasonably coherent whole, of a number of composites, moving successively further from Mishnah's substance. Chart 2 highlights the ubiquity and usage of structural formularies in Bavli. Rhetorical formularies appear frequently (at the left-hand margin) over the entire length of the first column, which charts Bavli. By comparison few formulae appear at the left margins of the second column.

The function of structural formularies and formulae in permitting the spinning out of lengthy series of analyses within an individual *sugya* is aptly demonstrated by that section of chart 2 which deals with Bavli II and its parallel at Yerushalmi IV. Both commence with a citation from m. AZ 1:6. Both open with a request for the reasoning behind the law. Bavli asks, "What is the reason?" while Yerushalmi inquires simply "Why?" Following in both texts is a dialectic analysis of some half-dozen steps. The resulting artificial debate is structured paratactically in both instances; the editors of Bavli and Yerushalmi have simply juxtaposed discrete units. Here Yerushalmi's elaborated composite ends, with 10 discrete units in all, including the Mishnah citation and the initial question. Bavli, however, introduces a series of structural formulae, 11 more in all. Each additional structural formula facilitates two to four more units of dialectical argument. The resulting *sugya* is 26 discrete units in length. The use of stock structural formularies is, therefore, fundamental to the rhetorical structure of the Bavli as devised by its (penultimate) redactors. Were further demonstration required of the relatively important role of structural formularies in Bavli, chart 4 provides relevant evidence.

CHART 4: Catalogue of structural formularies in b. AZ 14b-16a and y. AZ 1:6

b. AZ 14b-16a		**y. AZ 1:6**	
formulary	**#**	**formulary**	**#**
	Demanding a reason		
why?	1	why?	2
what is [the reason]?	1		
what is the reason?	9		
the reason that	1		
but according to your reasoning … what is the reason?	1		
	Challenge inviting further analysis		
but is it alright?	1		
but is it?	1		
is that to say?	1		

x challenged it	3		
and they rebuffed it	1		

Introducing an authoritative source to commence or resolve argumentation

and so we have learned	2	there we have learned	1
as it has been taught	1	as (\and) it has taught	3
for lo it is taught	1		
it is taught	2		
Our Rabbis taught	1		
but moreover it is taught	1		
as we have learned	1		
and/but we have learned	1		
come and hear	1		
lo you have said	1		
(said [x + citation opening elaborated structure])	2		
(said [x + rhetorical questioning or introduction of new view])	6		

Asking for/inviting (further) analysis/argumentation

it differs	1	what?	1
what is similar?	1	what is the difference among them	1
		what distinguishes	1
how are they similar?	1		
and here with what are we dealing? the case of	1		
well and good ... but...?	1		
it was asked of them ...what?	1	but they responded to him how?	1
ask of x, ask of y [as introduction to elaborated structure]	1		
ask of x [as introduction to substructure of elaborated structure]	1		

Introducing an alternative/hypothesis to spark further analysis

Or perhaps	1		
And if you say...then, lo	1	they should have said	1
rather	5		
and now that you have said	1	in accordance with his approach they	

		responded to him	1
and if it should occur to you	2		

Asking for some authoritative basis

and whence will you say that we have said?	1	and whence?	1
		who taught it?	1

Drawing interim or final conclusions

therefore	1		
always	1		
learn from this	1		
but x must have reversed	1		

(figures in parentheses include instances listed above in which "said" appears to function in the Bavli as a structural formulary)

For b: 38(40) structural formularies appear 55(63) times over 151 discrete units;
ratio of variety of formularies/no. of units = .25(.26)
ratio of occurrences/no. of units = .36(.42)

For y: 11 structural formularies appear 14 times over 95 discrete units
ratio of variety of formularies/no. of units = .12
ratio of occurrences/no. of units = .15

Simply put, in comparison with Yerushalmi, Bavli exhibits a far richer catalogue of stock structural formularies and formulae and uses them far more often.

Summary and interim conclusions

On the basis of analyses of b. AZ 14b-16a (in chapter one), of b. Bek. 2a-3b and 3b-5b (in chapter four) and of other passages of the Babylonian Talmud, I have distinguished two broad types of recurrent rhetorical formulaic language. Part and parcel of the grammar and syntax of many of the smallest units of Bavli, dialectical formularies (the subject of the next chapter) determine, even constitute, the modes of reasoning and argumentation within these discrete units. Structural formularies, the focus of this and the previous chapters, tend to stand outside and independent of the grammatical integrity of individual units of thought and argument. They invite the presentation of several discrete units of argumentation in a manner that makes these units seem the elaboration or extension of the antecedent analyses. Many structural formulae and formularies engender as well the introduction of "authoritative sources" other than phrases from the Mishnah passage that seemingly generates a composite "essay." These other "sources" offer points of departure for further analyses, either in relation to the Mishnah passage or in their own right. Hence, structural formularies and formulae facilitate the spinning out of an elaborated analytical composite or *sugya* of sometimes considerable length. Such rhetorical language, to be sure, along with other redactional strategies, permit the elaboration of successive *sugyot* within a larger composite. These *sugyot* will take up issues at nearer or further remove from those of the Mishnah passage ostensibly to be elucidated. Comparison with the Yerushalmi highlights the important role played by structural formularies and formulae in Bavli.

The rich but limited vocabulary of recurrent structural formularies and formulae pervades the Babylonian Talmud. These structural terms, therefore, are the vocabulary of Bavli's final or penultimate redactors. No other hypothesis concerning these formularies' provenance appears more probable, even if it is possible. That being the case, the individual elaborated composites or *sugyot* are also the creation of the final or penultimate framers of the Babylonian Talmud.[2] This must be the case for the larger encompassing composites as well. That the editors possessed traditions from the earlier centuries may be the case; so it is meaningful to talk perhaps of a talmudic tradition. But "talmud," in the generic sense as a mode of inquiry and analysis represented in Bavli's *sugyot* and larger encompassing composites, is the creation of the Talmud, that is, of Bavli's penultimate redactors—or perhaps, as it may now appear more appropriate—Bavli's authors.

The obvious question remains, To what ends, and in service of what social institutions, have the (probably sixth-century) framers of the Bavli undertaken to create "talmud" (a mode of religious virtuosity) through the production of "the Talmud?" What are the sets of meanings implicitly reflected and communicated in this way of going about matters? These issues we shall take up in chapter six, after we have examined in detail Bavli's dialectical formularies.

2. Weiss-Halivni (1986) would agree with this last point.

4

Bavli's Dialectical Formularies

This and the next chapter undertake to analyze the rhetorical formulae and formularies that help create Bavli's smaller literary units, the Talmud's individual statements. In comparison with the previous two chapters I adopt in these chapters a shorter focal length in order to examine the rhetoric of the Babylonian Talmud at the "micro-level." Again the goal is multiple. First, I identify stock rhetorical terms which bind together idiomatic items of content (conveyed in modified subjects, verbs and objects, individual phrases and clauses) into sentences, which themselves exhibit a stock pattern or structure. Second, I document the "types" of patterned sentences which result in terms of the modes of logic or reasoning which these formalized statements display. This two-staged analysis provides a sense of the editors' inventive use of their "authoritative data" in ways which they, and their intended readers, would have deemed cogent and compelling.

Chapter 5 pursues these issues further. By undertaking a similar analysis of representative passages of other, generally earlier rabbinic documents, I provide a number of comparative contexts for the assessment of Bavli's rhetoric at this "micro-level" and of the resulting modes of reasoning. I shall show that at this level Bavli is reminiscent of, or mirrors, much of the rhetorical patterns of these earlier rabbinic texts. This is hardly surprising; most of these texts constitute authoritative tradition for Bavli's editors, who liberally cite and expand upon these antecedent documents or similarly formulated materials. To use creatively these traditions, to extend or to challenge their reasoning and to incorporate them into its own analytic composite essays are part of Bavli's agenda. While at this "micro-level" of rhetoric Bavli often mirrors outright the rhetorical formulae and formularies of earlier rabbinic texts, it exhibits a decided tendency toward certain "types" of rhetoric, in particular in the service of constructing exploratory hypotheses, conjectural conclusions and trial arguments based on comparison and association. Integrated into the context of Bavli's composites, these exploratory and hypothetical argument-statements especially help create in Bavli the air of valuing ongoing critique and analysis. These conclusions, together with the discussions of chapters 2 and 3, pave the way for an examination (in chap. 6) of the social meaning of Bavli's rhetorical traits.

What I have called "dialectical formularies" generally operate at this "micro-level" of Bavli's rhetoric. In chapter one I differentiated two types of recurrent rhetorical formularies which pervade the Babylonian Talmud. One such type, the object of analysis in chapters two and three, I characterized with the adjective, "structural." As we have now seen, such formularies invite argument of a specific sort, but are only loosely connected grammatically to the argumentation which precedes or follows them. Rather they structure and order preceding and subsequent statements and arguments, joining individual parts and providing direction in the creation of a larger literary composition.

In what follows, I examine the character and use in Bavli of that other type of stock rhetorical language, what I have called "dialectical formularies." This class comprises a group of "logical operators" by means of which the very argumentation within an individual, small or primary unit of discourse takes place. These formulaic logical operators are the building blocks of individual argumentational units of thought—producing an argument-sentence.

Again I broach the subject at hand through a detailed charting and analysis of an extended passage of Bavli. But rather than returning to b. AZ 14b-16a, this chapter extends the reader's exposure to Bavli by presenting two other extended composites, b. Bekorot 2a-3b and b. Bekorot 3b-5b. Each passage appears below preceded by that section of Mishnah providing the point of departure for the Talmud's analysis. The presentations of b. Bek. 2a-3b and 3b-5b have been formatted in accordance with the same conventions as the translations in the preceding chapters of passages from the Bavli and the Yerushalmi. Structural formularies appear flush left; dialectical formularies are indented 2 centimetres; the remainder appears 4 centimetres from the left. Hebrew is is Roman type, with Aramaic in italics and Mishnah citations in capital letters.

Babylonian Talmud, Bekorot 2a-3b

Let me summarize the legal presuppositions informing m. Bek. 1:1, b. Bek. 2a-3b and b. Bek. 3b-5b. Underlying earliest rabbinic law on the sanctity and offering of the firstling is a harmonizing of scriptural verses at Ex. 13:2, 11-13; 22:28-29; 34:19-20; Lev. 27:26; Num. 3:13; 18:15-18; and Deut. 15:19-23. Mishnah understands that the firstborn males of all clean animals, that is, those species fit for food and sacrifice, must be given to the priest. If a clean firstling is unblemished the priest pours out its blood upon the altar and sacrifices the fatty portions of the animal.

The remainder is the priest's to consume (in a state of cleanness). If the animal has a blemish making it unfit for the altar, the animal is the priest's to do with as he wishes. The firstborn male of an ass—for Mishnah the only unclean species to which the law of the firstling applies—is redeemed with a sheep or goat. The latter is given to the priest. Should the owner not wish to redeem the ass foal, Scripture requires that the foal's neck be broken. The carcass is buried; no benefit may be derived from it. With this as background I turn to the texts at hand, commencing with m. Bek. 1:1a

m. Bek. 1:1a

1. He who purchases the foetus of an ass of a Gentile, [and the foetus when born will be a firstborn],
2. a. and he who sells to him [the Gentile, the foetus of an ass],
b. even though it [such a sale] is not permitted
3. and he who forms a partnership with him [the Gentile, so that they co-own the foetus],
4. and he who receives [a pregnant ass] from him [a Gentile],
5. and he who gives [a pregnant ass] to him [a Gentile] in trust—
6. is exempt from the law of the firstborn,
7. a. as it said, "Of an Israelite" (Num. 3:13),
b. but not of others.

b. Bek. 2a-3b

I

1. All of these—why would I [require them]?

2. They are required.

3. Since,
if it taught
BUYS,
I would say
that it is because (משום)
he causes her [the she-ass] to enter a state of holiness.

4. *But*
SELLS—
since (ד)
he releases her [the she-ass] from a state of holiness,

say,

"fine him."

5. *[Mishnah] informs us.*

---

6. AND HE WHO FORMS A PARTNERSHIP WITH HIM—

7. *Why would I [require m. to list this case]?*

8. *To exclude*
[the view deriving] from
R. Judah,

9. *who said:*

Partnerships with idolators [still] obligate [the Israelite partner to perform] the law of the firstborn.

10. *[Mishnah] informs us that*

IT IS EXEMPT FROM THE LAW OF THE FIRSTLING.

---

11. AND HE WHO RECEIVES—

12. *Why would I [require m. to list this case]?*

13. *Because*
since
[Mishnah] must teach [the case of]

HIM WHO GIVES TO HIM [THE GENTILE] IN TRUST, [we require its matched pair, the case of he who receives].

---

14. AND HE WHO GIVES TO HIM [THE GENTILE] IN TRUST—

15. *Why would I [require m. to list this case]?*

16. *It is required.*

17. *You might consider saying:*
since (הואיל)

the animal *in essence is the Israelite's,*

[then]

fine him,

18. *Lest* (דלמא)

[the animal] comes to be exchanged for another animal.

19. [Mishnah, therefore] informs us [explicitly concerning this case].

II

1. We learned there [in a m. Pes. 4:3 = m. AZ 1:6]:

2. R. JUDAH PERMITS [in the case of] A MAIMED ANIMAL;
3. BEN BATYRA PERMITS [in the case of] A HORSE.

---

4. It was asked of them:

5. [In the case of]
A FOETUS,
what [relevance] to me is:
"Said R. Judah [...]?"

6. The reason of
R. Judah
there,
[in] which [case]
he permitted
is because
[the animal] is MAIMED;
[here]
THE FOETUS
is MAIMED
also.

7.1. Or perhaps [one must reason as follows]:
7.2. [a case of] A MAIMED ANIMAL
is not
a common occurrence,
7.3. but (אבל)
[in the case of] A FOETUS—
because it is (כיון דהיינו)
a common occurrence,
[therefore]
[the foetus]
is not
[to be considered] MAIMED.

---

8. Come and hear:

9. HE WHO SELLS, EVEN THOUGH IT IS NOT PERMITTED—

10. And

R. Judah
does not dispute [this Mishnah].

11.1. And according to your [i.e., this] reasoning,

HE WHO FORMS A PARTNERSHIP WITH A GENTILE, HE WHO RECEIVES FROM HIM [AN ANIMAL], OR GIVES TO HIM [AN ANIMAL IN TRUST]—

[with regard to] which [cases
R. Judah] does not [explicitly] teach—

11.2. here too
[say that]
he did not dispute.

12.1. Rather [on the contrary,
just as there
[in the first case] he did dispute,
and
did not teach [his view],
so too here
[in the second case] he disputed,
and
did not teach [his view].

---

13. Come and hear [see t. Bek. 2:1]:

14. R. Judah says: He who sells an animal to an idolator, and it gave birth—they estimate its (masc.) value, and he gives half of its (masc.) worth to the priest.

15. And he who gives [an animal] to him [the idolator] in trust, even though it is not permitted—they fine him up to ten times its (masc.) value, and he gives all of its worth to the priest.

16. [For] what [does the penalty apply]?
Is this not [said] concerning
the foetus [a masc. noun]?

17. No, [rather] concerning
the animal [a fem. noun].

18. But lo והא,
it teaches
"its value" (masc.).

19. [Then]

let it [i.e., it should be emended to] teach
"its value" (fem.).

20. *But lo* והא,
it teaches,
"and he gives all of its worth to the priest."

21. *And if*
[it concerns] the animal,
what
has the priest *to do with it?*

21. *What [,then,] are we dealing with here [i.e., what is the case]?*

22. *It is as [in the following case]:*
he gave to him [the Gentile] a pregnant animal to be fattened;
since
we fine him on account of the animal,
[then]
we fine him [too] on account of the foetus.

---

23. *Said*
R. Ashi:
24. *Come and hear [see t. AZ 2:3]:*

25. R. Judah permits in [the case of] a maimed animal,
26. because
it cannot be healed.

27. *Lo,*
[when]
it could be healed,
[then]
he forbade.

28. *And lo*
a foetus
is also like
[an animal]
which
can be healed.

29. *Learn from this [what Judah would say with regard to the case in our Mishnah].*

III

1. Some taught it [the entire preceding text dealing with Judah's view elswhere in the Mishnah] with [direct] reference to our Mishnah[-text; i.e., rather than as given above].

2. AND HE WHO SELLS TO HIM, EVEN THOUGH IT IS NOT PERMITTED—

3. say:
the Mishnah is not in accord with
R. Judah,
4. as we have [been] taught [in m. AZ 1:6 = m. Pes. 4:3]:
R. JUDAH PERMITS IN THE CASE OF A MAIMED ANIMAL.

5. [Alternatively,] even say:
[our] Mishnah is in accord with
R. Judah,
6. [and]
A MAIMED ANIMAL *is not a common occurrence,*
but
A FOETUS *is a common occurrence.*

---

7. Come and hear [see t. Bek 2:1]:

8. R. Judah says: He who sells a animal to an idolator, and it gave birth—they estimate its (masc.) value, and he gives half of its (masc.) worth to the priest.

9. And he who gives [an animal] to him [the idolator] in trust, even though it is not permitted—they fine him up to ten times its (masc.) value, and he gives all of its worth to the priest.

10. [For] what [does the penalty apply] (מאי)?
Is this not [said] concerning
the foetus [a masc. noun]?

11. No, [rather] concerning
the animal [a fem. noun].

12. But, lo (והא),
it teaches
"its value" (masc.)!?

13. [Then]
let it [i.e., it should be emended to] teach
"its value" (fem.).

14.1. But lo (והא),
it teaches,
"and he gives all of its worth to the priest."

14.2. And if
[it concerns] the animal,
what
has the priest *to do with it?*

15. What [,then,] are we dealing with here [i.e., what is the case]?

16. It is as [in the following case]:
he gave to him [the Gentile] a pregnant animal to be fattened;
since
we fine him on account of the animal,
[then]
we fine him [too] on account of the foetus.

---

17. Said
R. Ashi:
18. Come and hear [see t. AZ 2:3]:

19. R. Judah permits in [the case of] a maimed animal,
20. because
it cannot be healed.

21. Lo,
[when]
it could be healed,
[then]
he forbade.

22. And lo, (emended to והא*, as above in sec II.28.)*
a foetus
is also like
[an animal]
which
can be healed.

23. Learn from this [what Judah would say with regard to the case in our Mishnah].

IV

1. It was asked of them:

2. One sold an animal for breeding [lit. for her foeti] —

What [is the law]?

3. [You must] ask of

R. Judah [and you will get one answer];

[you must] ask of

our rabbis [and you will get another].

---

4. [You must] ask of

R. Judah:

5. Hitherto

R. Judah permitted

only in the case of

A MAIMED ANIMAL,

[in] which [case

the issue of] it being exchanged does not enter [into consideration].

But [in the case of]

a whole animal,

which

might be exchanged,

he forbade.

6. Or perhaps [one might argue otherwise.]

Just as

[in the case of]

A MAIMED ANIMAL,

which

is [totally] removed from him [his ownership], [he permitted],

(w) all the more so

[in the case of]

a whole animal,

which

is not [totally] removed from him [his ownership, ie, our case], [he would permit].

7. You [must] ask

our rabbis.

8. Hitherto
our rabbis forbade
only [in the case of]
A MAIMED ANIMAL,
which
is [totally] removed from him [his ownership],
but [in the case of]
a whole animal,
which
is not [totally] removed from him [his ownership, which is the case at hand],
they permitted.

9. Or perhaps,

just as
[in the case of] A MAIMED ANIMAL,
which
does not come to be exchanged,
they forbid,
(ו) all the more so
[in the case of] a whole animal,
which
does come to be exchanged,
[they would forbid].

---

10. And the reason [for]
our rabbis' [view]
is because of this [baraita]:

11. But, lo, it has been taught [see t. AZ 2:3]:
they said to R. Judah: And do they not breed her and she gives birth?

12. Therefore,
it [the reasoning of the rabbis]
is on account of
its [the maimed animal's] offspring.

13. [And] thus they [the rabbis would have] said to him [R. Judah]:

13.1. our reason is
because
it [i.e., the foetus, might] come to be exchanged for [another] animal.

14. But [as regards] you [R. Judah]—
what is the reason

that you have permitted?

15. [Is it not] because
[since]
it [the maimed animal] cannot be healed,
it is like [the case of]
him who sells it [an animal] for slaughter?

16. But is it not [still the case that] (והלא)
they breed her and she gives birth,
17. And since
they breed her and she gives birth,
he retains it [and does not slaughter the animal].

18. And he[, Judah,] would have said to them:
And
would she give birth,
[seeing] that
she does not accept a male [mounting her]?

V

1. Come and hear:

2. HE WHO GIVES AN ANIMAL TO HIM [A GENTILE] IN TRUST.

3. And it did not teach,
EVEN THOUGH IT IS NOT PERMITTED. [Therefore, is it permitted!?]

4.1. But according to your reasoning,
HE WHO FORMS A PARTNERSHIP WITH HIM [THE GENTILE],
[in] which [case] it did not teach
[even though it is not permitted]—
4.2. here too [rule]
that
it is PERMITTED.

5. But, lo,
said
the father of Samuel:
It is forbidden for a person to form a partnership with an idolator, lest he obligate him [to swear] an oath, and he [might] swear to him in the name of his idol.

6. And the Torah said,

"[Do not mention the names of other Gods] and let it not be heard from your mouth" (Ex. 23:13).

7. Rather

[we conclude that the Mishnah] taught

[the law pertaining to] sale,

and so is

the ruling for partnership [with a idolator].

8. So too

[the Mishnah] taught

[the law pertaining to] sale,

and so is

the ruling for [giving over to an idolator in] trust.

---

9. And what is different about

sale

such that

[Mishnah] specified [with regard to it, EVEN THOUGH IT IS NOT PERMITTED]?

10. Since (ד)

the essence [of the legal proscription] is [with regard to] sale[, Mishnah taught the matter explicitly with regard to sale].

VI

1. Come and hear [see t. Bek. 2:1]:

2. R. Judah says: He who receives an animal from an idolator, and the animal gave birth, they assess its [the offspring's] worth and he gives half of its worth to the priest; and he who gives an animal [to a Gentile in trust], even though it is not permitted, they fine him up to ten times its worth, and he gives its entire worth to the priest.

3. And sages say: As long as an idolator has a hand in it, [the animal] is exempt (fem.) from the law of the firstborn.

4. [For] What [does the penalty apply] (מאי)?

5. Is this not [said] concerning
the animal?
6. No, [rather] concerning
the foetus.

7. Construe [the matter] as well
from that which it taught,
"they fine him up to ten times its worth (masc.)."

8. Learn from this [i.e., the argument is conclusive].

VII

1. It [the foregoing] supports [the view of]
Resh Laqish,

2. as
Resh Laqish
said:
He who sells a large animal to an idolator, they fine him up to ten times its value (fem.).

3. Exactly?
Or [perhaps] not
exactly [ten times the value of the animal]?

---

4. Come and hear
that which said
R. Joshua b. Levi:
5) He who sells his slave to an idolator—they fine him up to one hundred times his [the slave's] value.

6. It is different [with respect to]
a slave.
7. Since
daily he [the vendor] releases him [the slave] from [performance of] the commandments.

VIII

1. And there are those who say:

2. said
Resh Laqish:

He who sells a large animal to an idolator—they fine him up to one hundred times its [the animal's] value.

3. [But] we have learned [see above 2b, bottom, in name of R. Judah]:

4. and he who gives his animal in trust, even though it is not permitted—they fine him up to ten times its value.

5.1. [The difference is that]

selling *removes [it] from him [i.e., his jurisdiction,]*

5.2. [while]

placement in trust *does not remove [it] from him.*

---

6. Exactly [ten times],

or

not exactly?

7. Come and hear

8. that which said

R. Joshua b. Levi:

He who sells his slave to an idolator, they fine him up to ten times his value, [suggesting that exactly is intended].

9. [No.]

[The case of] a slave

differs,

[in] which [case

the slave] does not revert back to him.

---

10. [In the case of] an animal—

what is the reason [for the different amount of money]?

11. Because

[the animal] reverts back to him?

12. [In that case, then,]

we should fine him [only] one [unit] more.

13. [No.] Rather

[the issue is something else altogether; the minimal fine in the case of the slave is because the case of] a slave *is an uncommon occurrence.*

14. And [in] all [cases of]

uncommon occurrence, our rabbis did not decree concerning it, [and did not stipulate an increased sum].

IX

1. And the sages say: As long as the idolator has a hand in it, etc. [t. Bek. 2:1, cited above VI.1-3]

2. Said

Rabbi Joshua (Munich: Yohanan):
And both expounded the same verse.

[Namely, "Sanctify unto me] all the firstlings [whatsoever openeth the womb in Israel both of man and of beast is mine]" (Ex. 13:2).

3. Our rabbis

reasoned [as follows]:

"firstling" [alone]

implies

[even] part [ownership] of a firstling;

4.1. [but] the Merciful One wrote [in Scripture]

"all (כל)"

4.2. [in order to imply that one is not liable for the offering of the firstling]

until

he [the Israelite] has all of it.

5. And

R. Judah

reasoned [as follows]:

"firstling" [alone]

implies

[ownership of] the entire firstling;

6.1. [and] the Merciful One wrote [in Scripture]

"all"

6.2. [in order to imply that one is liable for the offering of the firstling]

even if

[one owns] any part of it (כל דהוא).

---

7. [And] If you question [my response], I could say [alternatively]:

8. that everyone [agrees]

"firstling" [alone]

implies

[ownership of] the greater part [of the animal]

9. [one] master (Munich: our rabbis) reasoned [that]

"all" *(משמע missing in Munich) comes to increase it [to complete ownership];*

10. [the other] master (Munich: R. Judah) reasoned [that]

"all" *[comes] to decrease it [to ownership of any part thereof].*

X

1. And to what

should the extent of the idolator's participation be, in order that [the animal] be exempt from the law of the firstling?

2. Said

R. Hunu:
Even an ear.

3. R. Nahman

objected to it:

4. Say to him:

take your ear and go, [that is, an ear is too inconsequential an amount, since the animal would still be alive and healthy, even without the ear].

---

5. It was said that

R. Hisda

said:

[The idolator must own] that which [if removed] would make it carrion [i.e., dead].

6. And

Rava

said,

That which would make it *trefah* (lit., an animal which has been mortally wounded by "tearing," i.e., other than by the slaughterer's knife).

7. About what do they dispute?

8. A living *trefah*.

9. The one who said:
That which makes it *trefah*,
reasoned:
[that the animal which is] *trefah* is not alive. [Therefore, that degree of co-ownership with a Gentile suffices to exempt the animal from the law of the firstling].

10. The one who said:
That which makes it carrion,
[reasoned:]
But
the *trefah* is [possibly still] alive [and therefore would remain subject to the law of the firstling, even if the idolator owned that part.]

---

11. [This is what]
the rabbis
said in the presence of
R. Pappa:
12. This [tradition] of
R. Huna,
(ו) *R. Hisda and Rava*
did not dispute
[Huna]—
13. [Rather]
one [i.e., Huna, deals with]
it [the foetus];
the other[s, i.e., Hisda and Rava deal with]
its mother.

14. Said to them
Rav Pappa:
What difference [does it make whether one deals with]
it [foetus]—
with respect to which we require
"All of the firstling" [to be owned by the Israelite],
and it is not [so],
[or with] its mother,
with respect to which we also require
"all of the flock producing males" [to be owned by an Israelite]
and it is not so?

15. Rather,
there is no difference.

---

16. Mar bar Rav Ashi

objected to it:

17.1. In what way does this differ from

miscarried foeti,

17.2. in which case (d)

even though

they are not living beings, they are sacred? [Therefore, the entire discussion regarding Gentile ownership of that part which if removed would kill the animal appears irrelevant.]

17.3. For the Master has said,

"That which opens the womb (שׁגר) of an animal" (Ex. 13:12),

[meaning anything] which

dwelt (שׁגר) in the the animal.

18. In the latter case

[i.e., Mar bar Rav Ashi's miscarried foetus],

since

profane stuff *is not mixed in [the animals],*

with respect to (ב)

the animal

it is deemed

"every (lit. all) first-born."

19. In the former case

[namely where the Gentile owns part of the animal],

since

profane stuff *is mixed in,*

it is not deemed

"every (lit., all) first-born." *[Therefore, we may learn nothing from the case of a miscarried foetus which is relevant to how much a Gentile may or may not own in partnership with a Jew so as to disqualify the foetus from the law of the firstling.]*

XI

1.1. [The following narrative is told:]

1.2. R. Eleazar [ben Pedat] did not enter the House of Study; he chanced upon R. Asi.

2. He [Eleazar] said to him [Asi]:

What did our rabbis say in the House of Study?

3. He said to him:
Thus said
R. Yohanan [bar Napahah]:
[Gentile ownership of a part which, if removed, would constitute] even a small blemish *[is sufficient to disqualify the animal from the law of the firstling]—*

4. and [as to] what we have learned [at m. Bek. 2:5] (והדתנן)*:*

A EWE WHICH GAVE BIRTH TO A GOATLIKE OFFSPRING, AND A GOAT THAT GAVE BIRTH TO A EWELIKE OFFSPRING, IS EXEMPT FROM THE LAW OF THE FIRSTLING. BUT IF IT [THE OFFSPRING] HAS SOME OF CHARACTERISTICS [OF THE PARENT'S SPECIES], IT IS LIABLE [TO THE LAW OF THE FIRSTLING]—*[What would Yohanan do with the latter clause?]*

5. *[Only when there is]* a permanent blemish *does [the priest] slaughter on account of it.*

---

6. Well and good
[Yohanan's teaching about] a small blemish;

7. it informs us
[of the ruling regarding a small blemish],
in accordance with [the view of]
R. Huna [who claimed that even the Gentile's ownership of a firstling's ear is sufficient to disqualify it],
8. and [comes] to exclude [the view] of
R. Hisda and Rava [who claim that the Gentile must own a part of the firstling upon which the animal's very survival depends, in order for the firstling to be disqualified].

9. But,
[with regard to requiring] a permanent blemish *[in order that the priest be permitted to slaughter the firstling for his own use]—*
10. why
[must the above tradition of Yohanan]
inform us [of the matter]?

11. [If to teach that]
since (דכיון)
[the firstling] is deformed,

it is [to be considered] (הוה ליה)
a blemish[ed animal],
12. [then] we have [already] learned [that from m. Bek. 6:8]:

13. [...] AND ITS MOUTH RESEMBLES THAT OF A SWINE—... LO, THIS IS A BLEMISH.

14. And if you want to say that
there [in m. Bek. 6:8],
[it comes to teach that in the case where] it is deformed with a trait
which
is not of a species
which
is holy
as regards to
the law of the firstling,
15. [while] here, [in the Mishnah above]
[it comes to teach the case of an animal which] is deformed with a trait
which
is of a species holy
as regards
the law of the firstling,

16. lo, we have also [already] learned [that in m. Bek. 6:10] (הא נמי תנינא):

17. [IF] ONE OF ITS EYES IS LARGE, AND ONE IS SMALL [...],

18. and [Mishnah also] taught [at m. Bek. 7:4] (ותנא):

19. LARGE LIKE THE LARGE EYE OF A CALF, AND SMALL LIKE THE SMALL EYES OF A GOOSE.

---

20. Well and good
[the Mishnah's teaching,] SMALL LIKE THOSE OF A GOOSE;
[since]
there is none among its [the goose's] species
which
is holy
as regards
the law of the firstling. *[Therefore Yohanan's teaching based upon Mishnah would still be required for the case of an animal deformed with a trait which is of a species holy as regards the law of the firstling.]*

21. But [it also teaches] (אלא)

LARGE LIKE A CALF'S,

[in which case] there is

among its species

which

is holy

as regards

the law of the firstling. *[Thus we seem not to require Yohanan's teaching based upon Mishnah to teach us the law in the same case.]*

22. But is it not rather (אלא לאו)
in order that we [might] say (משום דאמרינן):

because (כיון)

it is changed

[we consider it to be as though]

it has a blemish,

[and] not [simply] on account of

one having limbs of unequal length, *[and for this latter point we require Yohanan's expounding upon the Mishnah]?*

23. [But] this too may be reasoned [from elsewhere] (הכי נמי מסתברא),

24. as we have learned [in m. 7:1]:

25. THESE BLEMISHES [LISTED PREVIOUSLY WITH RESPECT TO ANIMALS], WHETHER PERMANENT OR TEMPORARY, RENDER [THE PRIEST] UNFIT [FOR TEMPLE SERVICE]: IN ADDITION TO THESE [I.E., THE FOREGOING] WITH RESPECT TO MAN [ADD THE FOLLOWING]: ... [m. 7:4] EYES [LARGE AS A CALF'S OR SMALL AS A GOOSE'S]—

26. [that is, if]

both of them are large [or] both of them are small [i.e., a change from the norm].

27. [But]

with respect to

humankind

it [the foregoing] is [taught,

and not animals],

28. as it is written:

"Any man of the seed (מזרע) of Aaron" (Lev. 22:4)—

29. [indicating] that we require

a man like unto Aaron in his limbs (בזרעו).

30. But (אבל) [as regards]
an animal,
[where]
both are large [or] both are small,
[one might suppose that] it would not in like manner be (נמי לא הוי)
a blemish. *[Therefore we require R. Yohanan's expounding of Mishnah with regard to such changes.]*

XII

1. [As regards the priest slaughtering a firstling if] ONE [EYE] IS LARGE AND ONE IS SMALL—
2. What is the reasoning?

3. If because of
[a simple] change *[from the norm],*
even [if]
both were large [or] both were small
[it would] also
[be considered a sufficient blemish].

4. Rather,
is it not
because
it has limbs of unequal size?

5. No.
Invariably *say:*
because of
[some] change *[from the norm] it is a blemish[ed animal].*

XIII

1. And [with regard to] that which is problematic for you,
[namely, do we require Yohanan's exposition of Mishnah, if] both were large [or] both were small?

2. There [in this latter case],
if on account of
[being] overly fat, both would have to be enlarged,
[and] if on account of
[being] overly thin, both would have to be shrunken [i.e., it is not in either case a genetic defect causing

a simple change, which must, however, be the case when one is large and one is small. Rabbenu Gershom: The question regarding needing Yohanan's exposition in cases of simple changes from the norm still stands].

XIV

1. [There is the case of]

a certain

woman proselyte to whom Achians [i.e., Gentiles] gave an animal to fatten.

2. She came before Rava.

3. He [Rava] said to her:
There are none who concern themselves with that [taught] by
R. Judah,

4. who said,

Partnerships with Gentiles [still] obligate [the Israelite with respect to] the law of the firstling.

5. [There is another case:]

Rav Miri bar Rachel had

these

[pregnant] animals the ears of whose [unborn firstlings] he sold to an idolator,

6.1. And

he forbad the shearing, or working *of them [of the firstlings],*

6.2. and

he gave them to the priests,

7. And

the animals of Rav Miri bar Rachel died.

8.1. And if (וכי)

given that

he forbad the shearing, or working *of them [the firstlings],*

and

he gave them to the priest,

8.2. why

did he sell their ears to an idolator?

9. Perhaps

[he feared that] he may come to [commit] some offence *on account of them, [such as shearing, or*

working firstlings].

10. If so
why

did the animals of Rav Miri die?

11. Because

he removes them from a state of holiness.

12. But, lo,

Rav Judah

said:

One may inflict a blemish in a firstling before it has emerged to [breathe] the world's air—[akin to Miri's sale of their ears before their birth].

13.1. There, [in the latter case,

it is] from the sanctity of the altar *[that] he excludes it;*

13.2. [but]

from the sanctity of the priest[ly dues] *he does not exclude it.*

14.1. Here, [in Miri's case,]
even

from the sanctity of the priest[ly dues] *he excludes it.*

15.1. And if you should question [my response], I could say [alternatively]:

Rav Miri knew how to contract a valid sale,

15.2. but

someone else [less knowledgeable] might see him,

and

might go and do [the same],

and

think [that] Rav Miri['s] words [alone] effected [a valid sale,

and

he would thereby come to [commit] an offence *[since the firstlings' ears would not have in fact become the property of the idolators and so would remain liable under the law of the firstling].*

Babylonian Talmud, Bekorot 3b-5b

m. Bek. 1:1b

1. Priests and Levites are exempt [from the law of the firstling (Rashi: as regards the firstling of an ass)]
2. from an argument *a fortiori*:
3. If [the Levites] redeemed that [animal] of an Israelite in the Wilderness, it is logical that they should [automatically have] redeem[ed] their own.

b. Bek. 3b-5b

I

1. They [themselves]

redeemed [the Israelites' animals]?

2. [No! Rather]

humankind, humankind [i.e., a Levite] redeemed;
3. an animal, a [Levite's] animal redeemed,

4. as it is written

[in Num. 3:45], "Take the Levites instead of each firstborn among the Israelites, and the animals of the Levites instead of their [i.e., the Israelites'] animals."

---

5. Said

Abbaye:

Thus it [should have] said:

[as regards] PRIESTS AND LEVITES—their animals ARE EXEMPT

6. FROM AN ARGUMENT *A FORTIORI*;

7. IF

the animals of the Levites released the animal OF AN ISRAELITE IN THE WILDERNESS,

IT IS LOGICAL THAT

[the Levites animal] should release those of THEIR OWN.

8. Said to him

Rava:

But lo,

THEY [the Levites] REDEEMED—

9. [i.e,] they themselves

it teaches;

10. and moreover,

if it is so,

[one would think that] even with regard to

a clean animal they are exempted.

11. Why [then] did we learn [in m. 2:1]:

12. THEY WERE NOT EXEMPTED REGARDING THE FIRSTLING OF A CLEAN ANIMAL;

13. RATHER [THEY ARE EXEMPT ONLY] REGARDING THE REDEMPTION OF THE FIRSTBORN SON AND REGARDING THE FIRSTLING OF AN ASS?

14. Rather,

said

Rava:

Thus [it should have] said (emended to הכי קאמר):

PRIESTS AND LEVITES redeemed themselves,

15. FROM AN ARGUMENT *A FORTIORI*:

16. IF

the sanctity of the [Rashi: ordinary] Levites released the sanctity OF [Rashi: the firstborn sons of] ISRAEL IN THE WILDERNESS, should they not [effect the]

(Munich: IT IS LOGICAL THAT THEY SHOULD)

RELEASE THEIR OWN [firstborn sons]?

---

17. We have found [an appropriate answer for]

humankind.

18. Whence [do we learn the case of]

the unclean animal?

19. Scripture said [in Num. 18:15 (and compare SifN. 118, ed. Horowitz)]

"But you shall surely redeem the firstborn of humankind, and redeem the firstborn of the unclean animal."

20. Whatever applies in the case of

the firstborn of humankind

applies in the case of

the firstborn of an unclean animal,

21. and whatever does not apply in the case of

the firstborn of humankind

does not apply in the case of

the firstborn of an unclean animal.

---

22. Said

Rav Safra

to

Abbaye:

According to your view,

23. in which you stated,

"their animals" [see section 5 above]—

24. a Levite *who had* a sheep

which (d)

[in the Wilderness] released [the firstling of an ass belonging to an Israelite]—

let it (l)

release [the Levite's own firstlings from requiring redemption];

25. [but

a Levite]

who

did not have a sheep

which

[in the Wilderness] released [the firstling of an ass belonging to an Israelite]—

let it not

release [the Levite's firstlings from requiring redemption].

26. [And]

whether [one considers] your view or

Rava's

[the same reductio ad absurdum holds].

27. [Since,

a Levite with a child] one month old

which

released [an Israelite's firstborn son]—

let it

release [the Levite's firstborn son from requiring redemption].

28. [But

a Levite with a child] less than one month old

which

did not release [an Israelite's firstborn son]—

let it not

release [the Levite's own firstborn son].

---

29. [And]

a woman Levite *[who had a son by an Israelite husband, such sons not having been used in the Wild-*

nerness to redeem Israelite firstlings,]

may not (לא ת)

release [her own firstborn son].

30. Why [then] did

Rav Adda bar Ahavah

say:

31. [Concerning] a Levite woman who gave birth [by an Israelite father to a firstborn son], [the father] is exempt from [payment of] the [redemption money in the amount of] five selas.

32. This [view of Adda's] is not a problem.

33. It is like (כר) [the view of]

Mar the son of Rav Joseph

who [said] in the name of

Rava,

who said:

34. "that which opens the womb" (Num. 3:12; see also Ex. 23:19)—

The Merciful One[, scripture's author,] makes the matter depend upon opening of the womb [of the woman rather than upon the father's eldest male progeny].

---

35. And

Aaron

who

was not [numbered] among the same group [as the Levites]

may not

release [his first firstborn son or the firstlings of his unclean animals]?

36. as it is taught (דתניא):

Why

do dots appear above [the name of] Aaron in the Pentateuch[al passage dealing with] the census [of the Levites]?

37. [To indicate] that

[Aaron] was not [accounted] among the same group.

38. [Rather]
said Scripture,

"The Levites" (Num. 3:41)—
39. [Scripture] likened all the Levites to one another [i.e., likening those who had sons one month old to those who had sons less than one month old, and this deals with all the subsequent cases mentioned above].

40. [And
concerning] priests,
whence [do we learn
the same]?

41. It is like [the view of]
R. Joshua b. Levi.

42.1. As said
R. Joshua b. Levi:
In twenty-one places [in Scripture the priests] are called, "the priests-Levites,"

42.2. and this is one of them:
"And the Priests, the Levites, the sons of Sadoq" (Ezek. 44:15).

43. And
[that this analogy holds] for the [subsequent] generations—
whence [do we learn that]?

44. Said Scripture,
"And the Levites shall be unto Me" (Num. 3:45)—
45. "shall be," [meaning,] in their future existences let them be [God's ministers].

---

46. And from what [do we learn] that
with a sheep *[the Levites redeemed the Israelite's firstlings of an ass]?*

47. Said
Rav Hisda:
Money
is stated (נאמר)
[as the ransom for firstborn sons] for future generations (see Num. 18:16)
and
a sheep
is stated

[as a ransom for the firstling of an ass] for future generations [see Ex. 13:11-16).

48. Just as
[concerning] the money
stated
for [ransom in] future generations—with it they ransomed for future generations [and] and with it they ransomed for that moment [in the Wilderness],
so too
[concerning] the sheep
stated
for [ransom in] future generations—with it they ransomed for future generations [and] with it they ransomed for that moment [in the Wilderness].

49. [No!]
[The analogy from the case of money to that of sheep does not hold.]
What of (מה ל)
money—
[in] which [case] indeed (שכן)
they redeem with it [also] Sanctified Things and Second Tithe!?

50. Rather,

said Scripture,
"You shall surely redeem the firstling of humankind, and the firstling of an unclean beast you shall redeem" (Num. 18:15).
51. Just as
[in the case of] the firstling of humankind you have not differentiated the future generations from that selfsame moment [in the Wilderness, in both of which instances the redemption was effected] with money,
so too
[in the case of] an unclean beast—you may not differentiate with regard to it the future generations from the selfsame moment [in the Wilderness, in which instance the redemption was effected] with a sheep.

---

52. Said
R. Hanina:
A single sheep of a Levite redeemed several firstlings of asses among Israel.

[How do we know this?]

53. Said

Abbaye:

Notice (תידע) that, lo,

Scripture numbered the remainder among humankind [i.e., those Israelite firstborn for whom there were no corresponding Levites were redeemed with money],

but (ו)

did not number the remainder among beasts, [indicating that the inferior number of Levites' sheep must have redeemed a superior number of Israelite beasts].

54. Wherefore (ממאי) [can one draw such a conclusion]!?

55. [For] perhaps

there did not belong to them [i.e., the Israelites] a greater number of animals.

56. It does not stand to reason (לא סלקא דעתך),

57. since it is written (דכתיב),

"Now the sons of Reuben and the sons of Gad had a very great multitude of cattle" (Num. 32:1).

58. [But] Perhaps

even so (אפילו הכי),

the [number of] common [beasts] of [all] the Levites [might have] stood up against these firstlings of Israel.

59. [No!]
Said Scripture,

"And [take] the beast of (read as singular-construct) the Levites instead of their beasts" (Num. 3:44)—[indicating] one beast instead of many beasts.

60. But say, [rather,

that it is like the verse],

"and many beasts" (Jonah 4:11), [in which the singular must be understood as referring to many beasts].

61. If so (אי הכי),

let Scripture have written

"a beast instead of a beast" [with both usages of "beast" understood to be plural],

or

"their beasts instead of their beasts."

62. [So] why,

[write]

"the beast of … instead of their beasts?"

63. Learn from this

[that] one redeemed many, [i.e., each beast of a Levite redeemed several Israelite beasts.]

---

64. Said

Rava:

Even so do we also teach (אף אנן נמי תנינא) [in m. Bek. 1:4]:

AND HE REDEEMS WITH IT MANY TIMES;

and

R. Hanina

[merely] interprets the reason for (טעמא ד...) the Mishnah.

65. And thusly he [should be understood to have] said:

66. What is the reason [for Mishnah's teaching,]

AND HE REDEEMS WITH IT MANY TIMES?

67. Because (משום ד)

A single sheep of a Levite redeemed several firstlings of asses among Israel.

II

1. It is said:

2.1. R. Yohanan

said:

They sanctified the firstlings [R. Gershom: born] in the Wilderness.

2.2. And

Resh Laqish

said:

They did not sanctify the firstlings [R. Gershom: born] in the Wilderness.

3.1. R. Yohanan

said:

They sanctified the firstlings [R. Gershom: born] in the Wilderness,

3.2. since
The Merciful One, [in Scripture] said
to sanctify them,
3.3. as it is written [in Ex. 13:2],
"Sanctify unto me every firstling."

4.1. And
Resh Laqish
said:
They did not sanctify the firstlings [R. Gershom: born] in the Wilderness,
4.2. from that which is written [in Ex. 13:11]:
"And it shall come to pass that when [the Lord your God] shall bring you [into the Land ...];"
4.3. and it is written thereafter [in Ex. 13:12]:
"And you shall cause to pass over [....]"
5. It follows that (מכלל ד)
from the outset (מעיקרא)
[the firstlings were] not holy.

6.1. R. Yohanan
answered
Resh Laqish:
6.2. UNTIL THE TABERNACLE WAS ESTABLISHED THE HIGH PLACES WERE PERMITTED AND [SO TOO WAS] SACRIFICIAL SERVICE BY THE FIRSTBORN (m. Zev. 14:4).

7. He [Resh Laqish] said to him:
[Only] by those [firstborn] who came out of Egypt.

---

8. [And] this also
is reasonable [i.e, self-evident];

9. since if (דאי)
you do not say so,
a one-year old *[firstborn] would be a performer of the sacrificial cult. [Therefore, Yohanan's use of the m. Zev. 14:4 carries no weight, and we learn nothing probative about firstborn born in the Wilderness.]*

10. And he [Yohanan] who raised it [the Mishnah], why did he raise it [altogether] (ודקארי לה מאי קארי לה)?

11. This [is what] was [actually] problematic for him (הכי קא קשיא ליה) [Yohanan, and for which his citing of m. Zev. 14:4 offers a solution]:

12. Well and good,

if you should say (emend to: בשלמא אי אמרת) [that]
since

their [the Egyptian-born firstborn's] holiness does not cease,

[then] these too

[the firstborn born in the wilderness]—from the outset their holiness also was not removed.

13. But (אלא)

if you should say:
that

their [the wilderness born firstborn's] holiness did cease,

[then] these too

[the Egyptian-born firstborn's]—from the outset their holiness [could have been] removed. [And m. Zev. 14:4 tells us that this is not the case, implying that the Wildnerness-born firstborn also were holy from birth.]

14. And the other [authority, Resh Laqish, what would his position be in this context]?

15. [He could say] that

The holy [i.e., Egyptian-born firstborn, remained] holy, and those not holy [i.e., the Wilderness-born firstborn did] not [become] holy [and this too would be consistent with m. Zev. 14:4, which therefore, tells us nothing about Wilderness-born firstborn].

16. He[, Yohanan, could have] replied to him (איתיביה) [citing a baraita from Seder Olam 9:]

The very day that the Tabernacle was set up [was the very day] those among Israel sacrificed [for the first time] vow-offerings and votive-offerings, sin-offerings and guilt-offerings, firstlings and tithes [thus indicating that animal-firstlings born in the wilderness were holy, since firstlings of animals were due for sacrificing when 30 days old and must have, therefore, been born in the wilderness.]

17. [And] so too with regard to (הכי נמי ב)

those [firstlings] who went forth from Egypt [must also have been holy.]

18.1. [And Resh Laqish could retort:]
but from it, [the baraita, one can conclude]

18.2. that very day *they were sacrificed;*
18.3. henceforth they were not sacrificed [—that is, in general firstlings born before entry into the Land were not holy]

19.1. There are those who say:
19.2. Replied
Resh Laqish
to
Rabbi Yohanan [citing a baraita from Seder Olam 9]:
19.3. The very day that the Tabernacle was set up [was the very day] those among Israel sacrificed [for the first time] vow-offerings and votive-offerings, sin-offerings and guilt-offerings, firstlings and tithes—
19.4. [meaning]
that very day,
yes,
henceforth,
no.

20. [No!]
say [the baraita's meaning is:]
from that day *and henceforth [supporting Yohanan against Resh Laqish]*

21.1. And what informs us (ומאי קמשמע לן) [that in reality it means]
from this day *[and henceforth]*
yes,
from the outset,
no—
21.2. [and] therefore
[personal] obligatory sacrifices were not sacrificed [by individual Israelites] on the High Places [before the Tabernacle's construction]?

22. Come and hear (see Mek. deR. Sim., Bo 13:12, eds. Epstein and Melamed, 42):

23.1. You find [from Scripture that] you [may] say:
23.2. In three places were the firstlings sanctified for Israel:
23.3. in Egypt,
23.4. and in the Wildnerness,
23.5. and upon Israel's entry into the Land.

24. 1. With respect to
Egypt,
what does it say?

24.2. "Sanctify unto me every firstling" (Ex. 13:2).

25.1. With respect to
the Wilderness,
it says:
25.2. "For mine is every firstling among the Children of Israel" (Num. 8:17).

26.1. With respect to
their entry into the Land,
it says:
"And it shall come to pass that when [the Lord your God] shall bring you [into the Land ...]; And you shall cause to pass over [...]" (Ex. 13:11-12)[—indicating, in accordance with R. Yohanan's view, that firstlings were indeed sanctified in the Wilderness].

27.1. Said
R. Nahman bar Isaac:
[From these scriptural passages one learns, rather, that] in three places they were exhorted concerning sanctifying the firstlings,
27.2. but they did not [necessarily] sanctify [them until later—supporting Resh Laqish's view].

28. And
in Egypt
also
[firstlings] were not holy?

29. Lo,
we have [had] stated [explicitly] that
they are holy!

30. [Rather,]
this [is what Nahman bar Isaac meant to have] said:

31. [In some] of those [three cases, i.e., Egypt] they sanctified [the firstlings],
32. and [in some] of those [cases, i.e., in the Wilderness], they did not sanctify [the firstlings, and only exhorted their sanctification at a later time—supporting Resh Laqish's view that firstlings were not sanctified in the Wilderness].

---

33. Rav Pappa
objected to it:

34. And

in the Wilderness they did not sanctify [the firstlings]!?

35. But, lo, it is written (והכתיב):

"Count every firstborn male among the Children of Israel" (Num. 3:40)!

36. Rather (אלא) ,
if it has been said (אי איתמר)

[that is, if Yohanan and Resh Laqish have expressed views concerning the sanctity of firstlings born in the Wilderness],

thusly, it has been said (הכי איתמר)

[that is, their views would have had to have been formulated thusly]:

37. R. Yohanan

said:

They sanctified [the firstlings in the Wilderness], and [the firstlings] did not cease [to be sacred].

38. And

Resh Laqish

said:

They sanctified [the firstlings in the Wilderness], and [the firstlings] did cease [to be sacred].

---

39. Well and good, [the reformulated view of]

Resh Laqish,

as (...כד)

he has stated [his] reasoning [above].

40. But with respect to (אלא ל)

R. Yohanan['s reformulated view],

what is the reasoning (מאי טעמא)?

41. Said

R. Eleazar:

R. Yohanan saw in a dream that [he] should give a better interpretation (מילתא מעליתא אמינא) [namely]:

42. Scripture said (אמר קרא):

"[...] shall be unto me" (Num. 3:13)—

43. in their very being they shall be, [that is, they shall continue to be].

44. And

R. Yohanan—

"And it shall come to pass ... and you shall pass over" [the verse supporting Resh Laqish's view]—

what does he do [with this verse]?

45. This [verse] he requires (ההוא מיבעי ליה)

46. in like manner as [that] which is taught by (לכדתניא)

the House [of Study] of R. Ishmael:

["And it shall come to pass ... and you shall pass over"—meaning] do this commandment, on account of which you shall enter [the Land] (see Mek. deR. Sim. Bo, 13:12, eds. Epstein and Melamed, 42).

---

47. Said

R. Mordechai

to

R. Ashi:

You teach it thusly [i.e., as above];

we teach it reversed, [as follows]:

48.1. R. Yohanan

said:

They did not sanctify the firstlings [R. Gershom: born] in the Wilderness.

48.2. And

Resh Laqish

said:

They sanctified the firstlings [R. Gershom: born] in the Wilderness.

49.1. He [Ashi] said to him [Mordechai]:

And did you also change the response [given above of Yohanan to Resh Laqish]?

49.2. And did you [also] change that [tradition] of R. Eleazar [given above]?

50. He [Mordechai] said to him [Ashi]:

[I understand the reformulated tradition as follows:] They did not sanctify [means] they did not have to sanctify [the firstlings as they were already holy] [i.e., the wording of Yohanan's view is preserved so the discussion which follows sections 1-2 above may stand as is.]

51. [Ashi said to Mordechai:]

If so,

it is [in accordance with

our [version] that [your version] comes to teach us [i.e., nothing is served by your more indirect, reversed version].

52. [Mordechai said to Ashi:]

One is obligated to state [a tradition] in the very words of one's teacher.

III

1.1. [The following story is told:]

Kontrokos, the governor,

asked

R. Yohanan b. Zakkai:

1.2. In

the census of the Levites [in Num. 3]

you find

twenty-two thousand, three hundred [Levites, when you add the figures for individual Levitical clans].

1.3. [But] in

totalling them [later on in Num. 3 for the purpose of redeeming Israelite firstborn],

you find

[Scripture giving the figure as] twenty-two thousand.

1.4. And

the [additional] three hundred—
whither did they go?

2.1. He [Yohanan b. Zakkai] said to him:
These

three hundred were firstborn,

2.2. and

a firstborn does not release a[nother] firstborn.

3. What is the reason?

4. Said

Abbaye:
It is enough that a firstborn [Levite] release his own sanctity.

5.1. And again

they [i.e., he, Kontrokos,] asked:
5.2. In

[the account in Ex. 38:25-26 of] the claiming of the silver-coin [i.e., the half-shekel of Temple poll-tax],

5.3. you [should] find

[Scripture giving the total as] two hundred and one talents and eleven maneh, [given the census-figures provided in Ex. 38:26],

5.4. as it is written (דכתיב),
"A beka a head, that is, a half-shekel, by the shekel of the sanctuary, etc" (Ex. 38:26).

5.5. And in
the [account in Ex. 38:27 of the] giving [of the totals] of the silver-coin,

5.6. you find
[Scripture giving the total as] one hundred talents,

5.7. as it is written (דכתיב),
"And the hundred talents of silver were for casting, etc." (Ex. 38:27).

5.8. [Therefore,]
Moses, your Rabbi, was [either] a thief, or a swindler, or he is not competent in calculations;

5.9. he gave half, and took half, and an entire half [of the latter, i.e., 25%] he did not return.

6.1. He [Yohanan] said to him:
Moses, our Rabbi, was a trustworthy treasurer, and he was competent in calculations;

6.2. And
the maneh of the sanctuary were double [the weight of the standard maneh].

7. Went at it [the foregoing] (הוי בה)
R. Ahai

8. What is the problem for him [Yohanan b. Zakkai](מאי קא קשיא ליה)?
9.1. "The one hundred talents of silver for casting, etc." (Ex. 38:27)—
9.2. these (הנך)
[funds were] for casting;
and those (ואינך)
[funds which remained constituted] a treasury [for subsequent use].

10. [But] another verse writes (כתב קרא אחרינא):
"And the silver from those of the congregation who were numbered was a hundred talents [and a thousand seven hundred and seventy-five shekels, by the shekel of the sanctuary]" (Ex. 38:25); [and here

nothing specifies that we are dealing with a one-half only to be used for casting; hence the need for Yohanan b. Zakkai's response as given above in 6.2.]

11. And that [which]

he [Yohanan] said to him [Kontrokos, namely:]

And a maneh of the sanctuary was double [the standard]—

whence does he get it (מנה ליה)?

12.1. If one says

from it [i.e., Ex. 38:28, cited below],

12.2. for lo, there is here [accounted for in Scripture

another] seventy-one maneh [which in standard measure would equal another talent and eleven maneh]—

12.3. "And of the thousand seven hundred and seventy-five he made hooks for the pillars" (Ex. 38:28),

12.4. and [note that]

Scripture counts [nevertheless] in [smaller] units [of a shekel]

only.

13. And if it were [the case]

[that Scripture were using standard measure],

one hundred and one talents and eleven maneh,

it [Scripture] would be required [to read].

14.1. [But] rather,

from the fact that (מדֹ)

Scripture counts [nevertheless] in [smaller] units [of a shekel]

only,

14.2. learn from this (שמע מיניה) [that]

a maneh of the sanctuary was double [the standard]

15.1. But perhaps [on the contrary] (ודילמא)

[for larger] sums [i.e, as for sums of one hundred talents, Scripture] counts in talents,

15.2. [but]

[for smaller] units [i.e., like one talent, Scripture] does not count in talents [but in the smaller units of a shekel, and, consequently, one cannot conclude from this that the maneh of the sanctuary was double the standard].

16. Rather (אלא),
from this (מהכא) [verse one may learn the matter]:

"And the bronze of the waive-offering was seventy talents and two thousand and four hundred shekels" (Ex. 38:29)—

17.1. for, lo,
there is here

[an amount of] ninety-six maneh,

17.2. and

Scripture counts [nevertheless] in [smaller] units [of a shekel]

only.

18. Learn from this

[that] a maneh of the sanctuary was double [the standard]

19.1. But perhaps [on the contrary]

many units [i.e., a significant proportion of one hundred talents, Scripture still] counts in talents,

19.2. [but]

a few units [i.e., a small proportion of one hundred talents, Scripture] does not count in talents.

20.1. Rather,

Said

R. Hisda:

from this [verse one may learn the matter]:

20.2. "And there shall be for you twenty gerah to the shekel, and twenty shekels, and twenty-five shekels, and fifteen shekels to the maneh" (Ezek. 45:12) [60 rather than the standard 25 shekels to the maneh].

21. And lo,

is this [not] two hundred and forty [Rashi, Gershom: dinari, i.e., whence the extra forty above the already doubled maneh]?

22. Rather,
learn from this

[that] a maneh of the sanctuary was double [the standard].

23. And learn from this [too]

[that] they may increase measures,

but

they may not increase [them] more than one-sixth.

24. And learn from this [too]

[that what is meant is] one-sixth of the [new figure] derived [after applying the increase, e.g., in the case above. Forty is one-sixth of 240, not one-sixth of 200, the figure before the increase]

IV

1.1. Said

R. Hanina:

I asked

R. Eleazar [emend to: אלעזר] in the *Great Court* (בבית מותבא רבה):

1.2. What is the difference between the firstlings of asses[, which must be redeemed,] and the firstlings of horses and camels[, which need not be redeemed]?

2. He said to him [in reply]:

It is an edict of Scripture [i.e., there is no logical reason for limiting the obligation to firstlings of asses].

3. And more[over],

[asses are singled out in this regard,]

since

they aided Israel in the hour of their exodus from Egypt;

4. for

each and every Israelite was accompanied by ninety Libyan asses laden with the silver and gold of Egypt.

5.1. And more[over],
I asked:

5.2. What is [meant] by the term, Refidim?

6. And he said to me [in reply]:

Refidim is [simply] its [place-]name,

7. As [two] tannaim [have differently taught] (כתני):

8. R. Eliezer

says:

Refidim is [simply] its [place-]name.

9. R. Joshua

says:

[The place is called Refidim],

since

[there] they loosed themselves from the words of Torah.

10. And so it says [in Scripture]:

"Fathers do not turn their thoughts toward their children—their hands let go" (Jer. 47:3).

11.1. And more[over],
I asked:

11.2. What is [meant] by the term, Shittim?

12. And he said to me [in reply]:

Shittim is [simply] its [place-]name,

13. as [two] tannaim [have differently taught]:

14. R. Eliezer

says:

Shittim is [simply] its [place-]name.

15. R. Joshua

says:

[The place is called Shittim],

since

[there] they occupied themselves with stupidity (see SifN. 131, ed., Horowitz, 170:12,20).

16. "And they called the people to [partake of] sacrifices of their gods" (Num. 25:2)—

17. R. Eliezer

says:

[this implies that] they came to them naked.

18. R. Joshua

says:

[this means that] they made them all unclean [as one who has had a nocturnal emission of semen].

Dialectical formularies in the Babylonian Talmud: B. Bek. 2a-3b and 3b-5b

I have defined dialectical formularies as those recurrent formalized terms which serve as the logical operators binding together discrete pieces of data into a single, coherent argument-statement. They tend to be syntactically part and parcel of the statements that they help constitute. On their own, dialectical operators are usually grammatically meaningless; but without them virtually no intelligible statements would remain.

Before proceeding with an analysis of Bavli's dialectical formularies as shown in my charting of b. Bek. 2a-3b and 3b-5b, I should first like to clarify at the outset what this analysis will not do. Fully appreciating the disclaimer is central to grasping the meaning of the evidence before us. My attempt to identify formularies which might be associated with this ideal type of formalized rhetorical operator in Bavli is intended to provide a useful *analytic* tool in the service of the overall goal of better understanding the use and meaning of formalized rhetoric in the Talmud. In no way do I wish to imply thereby that dialectical formularies, or the argument-sentences which they help constitute, either always or usually derive from one or more antecedent strata of materials which the penultimate redactors have subsequently incorporated, with the aid of their structural formularies, into elaborated composites (*sugyot*) and extended composite "essays." To be sure, other scholars (with other interests) have demonstrated that Bavli's editors have used, often whole hog, antecedent materials (see e.g., Neusner, 1986b). Equally evident, Bavli's redactors have often glossed and otherwise expanded upon antecedent materials (see e.g., Neusner, 1986b), imitating their style and rhetorical forms and formularies. Redactors have freely done this, even as they cite these passages as more ancient, authoritative traditions. All this has been shown, notwithstanding disputes about how and when this transpired, or whether this or that specific passage in the Bavli is an instance of such developments. Furthermore, I do not deny that an analysis of what I have called dialectical formularies can play a part in such literary historical work. My own discussions below can also provide a basis for showing that some of what appears in column 2 is language of materials expressly cited by the redactors as pre-existent authoritative sources. A comparison of the language of these citations with rhetorical forms in surrounding materials may often provide some warrant for accepting the redactors' claim that these cited traditions have been here reproduced (with or without substantial change) from some earlier corpus. However, questions concerning what the penultimate redactors had in their hands in the way of antecedent materials, legitimate as they may be, are not my principal concern. It does not directly serve my ends to decide with Weiss-Halivni (1986), against Kraemer (1990), that argumentative material dates from late fifth- and sixth-century anonymous rabbinic circles (Weiss-Halivni's *stama'im*) and does not represent a sustained mode of discourse which commenced a century or more earlier among the last two generations of Babylonian Amoraic authorities in the later decades of the fourth century. Suffice it to say that sorting out what among the individual units of Bavli's composites is earlier and what stems from later hands is a complex task, which at many junctures will not find a consensus. My own study remains focussed upon the character and meaning of the final product. All I need maintain is that such a final or penultimate product exists and exhibits sustained rhetorical characteristics, among which, to be sure, is the adducing of (modified, forged and real) antecedent sources. This suffices to ground our attempt to decode the meanings (implicitly) communicated in the Bavli's recurrent rhetorical patterns.

Why so assiduously preface my treatment of dialectical formularies by restating these disclaimers about a literary historical agenda that I might be perceived to have? The answer lies in the complexity and variety of rhetorical formularies and usages which my method has churned up in column 2 above. My way of identifying formalized language to be located in column 1 produced in the previous chapter a remarkably self-consistent body of data. Virtually all language in column 1 of the chart of b. AZ 14b-16a appeared in Aramaic (i.e., in italics in the translation). The repertoire and function of such language appeared strikingly limited and consistent, despite the obvious richness in comparison with Yerushalmi. And insofar as that langauge is pervasive in the Bavli, on the one hand, and serves to constitute successively larger elaborated units of the text, on the other hand, I may be confident that I am looking at a feature that communicates the meaning of the text *as a whole* as produced by its penultimate redactors. (A perusal of column 1 of the chart of b. Bek. 2a-3b and 3b-5b will, I might add, only confirm these impressions.) Finally, because items in column 1 are grammatically and syntactically separate from the argument-statements which precede and follow them, it has proven relatively easy to examine them in isolation; I have not yet had to confront the problem of the origin of formulaic language in what might be the Bavli's source-materials.

By contrast, even a quick perusal of column 2 suggests that what I have called dialectical formularies are in fact a variety of items, in Hebrew and Aramaic, appearing in both cited materials and in materials which are portrayed as the voice of the anonymous redactors. Much of the material in column 2 appears integral to, and engendered by, formulae in column 1; but other dialectical formularies seem quite independent, logically or literarily, of the surrounding structural formularies. I am more tempted with respect to many items in column 2 to ask, From what earlier texts and traditions did this come? In this and the subsequent chapter the question I wish to keep in the forefront is different, however: What character and meaning does this type of recurrent rhetoric give to the Bavli, having been located in, or formulated for, its current context?

With these issues in mind, I now wade into the materials in column 2 of the chart of b. Bek. 2a-3b and 3b-5b. In what follows I have regrouped all the materials constituting b. Bek. 2a-3b and 3b-5b with respect to a number of broad categories. These categories have emerged from the evidence of column 2 itself; they describe particular types of literary function discharged by the formulaic language of column 2. Thirteen such categories are suggested by this charted translation. They are:

1. attributional formulae/(contrived) debates;
2. conjectural analytic/argument-statements;
3. associative argument-statements;
4. deduction from stated reason/condition (if/since/because ..., [then] ...);
5. offering a reason for a previously stated view;
6. arguments from general to specific cases;
7. assigning a referent to a source's seemingly superfluous datum;
8. specification of information implicit in an authoritative source;
9. citing a scriptural verse as a prooftext in support of an antecedent position;
10. referring to the content of an authoritative source;
11. differentiating the application or referent of a previously stated opinion;
12. juxtaposing declarative sentences within an analytic argumentative context created by structural formularies;
13. narrative structures.

Since the language of column 2 frequently functions integrally with structural formularies—indeed, the latter often appear to have determined or engendered the former—I have in each instance presented language in column 2 with enough of the rhetorical setting to appreciate and assess the relationship obtaining in any given passage between structural and dialectical formularies. Because I focus upon an assessment of the recurrent formulaic language, I have in the subsequent presentation of passages eliminated altogether materials in column 3 (i.e., the idiomatic content) of the chart of b. Bek. 2a-3b and 3b-5b. Ellipsis points (i.e., ...) mark where these materials interpose among the rhetorical formulae. What remain are schemata of the sections constituting our talmudic text. In all other aspects the schemata replicate the conventions of the full charting of the text. That is, structural formularies appear leftmost (column 1); dialectical and other formularies are further indented 2 centimetres (column 2). As before Aramaic is represented by italics, Hebrew by Roman type.

1. Attributional formulae/(contrived) debates

Given the foregoing discussion, attributional formulae, used to link an opinion or statement to the authority of a named rabbinic sage, provide an apt point of departure. As we shall see, an examination of attributional formularies in column 2 immediately plunges us into the problem of Bavli's use of antecedent sources, for one would expect that the editor of the Bavli wishes us to understand the attributed material as an antecedent authoritative tradition.

As the reader will remember, in some very few instances in the charting and analysis (in chap. 1) of structural formularies in b. AZ 14b-16a, the formulary "said" appeared to play in and of itself a structural role not unlike "but, lo, it has been taught." Far more often, and perhaps by default, in column 2 I have located some half-dozen variations of the attributional formula. That is to say, in most instances the attributional formulae play no role in linking together argument-statements into elaborated composites. Yet they are undoubtedly formulaic and, therefore, to be distinguished from idiomatic content (in column 3).

Appearing in column 2 of the chart of b. Bek. 2a-3b and 3b-5b are:

> R. x says,
> said R. x,
> and R. x says,
> R. x said [that] R. y said,
> R. x said in the name of R. y, or
> as/for/that which/who said R. x.

These formulae may preface independent sayings attributed to authorities of either the tannaitic or amoraic periods. Even when the authority is an Amora, what is attributed to the rabbinic figure may be in Hebrew or in Aramaic. I will leave it to others to debate the incidence and meaning of the use of either language in sayings attributed to figures of the different amoraic generations. Sayings may stand alone as independent pronouncements or may appear as matched but opposing statements, that is, as disputes. With respect to the first four of the six versions of the attributional formula given above, only the context provides a basis for our identifying the formula as Hebrew (Roman type) or Aramaic (italics). Only the last two may be clearly identified as Aramaic. In the case of the fourth, "in the name of" (משמיה ד), Aramaic prevails. In the last of the six the presence of the telltale Aramaic particle, ד ("as"), rather than its Hebrew cognate, שׁ, serves to identify the formula as Aramaic. Here again the modal use is the Aramaic.

The attributions of "traditions" to rabbinic authorities is an obvious feature of rabbinic literature from Mishnah through the Babylonian Talmud and beyond. That is not to say, however, that its meaning and significance is the same throughout. Since the Bavli cites antecedent authoritative sources and traditions (real and, perhaps at times, invented), what is often replicated in the Bavli is the usage in the cited (or mimicked) authoritative source. Thus the terminology sometimes reflects usage in the Mishnah as cited, or in a citation of an extra-mishnaic tannaitic source (a *baraita*). In addition, as one might expect, the citation of amoraic authorities sometimes imitates the usage of attributional formulae in Mishnah or in *baraitot*. Since sorting out these usages will require us to become embroiled in the literary historical agenda, which I had hoped to avoid, I will finesse the issue for the moment in favour of a quite different and common use of attributional formulae in the Bavli. When in the next chapter I will have occasion to compare Bavli's dialectical formularies with the rhetorical formularies of other, and generally earlier, rabbinic documents, I may more profitably return to the nature and meaning of the most common usages in the Bavli of attributional language—this without being seriously sidetracked from our main purposes.

One of the six variations listed above deserves attention at this juncture, because it stands out in terms of its function as indicated by its relation to surrounding language in the Bavli. "As/for/that which/who said R. x," which in our passage appears exclusively in Aramaic, is often engendered by structural language in column 1 or by preceding dialectical formularies in column 2. Typical are:

1. *b. Bek. 3b-5b.I.33 and 41*:
It is like the [view of]
R. x
who said:

2. *b. Bek. 2a-3b.I.7-9*:
Why do I [require m. to list this case]?
To exclude [the view deriving] from
R. x
who said:

3. *b. Bek. 2a-3b.VII.1*:
It [the foregoing] supports [the view of]
R. x
as said
R. x

It is clear from these instances that the attributional formula does not stand alone merely linking the authority's name and cited view. Rather the attributional formula is part of a *structured sequence of formalized rhetoric* which together is *constitutive of, or furthers, an analysis or argument*. The presence in the patterned sequence of structuring language in column 1, that is, language which functions to create elaborated composites (*sugyot*), alerts us that the attributed material is cited, not so much for didactic purposes, that is, to preserve and transmit authoritative traditions, but rather, to analyze, argue and question for its own sake. In this respect, it is, in addition, interesting that in none of these examples furnished by b. Bek. 2a-3b and 3b-5b does "as said R. x" (followed by the attributed view) stand alone as a formula the intent or force of which is to provide an authoritative answer or solution to a question or problem. The attributed material seems not to have the force of precluding questioning or debate, such as might be the case in the following hypothetical structure for a self-contained pericope:

[statement of law]
as said R. x:
[attributed legal opinion as final and conclusive end to pericope].

Readers familiar with the Talmud would find such a pericope odd indeed. They would, I submit, expect something more, some prior and/or subsequent analysis or argument within the context of an elaborated composite. That expectation derives from prevailing characteristics of the items located in column 2 of our chart. Dialectical terms tend not to function as single "stand-alone" operators linking two items of content. Rather, like "... דאמר ר'" ("as said R.x" or "R. x, who said"), individual formulae in column 2 appear within a structured sequence of formulae, forming a formulary. Apart from these structured sequences individual dialectical terms seem mute or meaningless. These sequenced formularies together and almost invariably provide the force of argument or of analysis in the smallest syntactically and grammatically intelligible units—individual argument-sentences.

To be sure, some items in column 2 will not accord with this hypothesis about the norm. But in the majority of such exceptional instances, formulaic language in column 2 falls within cited antecedent sources, whether real or invented. Furthermore, as will emerge from comparative analyses undertaken later in this chapter, the use of formalized language and operators in these latter cases often corresponds to the use of language in other, for the most part earlier, rabbinic documents, the pericopae of which these citations in the Bavli closely resemble in style and character.

To take stock thus far, the use of attributional formulae in Bavli is a microcosm of the issues at hand. Integral to Bavli's purpose is the citation of earlier authorities and sources. Bavli at these junctures more or less faithfully repeats the use of language of the sources. In a more radical vein, one cannot preclude that Bavli "invents" at times such source materials; and when this is the case, Bavli tends to imitate the style and use of language of the mimicked corpus. (That in part is why the task of unravelling the antecedent literary history of Bavli's constituent parts has proven difficult and continues to be ground for considerable scholarly dispute.) On the other hand, the last in the list of variations of the attributional formula has pointed to another important sustained characteristic of the Bavli's use of language outside of cited sources, whether real or invented: formulaic language serves in structured sequences to constitute argument and analysis, with certain materials providing the appropriate grist for the analytic mill.

These very preliminary assertions about the nature and function of what I have called dialectical formularies in the Bavli prepare us for another formulaic use of "said," namely as signposts or joining language in (contrived) debate. Common in our evidence is the formulary,

> he said/would say to him/to you (אמר ליה/אמר לך),

as in the following:

4. *b. Bek. 2a-3b.XI:*
1.1. [The following narrative is told:]
1.2. R. ...did not ....
2. He said to him:
...?
3. He said to him:
Thus said
R. ...: ...—
4. and [as to] what we have learned [in the m. elsewhere] (והדתנן):

5. *b. Bek. 2a-3b.XIV:*
1. [There is the case of] a certain
....
2. X
came before
R ....
3. He said to her:
There are none who concern themselves with that [taught] by
...,
4. who said,
....

6. *b. Bek 3b-5b.I:*
Thus it [should have] said:
[reworded ver. of m. *ad locum*]
6. FROM AN ARGUMENT *A FORTIORI*;
7. IF
...,
IT IS LOGICAL THAT
....
8. Said to him
R.x ...:
But lo,
[citation of m. *ad locum*]—
9....

7. *b. Bek. 3b-5b.II:*
1. It is said:
2.1. R. f(Palestinian Amora)
said:
....
2.2. And
R. g(Palestinian Amora)
said:
....
3.1. R. f
said:
...,

3.2. since
The Merciful One, [in Scripture] said
to ...,
3.3. as it is written [in Ex. 13:2],
....

4.1. And
R. g
said:
...,
4.2. from that which is written [in Ex. 13:11]:
....;"
4.3. and it is written thereafter [in Ex. 13:12]:
...
5. It follows that (מכלל ד)
from the outset (מעיקרא)
....
6.1. R. f.
answered
R. g:
6.2. (m. Zev. 14:4).
7. He [g] said to him:
....

8. *b. Bek. 3b-5b.II:*
47. Said
R. k
to
R. Ashi(R. l):
You teach it thusly;
we teach it reversed:
48.1. (48.1-2 reformulate sec. 1-2 above)
R. f
said:
....
48.2. And
R. g
said:
....
49.1. He said to him:
And did you also ...?
49.2. And did you ...?
50. He said to him:
[I understand the reformulated tradition as follows:] ....
51. [He said to him:]
If so,
it is [in accordance with
our [version] that [your version] comes to teach us ....

52. [He said to him:]
One is obligated ... teacher.

9. *b. Bek. 3b-5b.III*
1.1. [The following story is told:]
m,
asked
R. n (Tanna):
1.2. In
...[in Num. 3]
you find
....
1.2. [But] in
... [later in Num. 3],
you find
....
1.3. And
....—...?
2.1. He [R. n] said to him:
These
...,
2.2. and
....
3. What is the reason?
4. Said
Abbaye:
....
5.1. And again
they [i.e.,m,] asked:
5.2. In
[Ex. 38:25-26] ...,
5.3. you [should] find
...,
5.4. as it is written (דכתיב),
(Ex. 38:26).
5.5. And in
[Ex. 38:27] ...,
5.6. you find
...,
5.7. as it is written (דכתיב),
(Ex. 38:27).
5.7. [Therefore,]
Moses ...;
5.8. [since] he ....
6.1. He [R. n] said to him:
Moses ...;
6.2. And

....

7. Went at it [the foregoing] (הוי בה)

R. o

8. What is the problem for him [R. n](מאי קא קשיא ליה)?

10. *b. Bek. 3b-5b.IV*:

1.1. Said

R. e(Tanna):

I asked

R. p(Tanna) in the *Great Court*:

1.1. ...?

2. He said to him:

....

3. And more[over],

...,

since

...;

4. for

....

5.1. And more[over],
I asked:

5.2. ...?

6. And he said to me:

...,

7. As [two] tannaim [have differently taught] (כתני):

In examining the seven passages cited, two quite distinct usages in column 2 of the formulary—"he (/I) said (/would say) to him (/you/me)"—immediately emerge. First, the language used within a narrative context. Here the verb, "said to," is part of the action and of the other stock devices which mark or establish the character of the passage as a narrative. These latter include some reference to a definite setting, time or protagonist. Thus "certain" persons "ask" R. x—that is, at a particular moment. Or an event took place "in the Great Court." Or R. x happened on a certain day not to attend the session with his master and encounters a fellow disciple. Thus where the "action" of a story includes a repartee, the formulary is part of the stock cues which maintain the narrative scenario. In the examples, this usage is internal to a largely independent unit (or to what is portrayed as an independent unit) incorporated by the redactors into the elaborated composite to serve the larger quite distinct ends of the latter. The tendency is to "tell stories" about tannaitic figures in Hebrew and about amoraic figures (especially of the latter generations) in Aramaic. I will return to narratives and their formulaic language later in this chapter.

The second usage of the formulary under discussion does not correlate at all with other linguistic patterns serving to mark the repartee as representing some historical encounter. Rather it serves, *together with more elaborate or explicit structural rhetoric* (which our charting would place in column 1), to emphasize the valence of what will follow as a counter argument or alternative analysis for one or another of two rabbinic figures whose opinions have already been reported in some cited tradition. In this sense, its provisional location in column 2 is a matter of default. For without accompanying structural formularies in column 1, I would have located such usages of "x said to y" together with what I have called structural formularies. Whether standing on its own to "spin out" a *sugya* from an antecdent cited tradition or, where such structural language is already present, providing additional valence as "rebuttal" to the analysis or argument to follow, it is clear that this formulary is part of the rhetoric establishing the Bavli's character as sustained argument and analysis. In this regard it is noteworthy that this "debate formulary" usually is in Aramaic (as indicated by the surrounding language), even when the initial views of protagonists have just been reported in a cited Hebrew source or tradition. It is as if the editors would alert us to a change in the "voice" of the unfolding analytic composite or *sugya*—as if to say, "Thus far the data was provided by the source, henceforth our own analytic agenda takes over and it is we, the talmudic redactors, who speak for the originally cited authorities." It is this change in voice that creates the urge to translate such uses of the debate formulary in the subjunctive mode. In other words, this is what R. x could have said in reponse to R. y.

My perusal of attributional formulae provisionally located in column 2 has highlighted the methodological and conceptual issues with which I commenced this chapter's discussion. Some of what is in column 2 speaks in the rhetoric of antecedent sources, cited (or mimicked) by the Bavli and incorporated into its *sugyot*. At other times, the voice of the Bavli's redactors is reflected in such rhetorical formularies. In the latter instances, overwhelmingly in Aramaic, formulae tend to act with others in a structured sequence providing the syntax of argument or analysis for a unit of discourse. Minimally, these formularies emphasize the tenor of that unit as argument or analysis. This characterization of the nature and function of the formulaic language which I have located in column 2 will be further borne out as I review of the remainder of the evidence provided by the chart of b. Bek. 2a-3b and 3b-5b.

2. *Conjectural analytic/argument-statements*

Common among Bavli's sequenced patterns of rhetorical formularies in evidence in column 2 are those which help constitute a conjectural statement. Such conjecture usually follows upon, and analyzes, some antecedent question or problem. The conjecture may build upon a hypothetical circumstance or upon a posited reason for an antecedent legal statement or source. Examples are:

1. *b. Bek. 2a-3b.I:*
   1. All of these —why would I [require them]?
   2. They are required.
   3. Since,
   if it taught
   ...,
   I would say
   that it is because (משום)
   ....
   4. *But*
   ...—
   since (ד)
   ...,
   say,
   ....
   5. [Mishnah] informs us.

2. *b. Bek. 2a-3b.I:*
   15. Why would I [require m. to list this case]?
   16. It is required.
   17. You might consider saying:
   since הואיל
   ...
   [then]
   ...,
   18. lest דלמא
   ....
   19. [Mishnah, therefore] informs us [explicitly concerning this case].

3. *b. Bek. 2a-3b.XI:*
   9. But,
   ...—
   10. why
   inform us [of the matter]?
   11. [If to teach that]
   since (דכיון)
   ...,
   it is [to be considered] (הוה ליה)

...,

12. [then] we have [already] learned [that from m. Bek. 6:8]:

13. ....

4. *b. Bek. 2a-3b.XI:*

30. But (אבל) [as regards]

...

[where]

...,

[one might suppose that] it would not in like manner be (נמי לא הוי)

....

5. *b. Bek. 2a-3b.XII:*

2. What is the reasoning?

3. If because of

...,

even [if]

...

[it would] also

[...].

4. Rather,
is it not

because

...?

6. *b. Bek. 2a-3b.XIII:*

1. And [with regard to] that which is problematic for you,

...?

2. There [in this latter case],

if on account of

...,

[then]

...

would have to be

...,

[and] if on account of

...,

[then]

...

would have to be

....

7. *b. Bek. 3a-5b.I:*

10. and moreover,

if it is so,

[one would think that] even with regard to

...

8. *b. Bek. 3a-5b.II:*

8. [And] this also
is reasonable [i.e, self-evident];
9. since if (דאי)
you do not say so,
....

9. *b. Bek. 3b-5b.II:*

11. This [is what] was [actually] problematic for him (הכי קא קשיא ליה):
12. Well and good,
if you should say (emend to: בשלמא אי אמרת) [that]
since
...,
[then] these too
....
13. But (אלא)
if you should say:
that
...,
[then] these too
....

10. *b. Bek. 3b-5b.III:*

11. And that [which]
he [R. n] said to him [m, namely:]
...—
whence does he get it (מנה ליה)?
12.1. If one says
from it [Ex. 38:28],
12.2. for lo, there is here
...—
12.3. (Ex. 38:28),
12.4. and [note that]
...
only.
13. And if it were [the case]
...,
it [Scripture] would be required [to read].

At first glance the ten items listed above might appear to comprise a rich and diverse array of types of arguments and analyses suited for quite different purposes, despite their common feature as conjectural. A closer look, however, reveals that whatever the varied duties and despite the quite different types of subject matter treated, most of the excised passages are dependent upon a remarkably limited, almost exclusively Aramaic vocabulary of formularies. Due to their appearance as a carefully and relatively consistently structured sequence, they constitute a single "core logic." This core is used with a considerable variety of content. The core formulaic vocabulary is:

one/you/I (might) say
if
since/because/on account of
it would/would not be
you/I would say
even/also/only

To be sure, not all of these formulaic logical operators are used in any one argument-sentence. The precise combination will depend upon the subject matter. Enough of the formulary must be present, however, in order to provide a sequence of logical operators which, with the idiomatic content, will produce a counterfactual conditional statement. That is, "if it were the case that ..., then it would be the case that ...." The use of the subjunctive in the English rendition indicates that the first condition is not in fact the case. If, for example, that condition is a reason or rationale for an antecedent opinion, then "since" or "because" will be required after "if."

When one isolates the "core" of such conjectural argument or analytic statements and the limited formulaic repertoire upon which it is built, one understands that the resulting statements cannot stand alone. They demand some previously defined problem, on the one hand, and some subsequent resolution, on the other, for which the counterfactual conditional is meant to be a false start. Such false starts cut off certain avenues, leaving open others in the contemplation of possible resolutions. The hypothetical conclusions of the counterfactual conditional sentence are either self-evidently absurd or contravene an allegedly unassailable source, such as a passage of Mishnah. Because the "core logic" constituted by this structured sequence of formulae assumes both antecedent and subsequent analyses, they now begin to appear to be integral to the dialectical or dialogical character of the immediate and larger composites in which they appear. That is to say, the counterfactual conditional argument-statements and the precise choice and variation of the formulary constituting the core logic of these statements seem dependent upon the redactor's plan for the encompassing *sugya* and upon the structural formularies which serve to construct the *sugya*. In virtually all instances these formularies are cast in Aramaic, in the text's own voice.

3. Associative argument-statements

The structured sequence of dialectical formulae most often encountered in the charted passages of the b. Bek. 2a-3b and 3b-5b serves to constitute an argument-statement which draws a conclusion from the comparison of two items. The general menu of formulae which generate the logic of such statements is:

> If/Just as
> there/with regard to [item a]
> which [characteristic b]
> [c is/is not the case],
> here too/with regard to/ this is also like [item a']
> which/because [characteristic b']
> [c' is/is not the case]
> also.

Either characteristics of a and a' bear a relation to one another such that a and a' are to be associated and treated alike. Or the traits of a and a' are sufficiently different that a and a' are to be treated differently. In other words, the association is either positive or negative. As with the previous class of sequenced formulae, it is difficult to conceive of such an argument-statement standing on its own. Minimally, the statement assumes antecedent data and some anterior problem (implicit or explicit) in order to be intelligible. The precise nature of the problem, together with the data supplied, will determine the choice made from the menu of available formularies. But whatever the choice deemed appropriate, one finds again a structured sequence of stock operators which together define the logical syntax of the unit of thought. I now review the examples provided by the charting of b. Bek. 2a-3b and 3b-5b.

1. *b. Bek. 2a3b.II (twice):*

4. It was asked of them:
5. [In the case of]
...,
what [relevance] to me is:
"Said R. ...?"
6. The the reason of
R. ...
there,
[in] which [case]
...

is because

…;

[here]

…

also.

7.1. Or perhaps [one must reason as follows]:

7.2. …

is not

…,

7.3. but (אבל)

…—

because it is (כיון דהיינו)

…,

[therefore]

[…]

is not

….

2. *b. Bek. 2a3b.II (twice):*

8. Come and hear:

9. [m. *ad locum*]

10. And

R. …

….

11.1. And according to your [i.e., this] reasoning,

…—

[with regard to] which [cases]

…—

11.2. here too

[say that]

…

12.1. Rather [on the contrary,

just as there

…

and

…,

so too here

…,

and

….

3. *b. Bek. 2a3b.II (repeated verbatim at III.18-23):*

24. Come and hear [see t. AZ 2:3]:

25. …,

26. because

….

27. Lo,

[when]

…,

[then]

....

28. And lo

...

is also like

[...]

which

....

4. *b. Bek. 2a3b.IV (twice):*

4. [You must] ask of

R. ....:

5. Hitherto

R. ...

only in the case of

...,

[in] which [case]

....

But [in the case of]

...,

which

...,

....

6. Or perhaps [one might argue otherwise.]

Just as
[in the case of]

...,

which

...,

(w) all the more so
[in the case of]

...,

which

....

5. *b. Bek. 2a3b.IV (twice):*

7. You [must] ask

our rabbis.

8. Hitherto

our rabbis ...

only [in the case of]

...,

which

...,

but [in the case of]

...,

which

...,

....

9. Or perhaps,

just as

…,

which

…,

…,

all the more so

…,

which

…,

[…].

6. *b. Bek. 2a3b.V (twice):*

1. Come and hear:

2. [m. *ad locum*].

3. And it did not teach,

….

4.1. But according to your reasoning,

…,

[in] which [case] it did not teach

[…]—

4.2. here too [rule]

that

….

5. But, lo,

said

R. …:

….

6. And the Torah said,

… (Ex. 23:13).

7. Rather

[we conclude that the m.] taught

…,

and so is

….

8. So too

[the m.] taught

…,

and so is

….

7. *b. Bek 2a3b.VII:*

1. It [the foregoing] supports [the view of]

R. …,

2. as

R. …

said,

….

3. …?

Or [perhaps] not

…?

---

4. Come and hear

that which said

R. …,

5. ….

6. It is different [with respect to]

….

7. Since

….

8. *b. Bek 2a3b.VIII:*

7. Come and hear

8. that which said

R. …:

….

9. [No.]

…

differs,

[in] which [case]

….

9. *b. Bek 2a3b.X (thrice):*

14. Said to them

R. …:

What difference [does it make whether one deals with]

…—

with respect to which we require

…,

and it is not [so],

…,

with respect to which we also require

…,

and it is not so?

15. Rather,

there is no difference.

16. R. …

objected to it:

17.1. In what way does this differ from

…,

17.2. in which case (d)

even though

…!?

17.3. For the Master has said,

(Ex. 13:12),

[meaning anything] which

….

18. In the latter case,

since

…,

with respect to (ב)

…

it is deemed

….

19. In the former case,

since

…,

it is not deemed

….

10. *b. Bek 2a3b.XI:*

14. And if you want to say that

there [in m. Bek 6:8],

…

which

…

which

…

as regards to

…,

15. [while] here, [in the m. above]

…

which

…

as regards

…,

16. lo, we have also [already] learned [that in m. 6:10] (הא נמי תנינא):

17. …,

18. and [m. also] taught [at m. 7:4] (ותנא):

19. ….

11. *b. Bek 2a3b.XI:*

20. Well and good

[m.'s teaching,] …;

[since]

…

which

…

as regards

…

21. But [it also teaches] (אלא)

…,

[in which case] there is

…

which

…

as regards

....

12. *b. Bek 2a3b.XI:*

23. [But] this too may be reasoned [from elsewhere] (הכי נמי מסתברא),

24. as we have learned [in m. 7:1,4]:

25. ...—

26. [that is, if]

....

27. [But]

with respect to

...

it [the foregoing] is [taught],

28. as it is written:

(Lev. 22:4)—

29. [indicating] that we require

....

30. But (אבל) [as regards]

...

[where]

...,

[one might suppose that] it would not in like manner be (נמי לא הוי)

....

13. *b. Bek 3b-5b.I:*

17. We have found [an appropriate answer for]

...

18. Whence [do we learn the case of]

...?

19. Scripture said [in Num. 18:15] (see t. Bek. 1:2; Sifre Num. 118; Sifre Zutta to Num 18:15)

[Num. 18:15].

20. Whatever applies in the case of

...

applies in the case of

...,

21. and whatever does not apply in the case of

...,

does not apply in the case of

....

14. *b. Bek 3b-5b.I (twice):*

22. Said

R. z

to

R. y:

According to your view,

23. in which you stated,

... [section 5 above]—

24. …

which

…—

let it

…;

25. [but]

…

who

…

which

…—

let it not

….

26. [And]
whether [one considers] your view or
R. x's
[…].

27. [Since,]

…

which

…—

let it

….

28. [But

…

which

…—

let it not

….

15. *b. Bek 3b-5b.I (three times):*
46. And from what [do we learn] that
…?

47. Said
R. d:

…

is stated (נאמר)

…(see Num. 18:16)

and

…

is stated

…(see Ex. 13:11-16).

48. Just as

…

stated

…,

so too

…

stated

....

49. [No!]

[...]

What of (מה ל)

...—

[in] which [case] indeed (שכן)

...!?

50. Rather,
said Scripture,

(Num. 18:15).

51. Just as

...,

so too

....

Over the course of b. Bek. 2a-3b and 3b-5b, such associative analytic statements appear 26 times in 15 separate passages. That is, there is a pronounced tendency for doublets. Where this is the case, structural formulaic language (in column 1) links two opposing similarly formulated associative argument statements. This fact may prove significant, especially when considered in light of the aforementioned observation that these statements generally require some antecedent data and statement of the problematic, again set out with the help of structural formularies. I take this to mean that once more the reader is intended to hear in the associative arguments the voice of the Bavli, with its now familiar penchant for the pursuit of analysis as much for its own sake as for reaching any final conclusion.

The overwhelming preference for Aramaic in these passages is related to our claim that in these associative arguments the reader is intended to perceive the final redactors' agenda. In 11 of the 15 passages, that is, in 20 of the 26 instances, associative analytic statements appear in Aramaic. Of the remaining six within four passages, one, number 13 (at b. Bek 3b-5b.I.17-21), might properly be said not to be an associative analytic statement at all. For that passage states that an association is to be made, but does not actually spell out the association and its upshot. Only the context provides the basis (which is in Scripture) for the assimilation of the two cases and the practical consequences of such an association. (Interestingly, b. Bek. 3b-5b.I.20-21 parallels language at t. Bek. 1:2 and SifN. {Korah} 118.) Perhaps it is significant that at example 15, another Hebrew passage in the list, Scripture again provides the basis for the triplet of associative argument statements. In the other two instances, the Hebrew relative pronominal prefix ("which"/ש) appears. However, the words to which they are prefixed are themselves Hebrew cultic *termini technici*. Perhaps it may have grated on the ear to use an Aramaic prefix with Hebrew terminology. In the final analysis the overwhelming tendency toward Aramaic remains, and may be related to other factors, already noted, which serve to alert the reader to the presence of the Bavli's own voice—and, therefore, agenda.

4. Deduction from stated reason/condition (if/since/because ..., [then] ...)

In the four passages displayed below, the text attempts to deduce the unknown from a stated premise where the latter is a reason or rationale. In a sense, such an argument may be viewed as a highly truncated and laconic version of an associative argument-statement. For inherent in the logic of the passages which follow is the association of the unknown aspect of the case at hand with some other case for which the comparable information is known. Since the same reason or rationale informs both cases, one may reliably associate or assimilate the two cases. Virtually everything that I have said earlier of associative arguments applies to the passages at hand, which I present without further discussion.

1. *b. Bek. 2a-3b.II (twice) (repeated at III.14-17):*

20.1. But lo והא,

it teaches,

....

20.2. And if

...,

what

...?

21. What [,then,] are we dealing with here [i.e., what is the case]?

22. It is as [in the following case]:

...;

*since (*דמיגו*)*

...,

[then]

....

23. Said

R. ...:

2. *b. Bek. 2a-3b.IV:*

14. But [as regards] you [R. ...]—

what is the reason

that

...?

15. [Is it not] because
[since]
…,
it is like [the case of]
…?
16. But is it not [still the case that] (והלא)
…,
17. and since
…,
….
18. And he [R. …] would have said to them:
And
…,
[seeing] that
…?

3. *b. Bek. 2a-3b.XI:*
22. But is it not rather (אלא לאו)
in order that we [might] say (משום דאמרינן):
because (כיון)
…
[we consider it to be as though]
…,
[and] not [simply] on account of
…?
23. [But] this too may be reasoned [from elsewhere] (הכי נמי מסתברא),
24. as we have learned [in m. 7:1,4]:
25. …—
26. [that is, if]
….

5. *Offering a reason for a previously stated view*

In eight passages a statement or opinion is married to a simple rationale or reason with "because" or "since." The relevant examples from b. Bek. 2a-3b and 3b-5b follow.

1. *b. Bek. 2a-3b.I:*
11. [citation of m. *ad locum*]—
12. Why would I [require m. to list this case]?
13. Because
since
[Mishnah] must teach [the case of]
….

2. *b. Bek. 2a-3b.IV:*
10. And the reason [for]

our rabbis

is because of this [baraita]:

11. But, lo, it has been taught [see t. AZ 2:3]:

…?

12. Therefore,

…

is on account of

….

13. [And] thus they [the rabbis would have] said to him [R. …]:

13.1. our reason is

because

….

3. *b. Bek. 2a-3b.V:*

9. And what is different about

…

such that

[m. specified] …?

10. Since (d)

….

4. *b. Bek. 2a-3b.VIII:*

10. …—

what is the reason?

11. Because

…?

12. [In that case, then,]

….

13. [No.] Rather

….

5. *b. Bek. 2a-3b.XII (twice):*

4. Rather,

is it not

because

…?

5. No.

Invariably *say:*

because of

….

6. *b. Bek. 3b-5b.IV:*

1.1. Said

R. e(Tanna):

I asked

R. p(Tanna) in the *Great Court*:

1.2. …?

2. He said to him:
....
3. And more[over],
since
...;
4. for
....

7. *b. Bek. 3b-5b.IV:*
7. As [two] tannaim [have differently taught] (כתני)*:*
8. R. q(Tanna)
says:
....
9. R. r(Tanna)
says:
...,
since
....
10. And so it says [in Scripture]:
(Jer. 47:3)

8. *b. Bek. 3b-5b.IV:*
13. as [two] tannaim [have differently taught]:
14. R. q(Tanna)
says:
....
15. R. r(Tanna)
says:
since
...(see SifN. 131).

16. (Num. 25:2)—
17. R. q(Tanna)
says:
....
18. R. r(Tanna)
says:
....

In five of the eight passages, formularies which aid in proffering a reason or rationale appear in Aramaic. In the last three, Hebrew prevails. In the latter passages, "since" appears within an independent source cited by the Bavli's redactors. The cited tradition in passage 7 and that of passage 8 match one another in form, language and issues. No doubt they have been previously formulated together, or one has spun out the other.

The literary characteristics of the last three passages contrast with the rhetorical traits in evidence in the first five. In no instance among the first five does one find simply a statement of view linked by "since" or "because" to the rationale. Rather, always immediately present and integral is structuring language (in column 1) which sets the reason in the context of some explicitly stated analytic problem. Furthermore, for the most part the rationale, once given, is never the end of matters. Rather, the rationale invokes further editorial comments regarding its sufficiency; sometimes this is achieved by providing an alternative solution (introduced by other stock formulaic language). In other words, providing a rationale with the formulary "since" or "because" seems integral to, and intelligible within, a context defined by other structural and dialectical rhetoric of the Bavli. Here rationales are not probative reasons glossing immediately antecedent opinions. They are, rather, part of the sustained analytic agenda of the unfolding composite.

This sharply contrasts with the last three (Hebrew) passages. In these latter pericopae, "since" is not immediately associated with any rhetorical language in column 1. Moreover, the only language appearing in the immediate vicinity in column 2 are attribitional formulae.

6. *Arguments from general to specific cases*

In one passage one finds the deduction of a stance with regard to a specific case by locating the latter within a more general encompassing category. The rule for the general is said to apply to the specific or subcategory. Little may be made from a single example.

1. *b. Bek. 2a3b.VIII:*
   13. [No.] Rather
   ....
   14. And [in] all [cases of]
   ....

7. *Assigning a referent to a source's seemingly superfluous datum*

In six instances within four passages, the Bavli engages in argument founded upon a type of source criticism. An apparently superfluous datum in the source is assigned a possible referent. The datum is understood either to limit or to extend the application of some law supported or enjoined elsewhere in the source. Authoritative sources may be Scripture, Mishnah or some other rabbinic tradition.

The general form of such argument is:

[source datum a]
implies
[conclusion b]
only
the Merciful One wrote
[source datum a']
implies/includes/excludes/learn from this
[conclusion b']

As we shall see in our schemata, the selection from among the dialectical operators listed above depends upon the nature of the source—for example, Scripture is cited with specific formulae—as well as the immediate larger context which the argument serves. As we have seen throughout this chapter, that context is constructed through the use of structural formulae which precede, follow and interpose between stock dialectical operators.

1. *b. Bek. 2a-3b.I:*

6. [citation of m. *ad locum*]—
7. Why would I [require m. to list this case]?
8. To exclude
[the view deriving] from
R. …,
9. who said
….
10. [Mishnah] informs us that
….

2. *b. Bek. 2a-3b.IX (three times):*

2. Said
R. …, "And both expounded the same verse."
[Namely,] ….
3. Our rabbis
reasoned [as follows]:
…
implies
…;
4.1. [but] the Merciful One wrote [in Scripture]
…
4.2. [in order to imply]
until
….

5. And

R. ...

reasoned [as follows]:

...

implies

...;

6.1. [and] the Merciful One wrote [in Scripture]

...

6.2. [in order to imply]

even

....

7. If you should question [my response], I could say [alternatively]:
8. That everyone [agrees]

...

implies

...;

9. [one] master (Munich: our rabbis) reasoned [that]

...;

10. [the other] master (Munich: R. Judah) reasoned [that]

....

3. *b. Bek. 2a-3b.XI:*

6. Well and good

[R. ...'s teaching] ...;

7. it informs us,

in accordance with [the view of]

R. ...,

8. and [comes] to exclude [the views] of

R. ... and R. ....

9. But,

...—

10. why
inform us [of the matter]?

4. *b. Bek. 3b-5b.III:*

14.1. [But] rather,

from the fact that (מדּ)

...

only,

14.2. learn from this (שמע מיניה) [that]

....

15.1. But perhaps [on the contrary] (ודילמא)

The rhetorical formularies throughout are Aramaic. In three instances, all contained in passage 2, the authoritative source is Scripture. The assumption is that *if* one's view relates to a biblical law, then one must use *all* relevant biblical passages for something. But the tenor of the rhetorical language, which once again includes dialectical terms integral to a context established with the aid of structural formularies, is decidedly one of theoretical or conjectural analysis. For no single meaning seems attached to any one verse. Rather, hypothetical scriptural grounds are explored for several rabbinic authorities' views, with an eye to seeing whether it is possible to impute to each authority a coherent position. The process is entirely academic, in the colloquial sense of the word. Even when one has constructed two coherent sets of use of Scripture for the two rabbinic protagonists, the elaborated composite immediately attempts to explore another possiblility of achieving the same.

A similar approach seems present in passage 1. Here Mishnah, not Scripture, is at issue. All of Mishnah's language is seen as both necessary and sufficient; the analytic agenda is to show how. At item 3, the necessity of a particular rabbinic (amoraic) tradition is considered. Indeed the entirety of the elaborated composite at b. Bek. 2a-3b.XI deals with possible alternative solutions to the problem posed by the seemingly superfluous character of a dictum attributed to the Amora, R. Yohanan.

The last example differs and is listed here by default. The datum in Scripture which provides the authoritative ground for the argument is not so much superfluous as overly (and therefore perhaps needlessly) specific. As with all of the other instances, the "proof" at hand is but one of a sequence of possible solutions to a problem, each one in turn subjected to criticism on one grounds or another. That sequence, constructed with the aid of structural formularies, comprises the larger context which this passage, with its dialectical language, has been formulated to serve.

8. Specification of information implicit in an authoritative source

Some 14 times in 11 passages a citation of a source (overwhelmingly Scripture) is followed by an interpretative gloss. The citation and the gloss support an antecedent argument, analysis or statement within some larger immediate context. In all these instances no logical operators or attendant argument is necessary to establish the legitimacy of moving from what Scripture says to what the gloss maintains Scripture means. That meaning is taken as *self-evidently* implicit in the Scripture. Stock joining language usually interposes between the citation and the interpretative gloss, giving us the form:

For the Master has said/as it is written/from that which is written
[Citation a]
which/that we require/it follows that from the outset/for lo there is here
[meaning b]
only.

As always, the choice of formulae to be used at any one instance depends to a great extent upon the larger, immediate content. As before, Bavli's structural formularies play a significant role in constituting that encompassing literary environment.

Of the 11 passages schematized below, nine appear in b. Bek. 3b-5b; only two may be found in b. Bek. 2a-3b. That this is the case hardly seems surprising. Virtually the entirety of the larger superordinating composite of b. Bek. 3b-5b emerges from an attempt to analyze the rabbinic laws pertaining to the firstling on the basis of not only biblical law but also the biblical narrative concerning the first redemption of the firstlings during the desert sojourn as described in Numbers. Let us review the examples at hand.

1. *b. Bek 2a3b.X:*

17.3. For the Master has said,
(Ex. 13:12),
[meaning anything] which
....

2. *b. Bek. 2a-3b.XI:*

23. [But] this too may be reasoned [from elsewhere] (הכי נמי מסתברא),
24. as we have learned [in m. 7:1,4]:
25. ...—
26. [that is, if]
....
27. [But]
with respect to
...
it [the foregoing] is [taught],
28. as it is written:
(Lev. 22:4)—
29. [indicating] that we require
....

3. *b. Bek. 3b-5b.I:*

29. [And]
...
may not

....

30. Why [then] did

R. a

say:

31. ....

32. This [view] is not a problem.

33. It is like the [the view of]

R. b

who [said] in the name of

R. x,

who said:

34. (Num. 3:12; see Ex. 23:19)—

....

4. *b. Bek. 3b-5b.I:*

35. And

Aaron

who

...

may not

...?

*36. as it is taught (*דתניא*):*

Why

...?

37. [To indicate] that

....

38. [Rather]
said Scripture,

(Num. 3:41)—

39. ....

5. *b. Bek. 3b-5b.I:*

43. And

...—

whence [do we learn that]?

44. Said Scripture,

(Num. 3:45)—

45. (citation of two words only of Num. 3:45 [meaning,] ....

6. *b. Bek. 3b-5b.I:*

59. [No!]
Said Scripture,

(Num. 3:44)—

[indicating] ....

60. But say, [rather],

7. *b. Bek. 3b-5b.II:*

4.1. And

R. g

said:

…,

4.2. from that which is written [in Ex. 13:11]:

…;

4.3. and it is written thereafter [in Ex. 13:12]:

….

5. It follows that (מכלל ד)

from the outset (מעיקרא)

….

8. *b. Bek. 3b-5b (twice):*

14. And the other [authority, R. g, what would his position be in this context]?

15. [He could say] that

….

16. He[, R. f, could have] replied to him (איתיביה) [citing a baraita from Seder Olam 9:]

….

17. [And] so too with regard to (הכי נמי ב)

….

18.1. [And R. g. could retort:]

but from it[, the baraita, one can conclude]

18.2. ….;

18.3. ….

19.1. There are those who say:

19.2. Replied

R. g.

to

R. f [citing a baraita from Seder Olam 9:]

19.3. …—

19.4. [meaning]

…,

yes,

…,

no.

20. [No!]

say [the baraita's meaning is:]

….

21.1. And what informs us (ומאי קמשמע לן) [that in reality it means]

…,

yes,

…,

no—

21.2. [and] therefore

…?

22. Come and hear

9. b. Bek. 3b-5b.II (twice):

39. Well and good, [the reformulated view of]

R. g,
as (כד...)
he has stated [his] reasoning [above].
40. But with respect to (אלא לֹ)
R. f,
what is the reasoning (מאי טעמא)?
41. Said
R. i:
R. f ...
42. Scripture said (אמר קרא):
(Num. 3:13)—
43. ....
44. And
R. f.—
(Ex. 13:11-12) [R. g]—
what does he do [with this verse]?
45. This [verse] he requires (ההוא מיבעי ליה)
46. in like manner as [that] which is taught by (לכדתניא)
the House [of Study] of R. Ishmael:
(see Mek. deR. Sim., Bo, 13:12):
....

10. *b. Bek 3b-5b.III:*
15.1. But perhaps [on the contrary] (ודילמא)
...,
15.2. [but]
....
16. Rather (אלא),
from this (מהכא) [verse one may learn the matter]:
(Ex. 38:29)—
17.1. for, lo,
there is here
...,
17.2. and
...
only.
18. Learn from this
...
19.1. But perhaps [on the contrary]
...,

11. *b. Bek. 3b-5b.IV:*
13. as [two] tannaim [have differently taught]:
14. R. q(Tanna)
says:
....
15. R. r(Tanna)
says:
since

...(see SifN. 131).

16. (Num. 25:2)—
17. R. q(Tanna)

says:

....

18. R. r(Tanna)

says:

....

We have before us relatively varied usages. Passage 11, in Hebrew, is an autonomous tradition cited by the Bavli. Here two disputants offer differing interpretative glosses on the same Scripture. None of the dialectical or structural language which has been common coin thus far is at hand in the immediate content of the interpretative gloss. By contrast, the exegesis at passage 10 is immediately prefaced by structural formularies which integrate the biblical interpretation into the immediate analytic context of the *sugya*. In passage 9 the integral relationship of the exegetical glosses to the analytic context of elaborated composite is even more apparent. The exercise at passage 9 strongly resembles in nature and purpose the agenda underlying the passages (listed earlier) which dealt with the problem presented by seemingly superfluous words or verses in Scripture; that is, a decidedly academic enterprise is undertaken to explore how all cited rabbinic authorities, with their differing views, might exhaust all relevant scriptural data. In passage 8 one gets a similar sense of the degree of integration of the exegesis into the immediate context of a *sugya*, unfolding through the use of stock structural and dialectical rhetoric. Here, interestingly, not Scripture but some other source (paralleling Seder Olam) is the object of exegesis.

In terms of the level of literary integration and unity with the encompassing analytic composite, most of our examples fall closer to the state of affairs in passages 8 and 9, this on a continuum of which passage 11 represents the other extreme. That is, notwithstanding whether these exegeses stem from antecedent exegetical traditions—and in a number of instances in addition to passage 11 that could certainly be the case—the editors have generally dissolved any original context, reformulated the selected, now atomized exegetical tradition and integrated it into its own analytic composites. In order to do so, Bavli's own formularies have been used. For the most part, little appears to remain of the rhetorical language of whatever original tradition may have furnished Bavli's editors with their exegetical material.

9. Citing a scriptural verse as a prooftext supporting an antecedent position

In six passages only does one find the citation of a scriptural verse as a prooftext. Of the six passages, five appear in the elaborated encompassing composite at b. Bek. 3b-5b, which, as mentioned above, is largely founded upon exploring possible associations between the biblical narrative in Numbers 3 and rabbinic law. I distinguish prooftexting from what we have seen in the previous category; in the passages below the scriptural citation glosses an antecedent statement. From the point of view of literary structure, Scripture is not interpreted in these passages. Verses are merely adduced, or appealed to, as support.

1. *b. Bek. 2a-3b.V:*
    5. But, lo,
        said
            R. ....: ....
        6. And the Torah said,
            ... (Ex. 23:13).
    7. Rather
        [we conclude that the m.] taught

2. *b. Bek. 3b-5b.II:*
            3.1. R. f
        said:
            ...,
        3.2. since
        The Merciful One, [in Scripture] said
            to ...,
        3.3. as it is written [in Ex. 13:2],
            ....
    4.1. And

3. *b. Bek. 3b-5b.II:*
    21.1. And what informs us (ומאי קמשמע לן) *[that in reality it means]*
            ...,
            yes,
            ...,
            no—
        21.2. [and] therefore
            ...?
    22. Come and hear (see Mek. deR. Sim., Bo 13:12, eds. Epstein and Melamed, 42):
        23.1. You find [from Scripture that] you [may] say:

23.2. ...:
23.3. ...,
23.4. ...,
23.5. ....

24. 1. With respect to
...,
what does it say?
24.2. (Ex. 13:2)

25.1. With respect to
...,
it says:
25.2. (Num. 8:17.

26.1. With respect to
...,
it says:
(Ex. 13:11-12).

4. *b. Bek. 3b-5b.III:*

5.1. And again
they [i.e.,m,] asked:
5.2. In
[Ex. 38:25-26] ...,
5.3. you [should] find
...,
5.4. as it is written (דכתיב),
(Ex. 38:26).
5.5. And in
[Ex. 38:27] ...,
5.6. you find
...,
5.7. as it is written (דכתיב),
(Ex. 38:27).
5.7. [Therefore,]
Moses ...;

5. *b. Bek. 3b-5b.III:*

19.1. But perhaps [on the contrary]
...,
19.2. [but]
....

20.1. Rather,
Said
R. d:
from this [verse one may learn the matter]:
20.2. (Ezek. 45:12)

6. *b. Bek. 3b-5b.IV:*

7. As [two] tannaim [have differently taught] (כתנאי):
8. R. q(Tanna)

says:
....
9. R. r(Tanna)
says:
...,
since
....
10. And so it says [in Scripture]:
(Jer. 47:3)

In all of the passages displayed above, scriptural prooftexts are joined to the antecedent statements for which they provide support by some stock citation formula. Aramaic citation formulae appear at passages 2, 4, and 5; they are:

the Merciful One said;
as it is written;
from this.

At 2, the scriptural citation is part of an elaborate analytical composite glossing the citation of an independent rabbinic source which provides the point of departure for the entire *sugya*. In that source two opposing and perfectly matched statements about biblical history are attributed to early Palestinian amoraic rabbis. The ensuing analysis (over 50 units long) explores the possible bases for the disputants' views. The analysis unfolds much at it would were legal tradition the object of the *sugya*'s explorations and proffered legal statements, arguments and cited legal sources the constituent units of the *sugya*. Hence the citation of Scripture in passage 2 schematized above occurs in the immediate presence of the Bavli's standard analytic rhetoric. The same holds for passage 5, part of an elaborate analysis taking as its point of departure an independent rabbinic story in which a Roman official is said to have challenged a (tannaitic) rabbi by alleging that Moses engaged in fraud in collecting donations from the Israelites for the construction of the desert Tabernacle. Passage 4 is curious, as the immediately surrounding context is the independent Hebrew narrative tradition about the Roman official's allegations. A closer look at the narrative indicates that the scriptural citations introduced by the Aramaic formulae do not belong in the source-tradition at all. The scriptural citations introduced by the Aramaic terminology seem redactional interpolations.

Three of the passages (1, 3 and 6) provide Hebrew citation formulae, namely:

and the Torah said;
with respect to ... what does it say?/it says;
and so it says.

In all three instances the citation formulae seem integral to a larger independently formulated tradition cited in whole by the Bavli's editors in the context of their own larger composite. The citation formulae at 3 and 6 appear part and parcel of the rhetorical style of the cited independent source. The independent tradition schematized in passage 1 is too concise to offer any judgments about the choice of citation formula.

10. Referring to the content of an authoritative source

In three cases passages refer to a scriptural source but do not cite it. All three instances occur within independent sources cited by the Bavli's redactors. Passages 2 and 3 below are a doublet. I present schemata of the three without further discussion.

1. *b. Bek. 3b-5b.II:*

22. Come and hear (see Mek. deR. Sim., Bo 13:12, eds. Epstein and Melamed, 42):

23.1. You find [from Scripture that] you [may] say:
23.2. ...:
23.3. ...,
23.4. ...,
23.5. ....
24. 1. With respect to
...,
what does it say?

2. *b. Bek. 3b-5b.II:*

1.1. [The following story is told:]
m,
asked
R. n (Tanna):
1.2. In
...[in Num. 3]
you find
....
1.2. [But] in
... [later in Num. 3],
you find
....

1.3. And

....—...?

2.1. He [R. n] said to him:
These

....

3. *b. Bek. 3b-5b.III:*
5.1. And again

they [i.e.,m,] asked:
5.2. In

[Ex. 38:25-26] ...,

5.3. you [should] find

...,

5.4. as it is written (דכתיב),

(Ex. 38:26).

5.5. And in

[Ex. 38:27] ...,

5.6. you find

...,

5.7. as it is written (דכתיב),

(Ex. 38:27).

5.7. [Therefore,]

Moses ...;

11. Differentiating the application or referent of a previously stated opinion

In two instances dialectical formularies in column 2, together with structuring rhetoric in column 1, serve first to define, and then to solve, an analytic problem by introducing finer distinctions or categorizations than is evident in previously adduced statements. Thus two opposing statements no longer differ with respect to some item a, but, it is argued, differ only with respect to some specific sub-category of that item. The rhetorical Aramaic formularies in evidence are

one/these ... the other/those.

The choice of one or another pair will depend upon the immediate context within the larger composite. Where attributed statements are the object of the finer differentiation, the named authorities are referred to with personal pronouns. Where the reference is to data themselves, demonstrative pronouns are called for. It is obvious that differentiating statements require some antecedent context for intelligiblity. And in both examples below, the statements offering the finer distinctions are immediately challenged. That is, in both instances the differentiating formulae are well integrated into a larger analytic context.

1. *b. Bek. 2a-3b.X:*
11. [This is what]
the rabbis
said in the presence of
R. ...:
12. This [tradition] of
R. ...a,
(ו) *R. ... and R. ...*
did not dispute
[R...]—
13. [Rather]
one [deals with]
...;
the other[s, deal with]
....
14. Said to them
R. ...:
What difference [does it make whether one deals with]
...—
with respect to which we require
....

2. *b. Bek. 3b-5b.III:*
7. Went at it [the foregoing] (הוי בה)
R. o
8. What is the problem for him [R. n](מאי קא קשיא ליה)?
9.1. (Ex. 38:27)—
9.2. these (הנך)
for ...;
and those (ואינך)
....
10. [But] another verse writes (כתב קרא אחרינא):

12. Juxtaposing declarative sentences within an analytic argumentative context created by structural formularies

In a limited number of instances one finds analysis and contrived debate in which the artificial repartee is achieved by interspersing structural formularies with simple declarative sentences. Often other formularies (in column 2) alert us to the nature or force of what follows in the statement. But these formularies cannot be said to be logical operators constituting the syntax of an analytic or argumentative statement. Following are schemata of passages exhibiting these traits.

1. *Bek. 3b-5b.II:*

28. And

...

also

...?

29. Lo,

we have [had] stated [explicitly] that

...!

30. [Rather,]

this [is what R. h meant to have] said:

2. *b. Bek. 2a-3b.III (III.7-13 repeats II.13-19; III.7-11 is repeated at VI:1-6):*

3. say: the Mishnah is not in accord with

R....,

4. as we have [been] taught [in m. AZ 1:6 = m. Pes. 4:3]:

....?

5. [Alternatively,] even say: [our] Mishnah is in accord with

R. ...,

6. [and]

...,

but

....

---

7. Come and hear [see t. Bek. 2:1]:

8.1....

9. ....

10. [For] what (מאי)?

Is this not [said] concerning

....

11. No, [rather] concerning

....

2. But, lo, (והא)

it teaches

...!?

13. [Then]

let it [i.e., it should be emended to] teach

....

3. *b. Bek. 2a-3b.X:*

5. It was said that

R. ...

said:

....

6. And

R. ...

said,

....

7. About what do they dispute?

8. ....

9. The one who said:

...,

reasoned:

....

10. The one who said:

...,

[reasoned:]

But

....

4. *b. Bek. 2a-3b.XIV:*

8.1. And if (וכי)

given that

he forbade ...,

and

he gave ...,

8.2. why

did he ...?

9. Perhaps

....

10. If so
why

...?

11. Because

....

12. But, lo,

R. ...

said:

....

13.1. There, [in the latter case],

...;

13.2. [but]

....

14. Here,

even

....

15.1. And if you question [my response], I could say [alternatively]:

R. ...

15.2. but

someone else ...,

and

might ...,

and

...,

and

would thereby ....

13. Narrative structures

Finally, to complete this survey of language located in column 2 of my charting of b. Bek. 2a-3b and 3b-5b, one notes three instances in which stock formularies constitute not logical operators at all, but rather are used to create historical narrative, albeit of the most skeletal or superficial (and perhaps also artificial) nature. These formulaic narrative signposts are a verb implying physical movement or action, adjectives such as "a certain" applied to an anonymous actor and dialogical attributional formulae such as, "he said to him" (discussed earlier). Our passages offer both Hebrew and Aramaic examples. All three passages schematized below are treated by the Bavli's editors as they would a cited authoritative source and are, therefore, points of departure for an elaborate analytic composite. In the final passage that process of spinning out a *sugya* is begun by interpolating questions and responses into the very presentation of the narrative tradition. This last example and others which I have examined would indicate that the Bavli's redactors are reluctant to let longer, especially narrative or aggadic, sources run on too long in their own right. I suspect that doing so would violate the literary style by which we recognize Bavli as "talmudic." That is, postponing excessively the analytic agenda of the composite is felt to undermine in some fashion the character, agenda and, therefore, the implicit meaning of the Bavli's enterprise. With these three schematized passages I have exhausted all evidence in column 2 of our chart of b. Bek. 2a-3b and 3b-5b.

1. *b. Bek 2a-3b.XI:*
1.1. [The following narrative is told:]
1.2. R. ...did not ....
2. He said to him:
...?
3. He said to him:
Thus said
R. ...:
... —

2. *b. Bek. 2a-3b.XIV:*
1. [There is the case of] a certain
...
who
...;
2. She came before
R ....
3. He said to her:

There are none who concern themselves with that [taught] by

…,

4. who said,

….

5. [There is another case:]

R. … had

these

…,

6.1. And

he forbade …,

6.2. and

he gave …,

7. And

….

3. *b. Bek. 3b-5b.III:*

1.1. [The following story is told:]

m

asked

R. n (Tanna):

1.2. In

…[in Num. 3]

you find

….

1.3. [But] in

… [later in Num. 3],

you find

….

1.4. And

….—…?

2.1. He [R. n] said to him:

These

…,

2.2. and

….

3. What is the reason?

4. Said

Abbaye:

….

5.1. And again

they [i.e.,m] asked:

5.2. In

[Ex. 38:25-26] …,

5.3. you [should] find

…,

5.4. as it is written (דכתיב),

(Ex. 38:26).

5.5. And in

[Ex. 38:27] …,

5.6. you find
...,
5.7. as it is written (דכתיב),
(Ex. 38:27).
5.7. [Therefore,]
Moses ...;
5.8. [since] he ....
6.1. He [R. n] said to him:
Moses ...;
6.2. And
....
7. Went at it [the foregoing] (הוי בה)
R. o
8. What is the problem for him [R. n](מאי קא קשיא ליה)?

Dialectical formularies in the Bavli: An interim synthesis of the data

In my survey of items in column 2, grouped under 13 headings, a number of pervasive traits emerge. First, in most of the categories formulae in column 2 do not function alone. Rather one finds *structured sequences of stock formulae, which together provide the logical syntax of an argument-statement*. The lion's share of these structured sequences are in Aramaic. In only a few categories one finds materials in which an individual rhetorical formula in column 2 effects on its own the appropriate logical operation. Similarly, one tends to find Hebrew formulae in column 2 in several categories only. Such stand-alone, often Hebrew formulae offer interpretative glosses of Scripture, link scriptural prooftexts to antecedent rulings, attribute statements to named figures or help construct narratives. These are the exceptions which prove the rule, since many passages in these categories are independent sources cited by the redactors. Where they are not, rhetorical formulae, which may not be part of a sequence of dialectical operators, are nevertheless closely linked with structural rhetoric in column 1. This leads to a second major interim observation.

In previous chapters it proved possible to examine structural formulae and formularies in their own right, without reference to dialectical rhetoric. The same may not be said of most of the rhetorical language in column 2. Excepting stock language within cited autonomous sources, language in column 2 is closely related to structural formulae and formularies in column 1. In many categories the appropriate choice from among an array of available dialectical terms is determined by the structural formularies, and, therefore, the unfolding agenda of the *sugya*. This is true even where certain questions and/or responses are attributed to a named figure. In other words, *much of the dialectical rhetoric of the Bavli text examined is part and parcel of the elaborated composites in which individual argument-statements appear.* No doubt this is a contributing factor to the sense of literary uniformity within Bavli's elaborated composites, allowing one to recognize a composite as typically talmudic. No doubt it is this same feature which permits Bavli to communicate forcefully (albeit implicitly) a consistent set of meanings. As discussed more fully in the introduction, it is in the consistent ordering of things with respect to one another that a document conveys a map or a model of how such things (and, to some degree, things in general) ought to be ordered.

I hesitate to proceed further at this point with interpreting the meaning of the Bavli's dialectical language (in column 2). Before returning to these issues, as I shall toward the close of this study, it is worthwhile gaining some perspective, some increased purchase upon, the data by comparing language in column 2 of b. Bek. 2a-3b and 3b-5b with linguistic usages in other, generally earlier, rabbinic works, against which backdrop the Bavli's dialectical rhetoric may be more profitably assessed. There is a double advantage to such comparison. First, the use of language in other documents will only serve to highlight usage in the Bavli and, therefore, further elucidate for us Bavli's rhetorical formularies and their meaning. Second, there is good reason to suspect that the Bavli's editors were aware of these documents or (in some cases) of sources like them in literary style and content. Therefore, the Bavli's own choices in its use of language may be viewed against models available to Bavli's editors. Let us turn then to *possible* linguistic correlates of the Bavli's dialectical formularies.

5

Bavli's Dialectical Formularies in Comparative Relief

This chapter completes the agenda set out at the beginning of chapter 4: to analyze the rhetorical formulae and formularies that help create Bavli's smaller literary units. In chapter 4 I identified stock rhetorical terms that bind together idiomatic items of content into stylized statements. These rhetorical terms I called dialectical formularies. Chapter 4 documented as well the "types" of patterned sentences that resulted with reference to the modes of logic and reasoning in evidence at this "micro-level" of the Bavli. The current chapter furthers this agenda by providing a number of comparative contexts for the assessment of Bavli's rhetoric at this level. In order better to understand the Bavli's use of dialectical formularies and to appreciate the place of the dialectical argument and analysis created in the Bavli by means of these stock rhetorical operators, I will once again refer to the evidence of the Talmud and other early rabbinic documents.

As I have demonstrated with respect to structural formularies and the elaborated composites that structuring rhetoric help constitute, the Bavli's programme and organization differs from that of the Yerushalmi. Close parallels between the Bavli and Yerushalmi result most often from their mutual, independent reliance on common source materials, Mishnah being the most obvious and basic (see Jaffee, 1989). Tosefta or toseftan-like materials constitute a second, important repository. The Bavli also draws extensively upon, or replicates the modes of analysis of another significant body of materials extant from early Rabbinism, the halakic midrashim. Of this corpus, Sifra on Leviticus, Sifre on Numbers and Sifre on Deuteronomy constitute the major, pre-talmudic late antique documents. To gain appropriate purchase upon the Bavli's dialectical formularies, therefore, I attempt in what follows a comparison of the Bavli's dialectical argumentation, as constituted by its dialectical formularies, and evidence from Mishnah, Tosefta and Sifre on Numbers respectively. Although, as the analyses in chapter 3 suggest and as Neusner (1986b) has demonstrated on independent grounds, the Bavli either does not depend upon, or does not limit itself to, the agenda of the Yerushalmi (see Jaffee, 1989), the evidence of that other, cognate "Talmud" also provides a valuable point of comparison in assessing the nature, meaning and significance of dialectical formularies and argumentation in the Babylonian Talmud.

Viewed in the comparative contexts provided in this chapter, it is evident that Bavli's modes of rhetoric and the agenda which they serve differ substantially from those of earlier rabbinic texts—especially from those of Mishnah, *the* canonical rabbinic document for Bavli's editors. In the main, Mishnah uses its rhetorical tools to construct hierarchically organized lists of cases or an inventory of circumstances defining a single case. For example, characteristic of Mishnah's rhetoric is the use of "and" to join several cases, and of "and" or "which" to concatenate the states of affairs defining a complex case. The rules pertaining to cases effect a "classification" of the things of this world. Bavli's rhetoric and modes of reasoning, in contrast with those of Tosefta and Yerushalmi, serve less to explain, to explicate and to supplement Mishnah than to pursue for their own sakes analysis and critique, for which Mishnah, other rabbinic sources and Scripture provide data. As I stated at the outset of chapter 4, while at this "micro-level" of rhetoric Bavli is often reminiscent of, or mirrors outright, the rhetorical formulae and formularies of earlier rabbinic texts, Bavli in particular exhibits "types" of rhetoric serving to construct exploratory hypotheses, conjectural conclusions and trial arguments based on comparison and association. Integrated into the context of Bavli's composites, these exploratory and hypothetical argument-statements especially help create in Bavli the air of valuing ongoing critique and analysis.

Points of comparison in Mishnah

I turn, first, to a charting of one complete chapter of Mishnah, m. Bekorot 1, as the point of departure for our comparative analyses. I apply the same conventions for differentiating and presenting the text's use of rhetorical formularies as used earlier in charting sections of the Babylonian Talmud. That is, structural formularies appear flush left; Dialectical formularies are indented 2 centimetres; the remainder of the text is indented 4 centimetres. For the purposes of the charting of Mishnah, I have relied principally upon the translation by J. Neusner, with two notable exceptions. M. Bek. 1:1a and b follows my own translation as presented earlier in the context of the charting of b. Bek. 2a-3b and 3b-5b. I have altered Neusner's translation of m. Bek. 1:6(A-C) to accord with my own, quite different, understanding of its meaning.

By way of anticipating what follows, I should point out that applying this methodology for differentiating types of language, when applied to Mishnah, proves not only difficult but produces at many junctures quite ambiguous, even bizarre, results; the method fails us at many junctures, because the very definitions which underlie this method of charting texts, so useful with the Bavli, do not accord with how Mishnah uses language. I will return to this point.

Mishnah Bekorot, Chapter 1

1:1

A.(1) He who purchases the foetus of an ass of a Gentile[, and the foetus when born will be a first-born],

A.(2.1) and

he who sells to him [the Gentile, the foetus of an ass],

A.(2.2) even though

it [such a sale] is not permitted

A.(3) and

he who forms a partnership with him [the Gentile, so that they co-own the foetus],

A.(4) and

he who receives [a pregnant ass] from him [a Gentile],

A.(5) and

he who gives [a pregnant ass] to him [a Gentile] in trust—

C. is exempt from the law of the firstborn,

D.(1) as it said,

"Of an Israelite" (Num. 3:13),

D.(2) but

not of others.

1:1b

A. Priests and Levites are exempt [from the law of the firstling (Rashi: as regards the firstling of an ass)]

B. from

an argument *a fortiori*:

C. If

[the Levites] redeemed that [animal] of an Israelite in the Wilderness,

it is logical that

they should [automatically have] redeem[ed] their own.

[1:1a&b, charting and trans. my own]

1:2

A. A cow
which
bore [an offspring] like an ass,
or
an ass
which
bore [an offspring] like a horse—
B. it [the offspring is exempt from the law of the firstling,
C. since it is said,
"The firstling of an ass" (Ex. 13:13), "The firstling of an ass" (Ex 34:20)—
D. two times,
[meaning]
only when
that which
gives birth is an ass
and
that which
is borne is an ass.
E. And what is
their rule as to eating?
F. A clean beast
which
bore [an offspring] like an unclean beast—
it [the offspring] is permitted as to eating.
G. And an unclean beast
which
bore [an offspring] like a clean beast—
it [the offspring] is prohibited as to eating.
H. For
that which
comes forth from the unclean is unclean
and
that which
comes forth from the clean is clean.
I. An unclean fish
which
swallowed a clean fish—
it [the clean fish] is permitted as to eating.
J. A clean fish
which
swallowed an unclean fish—
it [the unclean fish] is prohibited as to eating,
K. for
it is not its product.

1:3

A. An ass
which
had not given birth
and
[which]
bore two males [and it is not known which of them came out first]—
B. One gives a single lamb to the priest.
C. [If
it bore] male and female [and it is not known which of them came out first]—
D. One separates a single lamb for himself.
E. Two asses
which
had not given birth
and
[which]
bore two males—
F. one gives two lambs to the priest.
G. [If
they bore] a male and a female
or
two males and a female,
H. One gives a single lamb to the priest.
I. [If
they bore two females and one male,
or
two males and two females,
J. there is nothing here for the priest.

1:4

A. [Two asses], one
[of which]
gave birth,
and
one
which
had not given birth,
and
which
bore two males—
B. one gives a single lamb to the priest.
C. [If
they produced a male and female,
one separates a single lamb for himself.

D. For it is said,

"And every firstling of an ass you shall redeem with a lamb" (Ex.34:20)—

E.(1) [a lamb deriving] from sheep

or (ו)

from goats

F.(2) male

or

female,

G.(3) large

or

small,

H.(4) blemished

or

unblemished.

I.(1) And

one redeems with it many times.

J.(2) And

it enters the fold to be tithed.

K.(3) And

if

it dies,

they derive benefit from it.

1:5

A. They do not redeem [firstling of an ass] with

(1) a calf,

and

(2) not with a wild beast,

and

(3) not with an animal

which

has been properly slaughtered,

and

(4) not with an animal

which

is terefah,

and

(5) not with a hybrid [of a he-goat and a ewe],

and

(6) not with a koy [the offspring of a he-goat and a hind].

B. R. Eleazar permits in the case of a hybrid,

because

it is deemed a lamb,

and

prohibits in the case of the koy,

because

it is a matter of doubt [whether it is deemed a lamb].

C. [If]

one gave it [the offspring of an ass] to the priest,
the priest is not permitted to keep it,

until

he will separate (set aside and designate] a lamb in its place.

1:6

A. He who separates a redemption lamb for a firstborn of an ass

and

[the lamb] died—
B. R. Eliezer

says:

(1) They [the owners] are responsible for it [to give another redemption lamb to the priest],

(2) as

[the one is liable for] the five selas [paid in the redemption of the firstborn] son.

C. And

sages

say:

(1) They are not liable for it [to give another redemption-lamb to the priest],

(2) as

[the owners are not liable in the case of] the redemption of second tithe.

D. Testified

R. Joshua and R. Sadoq

concerning

the redemption-lamb

which

was set aside for the firstling of an ass

[and]

which

had died,

that

E. there is nothing whatsoever for the priest here.

F. [If]

the firstling [of an ass] died,
G. R. Eliezer

says:

It is to be buried.

And

[the owner] is permitted to derive benefit from the lamb [which had been set aside to redeem it].

And

sages

say:

It need not be buried.

And

the lamb belongs to the priest.

1:7

A. [If]

one did not want to redeem it [the firstling of an ass],
he breaks its neck from behind with a hatchet,

and

buries it.
B. The requirement of redemption takes precedence over the requirement of breaking the neck,

since it is said,

"And if you will not redeem it, then you will break its neck (Ex. 34:20).
D. The requirement of espousing [a Hebrew bondswoman] takes precedence over the requirement of redemption.
E. The requirement of Levirate marriage takes precedence over the requirement of *halisah*—

G. at first
when

they would consummate the Levirate marriage for the sake of fulfilling the commandment.

H. But

now
that

they do not consummate the Levirate marriage for the sake of fulfilling the commandment,
I. the requirement of *halisah* takes precedence over the requirement of Levirate marriage.
J. The requirement of redeeming [an unclean beast dedicated to the Temple] is incumbant upon the master.
K. He takes precedence over every other person,

L. since it is said,

"[Then he shall ransom it ...] or if it is not redeemed, then it shall be sold according to thy estimation (Lev. 27:27).[1]

1. The charting of the m. Bek. 1 is my own; the translation of m. Bek. 1:2-7 is J. Neusner's from *A History of the Mishnaic Law of Holy Things: Part Three,* (Neusner, 1979:144-55); variation from the translation by Neusner at m. Bek. 1:6.A-C is based on my own, differing reading of the meaning of the text.

The attempt to apply to Mishnah the definitions and methodology used to chart texts from the Bavli fails in a number of significant instances. How so? For the most part the column flush left, reserved for structural formularies, contains to all intents and purposes only a single formula, if we can call it a formula at all. With two exceptions only, various lexical meanings of the Hebrew conjunction, *vav* (ו), account for everything in column one in the chart as currently organized. The fact that *vav* can be variously rendered as "and," "or," or "but" seems to me to be insignificant. But in what way are the instances of *vav* in the first column structural? True, in the most minimal sense, they link individual items together. But they do not, as do structural formularies in the Bavli, help create and order particular structures with particular programmatic or analytic agendas. In the Bavli, as we have seen, the structural formulary, "ask of R. x, ask of R. y," served to shape a particular elaborated analysis. Even *vav*, whether understood as "and" or "but," often functioned in the Bavli to introduce an analysis which we came to expect would significantly challenge or differ from the reasoning that had immediately preceeded it. By contrast, *vav* in the Mishnah passage before us serves as joining language only. For the most part, *vav* serves either to build simple lists of items or cases that the law of Mishnah will classify together or, alternatively, *vav* joins a list of circumstances in the service of defining a single case. Of the former usage m. Bek. 1:1 offers examples at A(2.1,3,4 and 5). The use of "and" to link the individual circumstances that constitute a single case is evident at 1:3:A, E, 1:4:A (twice) and 1:6:A. Neusner (1981; 1983b) and Green (1983) have characterized Mishnah as a document preoccupied with the "science of lists." That is, most of Mishnah lists cases for the purpose of defining whether one or another rule applies to each. Mishnah will, in addition, permutate lists of circumstances in order to produce a series of cases, each requiring classification under one rule or another. (Of this m. Bek. 1:3 and 1:4 offer striking examples.) *Vav*, virtually the sole occupant of column 1, appears to be, therefore, an aspect of Mishnah's pervasive *Listenwissenschaft*.

Two items in column 1 remain, after consideration of Mishnah's concatenating *vav*, "even though" at 1:1:A(2.2) and "And what is" at 1:2:E. After our exposure to the Bavli, we are predisposed to find in these two phrases something akin to the Bavli's rhetorical formularies inviting or helping build analyses. But again our expectations, and our typological method and definitions, come to nought. "Even though" also is joining language permitting the editor to gloss the case at hand with a secondary ruling. The use of "And what is" at 1:2:E appears similar in function, permitting the case at hand (1:2:A), already classified with respect to the law of the firstling (at B), now to be classified with respect to a different legal domain, fitness for consumption. A sublist on this latter issue is thereby occasioned at 1:2:F, G and J. Thus we have exhausted the contents of column 1 and found little that significantly parallels the structural formularies of the Bavli. This is so because just as Mishnah's purposes differ from the Bavli's, so too does Mishnah's use of language differ from the Bavli's in a most fundamental manner. The hypothesis we are moving towards in this comparison is that rhetorical formularies and formulae, that is, the recurrent formulaic use of items of language, either reflects, or helps constitute and convey, the fundamental meaning and significance of the document. For Mishnah, that meaning and significance has intimately to do with its *listenwissenschaftliche* and classificatory agenda. The repeated use of *vav* as much drives home, implicitly, to be sure, that fundamental message as does Mishnah's idiomatic content.

If we now examine the contents of column 2, containing what provisionally we have attempted to identify as dialectical formularies in Mishnah, the foregoing hypotheses will be further confirmed. Again we see that significance lies precisely in our failure to have classified satisfactorily items using the definitions applied in the analysis of the Bavli. The telltale error is the appearance of "which" (שׁ) in column 2. "Which" more often than not serves a function in Mishnah directly cognate to *vav*. That is, the relative pronoun frequently enables the concatenation of clauses. This serves to build another type of list. But it is not a list of cases. Rather "which" serves to specify a list of circumstances that define a single case which Mishnah may then classify with respect to a particular law. Mishnah 1:2.F-G offers two simple examples:

F. A clean beast
which
bore [an offspring] like an unclean beast—
it [the offspring] is permitted as to eating.
G. And an unclean beast
which
bore [an offspring] like a clean beast—
it [the offspring] is prohibited as to eating.

Here the relative pronouns, "which," are both syntactically and logically—although not grammatically—conjunctive. A dramatic indication of this fact is that the relative pronoun could be replaced with "and it" with no loss of meaning. Thus:

F. A clean beast,
and it
bore [an offspring] like an unclean beast—
it [the offspring] is permitted as to eating.
G. And an unclean beast
and it
bore [an offspring] like a clean beast—
it [the offspring] is prohibited as to eating.

Such a substitution not only works in principle, which is all I must demonstrate, but is also at times preferred mishnaic usage and style. Witness, for example, m. Bek. 1:3.A-B:

A. An ass
which
had not given birth
and
[which]
bore two males [and it is not known which of them came out first]—
B. One gives a single lamb to the priest.

The first appearance of the relative pronoun parallels what we have seen. The second is an interpolation, which the translator, here Neusner, has supplied in response to the demands of English-language style. The Hebrew text of the Mishnah has in fact joined the second and third circumstances making up the case with "and it"—in accordance with the redactor's sense of *Hebrew* style. Functionally "which" and "and it" are equivalent.

That "which" and "and it" are interchangeable as to meaning and purpose, and that the choice is based on quite other stylistic considerations is aptly demonstrated by appealing to 1:6A.

A. He who separates a redemption-lamb for a first-born of an ass
and
[the lamb] died—
B. R. Eliezer
says: ....

In this instance, the redactors commence the pericope with the quite common formulary, "he who ..." (*heh*, plus the present participle), in order to cue the reader to a change in the problematic to be addressed. Neusner (1977) has demonstrated that this cue represents a standard redactional device in Mishnah. Only the participial opening generates the use of "and." Equally commensurate with mishnaic style and formularies would be:

	[Concerning] the redemption-lamb for the firstling of an ass
which	
	died—
	R. Eliezer
says:	

(Indeed, precisely the use of "he who ... and ..." has generated the exegetical problem, What or who has died. Our revised version lacks the ambiguity and, at least in this one respect, would have been preferable.)

To sum up our discussion thus far of what we have provisionally identified as Mishnah's dialectical formularies, column 2 is largely populated with the relative pronoun "which." The relative pronoun, however, plays virtually no dialectical function as a logical operator in a unit of argument, reasoning or questioning, as is so often the case in the Bavli. Rather, in the vast majority of cases in Mishnah, "which" appears as the functional equivalent of "and" and serves in the concatenation of items. The relative pronoun seems part and parcel of Mishnah's *Listenwissenschaft*.

Among those linguistic formularies provisionally identified as dialectical only a few now remain. They are:

1. m. Bek. 1:1a.D

since/as/for it is said	
	[scriptural citation],
but (אבל)	
	[exegetical gloss] (1:1.D)

2. m. Bek. 1:2

since/as/for it is said	
	[scriptural citation(s)]
	[statement of fact about Scripture]
only when	
	[concatenation of conditions supporting previously stated law]

3. m. Bek. 1:4.D.

since/as/for it is said	
	[scriptural citation]

[concatenation of items allegedly satisfying the requirements of the verse]

4. m. Bek. 1:7.B. and L.

since/as/for it is said

[scriptural citation (standing in and of itself as sufficient support for antecedent law]

5. m. Bek. 1:1b

[declarative statement of law]

from

an argument *a fortiori*;

if

[declaration of 'stronger' fact]

is it not logical that

[declaration of weaker proposition supporting law]

6. m. Bek. 1:2.H and K

for (לפי ש/ש)

[statement of general principle]

7. m. Bek. 1:5.B (twice)

because (מפני ש)

[simple statement of fact, which is intended as sufficient reason for law]

8. m. Bek. 1:6.B and C

as

[statement of other case, allegedly providing a probative analogy for antecedent ruling]

9. m. Bek. 1:7.E-I.

[declarative statement of law]

at first

when

[historical circumstances]

But

now

that

[contemporary circumstances]

[declarative statement reversing law]

10. m. Bek. 1:6.B-C and G-H.

R. x/sages

says/say

[ruling]

11. m. Bek. 1:6.

testified

R. x/x and y

concerning
[statement of case]
that
[ruling]

Let us briefly analyze each of these eleven items. Among them only item 10 ("R. x/sages says/say") is a sustained trait of Mishnah. However, while the use of this attributional formula is central to interpreting the underlying intent and purpose of Mishnah's editors generally, it is, among the 11 items, the least relevant to our quest for possible antecedents in Mishnah of the Bavli's use of dialectical formularies.

Numbers 1 through 4 offer several variations of the formulary for proferring scriptural backing for an antecedent ruling. While "but" (item 1) and "only when" (item 2) appear to be logical operators resembling dialectical formularies in the Bavli, they play the less modest role, in my view, of aiding in the identification of those salient features of the scriptural evidence which support the legal opinion in question. Item 3 manages the same without the help of such facilitative language. In item 4 the probative force of the Scripture is taken to be self-evident, and therefore no amplification glosses the citation. The frequency and nature of appeals in Mishnah to Scripture have been extensively treated by Neusner (1981); it is not a sustained trait of Mishnah's authorship, with some notable exceptions.

Item 11 is an example of the testimony form. Like the citation of Scripture and the brief precedent narrative (introduced by מעשׂה ב or מעשׂה שׁ), of which we have no example m. Bek. 1, the testimony aims to provide not a rationale or supporting argument but the force of some recognized authority for a previously articulated ruling. Only one tractate of Mishnah, Eduyyot, is based on the use of the testimony form. Its use outside that tractate is relatively rare, and in such instances a parallel almost always is to be found in Eduyyot. We need not commit ourselves to solving the problem of whether in such instances Eduyyot is always or usually the original context. The more salient point is that within Eduyyot the testimony form functions simply as an attributional formula, linking a particular ruling to one or more rabbinic figures, functionally similar to "R. X says," followed by an independent legal statement. Outside Eduyyot the testimony form plays a quite different role, to provide authoritative backing for an opinion already registered. Even less so than citations of Scripture and precedent narratives, the testimony form is not (outside of Eduyyot) a sustained and pervasive characteristic of Mishnah.

In Item 6, "for" is used to join an antecedent ruling and a general principal, of which the ruling is a mere instance. It is a redactionally simplified cognate, therefore, of the formulary "this is the general principal (זה הכלל)," followed by a generalized description of circumstances and the ruling that pertains to them. In this simplified version, the ruling itself need not be repeated. When it occurs, the stipulation of general principles in Mishnah can be related to Mishnah's enduring interest in locating items within one category or another, and in contemplating ever more complex, hybrid cases to submit to the operating classificatory criteria. It is only remotely related to offering, let alone to arguing about, a rationale for a ruling, a sustained trait of the Bavli.

Item 9 offers a formulary pattern which appeals to a change in historical circumstances to support a revised version of the law in question. It is undoubtedly a form of rationale, but it is not one resembling dialectic argument. Such appeals to historical circumstances are relatively rare, although a few mishnaic tractates (e.g., Yoma) or chapters cast their presentation of the law as a rather thin historical reminiscence by liberally using verbs in the perfect tense.

We are left with three items (5, 7 and 8) which, in my view, are thinly argumentative. Neither number 7 ("because ...") nor 8 ("as [in the case of] ...") offer support from some authoritative source, the case in virtually all instances discussed thus far. Rather, 7 and 8 appeal to alleged facts or premises. The latter could form the basis of an *implied* argument providing a rationale for the antecedent ruling. The unspecified or implied argument of item 8 is founded upon an appeal to an allegedly probative analogy. (And as we have seen, the offering and rebutting of analogies of one form or another abounds in the Bavli's dialectical argumentation.) Only at 5, the argument *a fortiori* based upon an accepted datum, do we have in m. Bek. 1 an item in which the supporting argument and rationale is articulated. Here only do we actually encounter language which approximates the Bavli's ubiquitous and sustained use of dialectical formularies.

On the whole, then, a study of linguistic formularies in m. Bek. 1 isolated language which only appeared to parallel in function structural and dialectical formularies of the Bavli. Virtually all of the terms found in column 1 in our chart of m. Bek. 1 are conjunctive and serve Mishnah's *listenwissenschaftliche* orientation. The use of the relative pronoun as documented in column 2 serves in Mishnah ends similar to those served by its conjunctions, namely the concatenation of items defining a complex case requiring a ruling. This seems a far cry from the Bavli's use of the relative pronoun in frequent challenges based on arguments from analogy, such as

> No!
> ... differs
> If you say ...
> with respect to ...,
> which ...,
> would you say ...
> with respect to ...,
> which ....

Apart from the relative pronoun, what dominates in column 2 of our chart of m. Bek. 1 is a simple appeal to some authoritative source as support for an antecedent ruling. In addition, Mishnah can, it seems, appeal to allegedly probative facts using the conjunction "because." We have found one appeal to analogy, but the force of the analogy is not articulated in an argument. We are left, in the end with one set of linguistic formulae serving a mishnaic argument *a fortiori*, which reminds us of the Bavli's use of language generally. The reason for this state of affairs in Mishnah is, to my mind, obvious. To have allowed more fully articulated argument an important, even if not dominant, role in Mishnah would have totally undermined its *listenwissenschaftliche* character, a trait which implicitly bolsters its claim to authority, its implied assertion to have portrayed matters simply "as they are."

This study of m. Bek. 1 cannot of course allow me to make assertions about Mishnah's use of linguistic formularies generally. That is not my interest in any case, and Neusner (1977; 1981) has extensively documented forms and formulary patterns in Mishnah. Rather my perusal in detail of m. Bek. 1 for possible linguistic correlates in m. Bek. 1 of the Bavli's structural and dialectical formularies serves to highlight and to place in a meaningful context Bavli's rhetoric. To be sure, the editors of the Bavli may have learned a thing or two from Mishnah where the latter's editors have departed from their predominant taxonomic preoccupation of classifying lists of cases with respect to one ruling or another. But whatever the debt owed by the Babylonian Talmud to Mishnah, the Talmud's propensity to set matters in a dialectical analytic context with the help of its recurrent rhetorical formularies remains pre-eminent, and starkly so, following this brief treatment of Mishnah, the base-text and authoritative source par excellence of the Babylonian Talmud.

Points of comparison in Tosefta

Mishnah, as the base-text with respect to which the Bavli is organized in the semblance of commentary, provided the most obvious point of comparison for bringing into relief the Babylonian Talmud's use of rhetorical formularies. Two other early rabbinic documents, Tosefta and Sifre on Numbers, may serve similar ends. I turn to Tosefta first.

Tosefta, literally, "The Supplement," contains extra-mishnaic materials bearing upon the further elucidation of Mishnah and organizes these materials, like the Bavli, with respect to the tractates, chapters and individual pericopes of Mishnah. Tosefta, probably edited sometime between 240-300 CE represents, therefore, the first attempt to formulate a comprehensive commentary on Mishnah. As is evident from my presentation earlier in this chapter of b. Bek. 2a-3b and 3b-5b and from the charting in the previous chapter of b. AZ 14b-16a, the Babylonian Talmud often cites extra-mishnaic, (allegedly) tannaitic materials (i.e., *baraitot*) which parallel pericopes in Tosefta. The problem of the relationship obtaining between these *baraitot* in the Bavli (and for that matter in the Yerushalmi) and the Tosefta as we have it is complex. For my purposes, I need not commit myself on the question. My impression, however, is that the Bavli uses Toseftan materials and modifies them to suit its immediate needs. I shall examine a chapter of Tosefta in the same fashion and to the same ends as the analysis of a chapter of Mishnah.

Neusner (1977) has classified Tosefta's pericopes in terms of the relationship which materials bear to Mishnah. Toseftan passages either comment upon, complement or supplement Mishnah. In commenting upon Mishnah, a passage will often cite sections of the relevant mishnaic pericope and gloss or comment upon it. Complementary materials will extend a problem in a given mishnaic passage, left uncited but undoubtedly assumed. Supplementary materials will introduce issues which are related to the subject matter of Mishnah, but which are not explicitly or implicitly part of Mishnah's problematic. As Neusner has shown, roughly 66 percent of Tosefta comments upon, or complements, Mishnah. The language of these materials, their forms and formulary patterns generally replicate those of Mishnah. The language of supplementary materials seems less constrained by Mishnah's models. I leave it to others to pronounce on the historical and literary provenance of Tosefta's supplementary pericopes.

In what follows, I have again organized formulaic or rhetorical language in accordance with criteria that served so well in charting the text of the Babylonian Talmud (see p. 26). The general lack of success in similarly attempting to classify Toseftan language rebounds upon our understanding of the Bavli. I need only add that in the presentation of t. Bek. 1, verbatim citations of Mishnah appear in boldface type.

Tosefta Bekorot, Chapter 1

1:1

A.(1) He who purchases the foetus of an ass of a Gentile[, and the foetus when born will be a firstborn],

A.(2.1) and

he who sells to him [the Gentile, the foetus of an ass],

A.(2.2) even though

it [such a sale] is not permitted

A.(3.1. and

he who forms a partnership with him [the Gentile, so that they co-own the foetus]

A.(3.2.) [that is,] he who gives to him within a partnership

A.(4) and

he who receives [a pregnant ass] from him [a Gentile],

A.(5) and

he who gives [a pregnant ass] to him [a Gentile] in trust—

C. is exempt from the law of the firstborn,

D.(1) as it said,

"Of an Israelite" (Num. 3:13),

D.(2) but

not of others.

1:2

A. And

so you [must] say

in the case of

priests

and

in the case of

Levites.

B. Because,

since

the priests and the Levites are liable

in the case of

a clean animal,

one might [think]
them to be liable
in the case of
an unclean animal.
C. Scripture [however] says:
"Of humankind and of beast" (Ex. 13:2; Num. 18:15)—
D. that which
applies to you
in the case of
humankind
applies to you
in the case of
an animal.
E. That which
does not apply to you
in the case of
humankind
does not apply to you
in the case of
an animal.
F. [Thus]
they exempted the Levites from the law of the firstling of an unclean beast.
G. But (אבל)
they give the redemption for firstborn son
and
the redemption for the firstling of an ass to the priests only [despite priests and Levites being similarly exempted as stated above].

1:3

A. Among all
unclean animals,
that which
is liable for you under the law of the [redemption of the] firstling
is the firstling of an ass
only.

B. Among all
wild animals,
that which
is forbidden to you the price [received therefrom]
is [the price received for] the dog
only.

1:4

A. R. Meir

used to say:

[Concerning] whoever fulfills the commandment [with respect to] the [redemption] of the firstling of an ass—
they account him as if he has fulfilled the commandment of [the redemption] of all [other] unclean animals.
B. [Concerning] whoever abrogates [for himself] the commandment [with respect to] the [redemption] of the firstling of an ass—
they account him as if he has abrogated [for himself] the commandment of [the redemption] of all [other] unclean animals.

1:5

A. R. Yose the Galilean

says:

"But the firstling of an ox, or the firstling of a sheep, or the firstling of a goat you shall not redeem; they are holy" (Num. 18:17)—
B. "The firstling of an ox" [indicates that the offspring is not holy]

unless it be [the case] that (עד ש)

the offspring and the bearer are both an ox.
C. "The firstling of a sheep" [indicates that the offspring is not holy]

unless it be [the case] that (עד ש)

the offspring and the bearer are both a sheep.
D. "The firstling of a goat" [indicates that the offspring is not holy]

unless it be [the case] that (עד ש)

the offspring and the bearer are both a goat.

E. And

if

[the offspring] exhibits some of the traits characteristic of [the species] of its mother,
it is liable under the law of the firstling.

1:6

A. A clean animal

which

bore [something looking like] a species of an unclean animal—
[the offspring] is permitted as regards eating.

B.And
if
[the offspring] exhibits some of the traits characteristic of [the species of its mother],
it is liable under the law of the firstling.

C. And
the unclean which bore something like **the clean—**
[the offspring] is prohibited as regards eating.
D. For
that emerging from the unclean is unclean.

E. And
that emerging from the clean is clean.

1:7

A. An unclean fish
which
swallowed a clean fish—
[the fish swallowed] is permitted as regards eating.

B. And
A clean fish
which
swallowed an unclean fish—
[the fish swallowed] is prohibited as regards eating.
C. Because (לפי ש)
[in either case the fish swallowed] is not its progenitor.

1:8

A. Because of what [reasoning] (מפני מה)
did they say:
B. The honey of bees is permitted [as regards eating—given that the honey is produced by an unclean swarming thing]?
C. Since (ש)
they do not produce it;
but only
gather it.

D. And
the 'honey' of spider-mites is prohibited.
E. Since (ש)
it is its saliva
only.

1:9

A. R. Simeon
says:
Why does Scripture say:
"a camel" (Lev. 11:4) and [again elsewhere] "a camel" (Deut. 19:7)—[that is,] twice?
B. [It does this] in order to (לְ)
include [within the category of that which is prohibited for eating] the camel[-like offspring] borne by a cow,
just as (כ)
one borne from a camel-dam [is prohibited].
C. And
if
its head
and
the greater part of it[s body] resembles its mother,
it is permitted as regards eating.
D. And
the sages
say:
And
that emerging from the unclean is unclean.
E. And
that emerging from the clean is clean.
F. Since (שׁ)
an unclean animal does not bear [young] by a clean [animal],
and
a clean [animal] does not bear [young] by an unclean [animal],
and
not large cattle [e.g., oxen] by small cattle [e.g., sheep],
and
not small cattle by large cattle,
and
not humankind by any of them,
and
not any of them by humankind.

1:10

A. clean small cattle bear [young] after five months [of pregnancy] (emend to remove: even … they have said; see Neusner, *Holy Things* {1979:148});
B. clean small cattle [bear young] after nine months [of pregnancy];

C. unclean large cattle [bear young] after twelve months [of pregnancy];
D. the dog [bears young] after fifty days [of pregnancy];
the cat [bears young] after fifty-two days [of pregnancy];
E. swine [bear young] after sixty days [of pregnancy];
F. fox

and

all that run [bear young] after six months [of pregnancy];
G. the wolf

and

the lion

and

the bear

and

the tiger

and

the leopard

and

the elephant

and

the monkey

and

the long-tailed ape [bear young] after three years [of pregnancy];

H. and

the snake [bears young] after seven years [of pregnancy];

1:11

A. The dolphins bear [young]

and

raise [them]

like

humankind.
B. An unclean fish spews out [living] young;
C. a clean fish lays eggs.

1:12

A. The guts of fish

and

[its] foetus are eaten only [upon a decision] from the expert [in clean and unclean things].

B. the fowl is eaten on the basis of (ב) [the judgment of anyone knowing relevant] tradition;
C. [e.g.] a hunter is trusted to say: This fowl is clean.

1:13

A. [Concerning] a cow
which
bore [something looking] like the sheep species—
They do not redeem with it the firstling of an ass.
B. Since (emend to delete שׁ)
everywhere [in Scripture]
that is it said:
"a lamb" (as in Ex. 34:20),
C. it encompasses **sheep**
and
goats,
large
and
small,
males
and
females,
unblemished
and
blemished;
D. One redeems with it;
one repeats a second time [using the same sheep],
and
one repeats a third time [using the same sheep];
E. and
one brings it [the same animal] as a vow-offering
and
a free-will offering,
and
for one's sin-offering
and
for one's guilt-offering;
and
it is liable under the law of the firstling [should it give birth to a firstling],
and
[for] the priestly gifts [should it be slaughtered as food].

F. R. Eleazar
says:

[Concerning] **the mixed-kind** [borne] from [the union] of a ewe and a goat—
they redeem with it the firstling of an ass;
G. [concerning] a *koy* (emended to delete: from)—
they do not redeem with it.

1:14

A. Just as (כשם ש)
they do not redeem with a slaughtered [lamb]
so (כך)
they do not redeem the firstling of an ass
which
has died (emended, as per Lieberman, *Tosefet Rishonim*, II, 262, to read: פתר חמור).
B. [Concerning] the firstling of an ass—
the commandment with respect to it [requires] sustaining it for thirty days;
C. henceforth [either] one redeems it
or
one breaks its neck.

1:15a

A. Below (lit. from) what
[value] may one not go [in choosing a redemption-lamb]?
B. R. Yose b. R. Judah
says:
One may not go below a shekel's worth.
C. What
is [the case involving] the redemption-[lamb] for the firstling of an ass
that (ה)
re-enters [among] the pen[ned flock] to be tithed (i.e., in m. Bek. 1:4:J)?
D. [The case concerns] an Israelite
who
had [ass-foals whose status as firstlings was] in doubt [i.e, the case of m. Bek. 1:4:C];
and
he undertook to redeem them [with the said redemption-lamb].
E. And
so too
[in the case of] a priest
who
inherits [the estate] of his mother's Israelite father (as emended by Lieberman, *Tosefet Rishonim*, II,

266) [and the estate included the firstling of an ass],

F. or,

[an Israelite] gave him as a gift the firstling of an ass [still needing] to be redeemed [and the priest redeemed either ass-foal with a lamb]—
G. this is the redemption-[lamb] for the firstling of an ass (as per Lieberman's emendation above)

that

re-enters [among] the pen[ned flock] to be tithed.

1:15b-16

A. Lo,

[in the case of an Israelite]

who

has the firstling of an ass,

[and]

does not have [a lamb] to redeem it [with] (as per Lieberman's emendation above)—
B. [Should] a priest say to him:
Give it to me,

and

I will redeem it,

lo,

this [Israelite] shall not give it to him,

unless

he is certain

that

he [the priest] will redeem it.

1:17

A. **He breaks its neck from behind with a hatchet,**

and

buries it (m. Bek. 1:7:A, trans. Neusner, *Holy Things*, III, 154),

B. and

it is forbidden to derive benefit [from it].

C. One shall not kill it [in any other manner];
not with a staff,

and

not with a cane,

and,

one shall not lock the door before it [i.e., shut it in or out]

so that

it might die [of starvation or neglect].

D. And
if
one did so,
lo,
this one has fulfilled (Lieberman, *Tosefet Rishonim*, II, 266, emends to: has not fulfilled] [one's obligation].

1:18

A. While yet (ב)
alive
[the unredeemed firstling] is forbidden
as regards (ב)
shearing
and
as regards
working.
B. And
R. Simeon
permits [this].
And
the firstborn son is permitted
as regards
all of them.

1:19

A. [In the case of] a she-ass
which
had not [yet] borne offspring,
and
she bore two males [but one does not know which emerged first]—
B. one gives one lamb to the priest;
C. [If she bore] a male
and
a female [but one does not know which emerged first],
D. one separates out a [redemption]-lamb,
and
it remains **one's own.**
E. [In the case of] two [she-]asses,
which
had not [yet] borne (see Lieberman, *Tosefet Rishonim*, II, 266),
and
they bore two males,
F. one gives two [redemption]-lambs to the priest.

	G. [If they bore] a male
and	
	a female,
H. or	
	two males
and	
	a female,
	I. one gives one [redemption]-lamb to the priest.
	J. [If they bore] two females
and	
	a male,
K. or	
	two males
and	
	two females,
and	
	one does not know [who gave birth to what],
	L. **there is nothing here for the priest [to claim]** (m. Bek. 1:3).
M. But	
	one separates out a single lamb
and	
	redeems with it each and every [male].[2]

The imposition upon Tosefta of analytic categories so useful in analyzing the Bavli is not very successful. I need not concern myself with Tosefta's citations (in boldface type) of Mishnah, as I have already examined Mishnah in its own right. Of interest is the Tosefta's use of language where it glosses, comments upon, or complements Mishnah, and where Tosefta has added supplementary materials which depart from Mishnah's agenda. Discounting, then, all materials appearing in boldface in column 1, one gets the following tally:

-"and" appears 46 times;
-"or" is used 2 times;
-some other term appears in only 6 instances, as follows:
- "But (אבל)," 2 times (at 1:2:F and 1:19:M);
- "Because of what (מפני מה)," 1 time (at 1:8:A);
- "Why does Scripture say (מה תלמוד לומר)," 1 time (at 1:9:A);
- "Below (lit. from) what [value] (מכמה)," 1 time (at 1:15a:A);

2. The charting and translation of t. Bek. 1 (ed. Zuckermandel) are my own, unless otherwise noted.

"What is [the case of] (איזה הוא)," 1 time (at 1:15a:C);

For the most part, structure and order in t. Bekorot 1, when not deriving from simple juxtaposition of cases and rulings, results in an overwhelming number of instances from the use of "and" (and sometimes "or") to concatenate items. Here Tosefta shows a propensity for mimicking Mishnah's use of language and can be said to be preoccupied with serving and extending Mishnah's *listenwissenschaftliche* agenda. This is the case in a full 48 out of 54 entries (in Roman type) in column 1.

The concatenation of items by juxtaposition or by the use of "and" (or "or") is, moreover, a feature regardless of whether the passages comment upon, complement or supplement Mishnah, to use Neusner's classification. Witness in this regard t. Bek. 1:13D, which offers a typical example of toseftan commentary upon Mishnah (m. Bek. 1:4.I.1.):

m. Bek. 1:4.I.1.

And	
	one redeems with it [the redemption-lamb] many times.

t. Bek. 1:13.D.

	One redeems with it;
	one repeats a second time [using the same sheep],
and	
	one repeats a third time [using the same sheep].

Tosefta now moves forthwith from commentary at t. Bek. 1:13.D to providing complementary material at t. Bek. 1:13.E:

t. Bek. 1:13.E.

E. and	
	one brings it [the same animal] as a vow-offering
and	
	a free-will offering,
and	
	for one's sin-offering
and	
	for one's guilt-offering;
and	
	it is liable under the law of the firstling [should it give birth to a firstling],

and

[for] the priestly gifts [should it be slaughtered as food].

An apt example of the use of a Mishnah-like list form in Tosefta's supplementary materials appears at t. Bek. 1:10 (supplementing both m. Bek. 1:2:H as well as its commentary at t. Bek. 1:9.F.)

m. Bek. 1:2.H:

H. For
that which

comes forth from the unclean is unclean

and

that which

comes forth from the clean is clean.

t. Bek. 1:9.F and 1:10:

F. Since (שׁ)

an unclean animal does not bear [young] by a clean [animal],

and

a clean [animal] does not bear [young] by an unclean [animal],

and

not large cattle [e.g., oxen] by small cattle [e.g., sheep],

and

not small cattle by large cattle,

and

not humankind by any of them,

and

not any of them by humankind.

1:10

A. clean small cattle bear [young] after five months [of pregnancy] (emend to remove: even … they have said; see Neusner, *Holy Things* {1979:148});
B. clean small cattle [bear young] after nine months [of pregnancy];
C. unclean large cattle [bear young] after twelve months [of pregnancy];
D. the dog [bears young] after fifty days [of pregnancy];
the cat [bears young] after fifty-two days [of pregnancy];

E. swine [bear young] after sixty days [of pregnancy];
F. fox

and

all that run [bear young] after six months [of pregnancy];
G. the wolf

and

the lion

and

the bear

and

the tiger

and

the leopard

and

the elephant

and

the monkey

and

the long-tailed ape [bear young] after three years [of pregnancy];

H. and

the snake [bears young] after seven years [of pregnancy];

Mere juxtaposition is used at t. Bek. 1:10A-F; thereafter "and" serves to build lists.

I turn now to the six other items provisionally placed in column 1. "But" at both t. Bek. 1:3 and t. Bek. 1:19 serves exactly the same functions, in both instances, as joining language. In the first, a supplementary ruling is melded to the preceding law. At 1:19 the coordinating conjunction joins complementary toseftan rulings to an antecedent citation of Mishnah. In sum, "but" functions too to concatenate rulings in listlike fashion.

The four remaining items in column 1 all ask direct questions. At t. Bek. 1:9, "What does Scripture say" introduces a legal exegesis of the biblical text. The question is structural; of necessity it draws in its wake several items, namely, a citation of Scripture integrated into the question, a response to the question, a probative analogy or reason (here an analogy) which, implicitly at least, flows from particuliar (apparently idiosyncratic) features of the scriptural verse. In fact, the question is needed only because the feature of the verse must, in the formulator's view, be explicitly identified. Otherwise, the scriptural citation could stand alone as the opening to the midrashic pericope (commencing, "'A camel,' 'A camel'—[is stated twice] in order to ...").

From a literary perspective, the exegetical unit as a whole is entirely independent of Mishnah. It is intelligible on its own, reflects nothing of Mishnah's language, and assumes Scripture as its base-text, rather than Mishnah. Indeed, 1:9.A-B(+C) directly contradicts m. Bek. 1:2.E-H. What the toseftan editors have done is to juxtapose the exegesis with the Mishnah ruling in question. By providing attributions for each (Simeon for the exegesis, the sages for the Mishnah's anonymous ruling) the editors have created a semblance of a dispute. The dispute, of course, shows none of the features, such as the careful balance of stichs and use of parallelism, which characterize that form as typically used in Mishnah.

But as much as t. Bek. 1:9.A-B(+C) is in literary terms distant from Mishnah, it is not entirely Bavli-like either. To be sure, the Bavli incorporates into its analytic composites just such legal exegeses as *baraitot*, extra-mishnaic sources of purported tannaitic origins. But the Bavli's structural formularies, even its structuring questions, differ substantially from the type of interrogative formulary in evidence in the legal exegesis here incorporated by the toseftan editors into a poorly formulated dispute. For clearly the question here plays no role in the larger task of formulating extended analytic composites. For the Bavli's structuring questions usually refer, so to speak, both backwards and forwards. That is, they challenge or seek expansion upon an antecedent analysis and draw in their wake a subsequent discussion. Here the admittedly analytic questioning plays no such role. Its structuring function is contained totally within the discrete pericope of legal midrash. When I turn to a legal midrashic document, Sifre on Numbers, we shall see much that is similar. Suffice it to say, that t. Bek. 1:9.A-B(+C) differs in its rhetorical formularies from most of what we have found in column 1 of Tosefta, which thus far shows a propensity to imitate Mishnah's use of conjunctions to build lists.

t. Bek. 1:15 provides the last two items in column 1 requiring attention. "Below (lit. from) what [value]" asks a straightforward question which functions as a legal protasis for the ruling which follows. Like questions in Mishnah (e.g., m. Bek. 1:2.E.: "What is their ruling as to eating?"), the question here at A permits turning to a new issue, for which none of the preceding phrases provide an adequate literary antecedent. One may say the same for the question, "What is [the case] ...?", at C, which produces a Mishnah-like list of three appropriate, complex cases.

In sum, items in column 1 of Tosefta, spanning materials which comment upon, complement and supplement Mishnah, generally mimic Mishnah's use of conjunctions and of the occasional question to concatenate rulings and lists. Thus far, Tosefta seems to use language in a manner similar to its base-text, Mishnah.

Let me now review the foiled attempt to locate in column 2 toseftan linguistic formularies cognate to the Bavli's dialectical formularies. As was the case with Mishnah, I cannot hope to deal in detail with the role in Tosefta of attributional formulae such as "R. x says" or "said R. x." One would expect Tosefta, following Mishnah, to use attributions to append several different legal rulings, or apodases, to a single statement of case, or protasis. Such disputes, frequent in Mishnah, appear as well throughout Tosefta (see Neusner, 1977). Oddly, t. Bek. 1 offers only one clear example of this usage of "said/says," at t. Bek. 1:6.F-H. T. Bek. 1:13.F. would provide another instance, if one were to append F to m. Bek. 1:5.A as a replacement of m. Bek. 1:5.B, of which Tosefta proffers an alternate wording. Otherwise, all other instances of attributional formulae in t. Bek. 1, including t. Bek. 1:13.F, serve to link named authorities to independent rulings, that is, rulings which do not dispute another legal statement on the same issue. If in Mishnah "says" is in part a redactional concatenating device to offer several apodases to a single protasis, in t. Bek. 1 quite another function may be served by the attributional formulae, namely supplying an authoritative voice for a ruling, even when that ruling does not dispute another legal opinion. In this respect the use of "says/said" in Tosefta's independent sayings parallels one frequently used mode of attribution in the Bavli. That mode is evident in the Bavli not only when it cites what it deems to be tannaitic authorities but also in its citation as *authoritative source material* of sayings attributed to amoraic authorities, whose views are submitted to query and analysis or cited as proof of some stated proposition.

As with Mishnah, one finds in Tosefta the relative pronominal prefix, שׁ (variously translatable as "which," "who" or "that"), used to concatenate circumstances comprising a complex case. We find in Tosefta, however, quite another usage of the pronominal prefix, שׁ, one which recalls strongly the recurrent dialectical rhetoric of the Bavli. In these latter instances, "which" does not stand alone in column 2, merely joining two circumstances of a case. Rather, "which" appears as part of a sequence of operators specifying the precise logical relationship which obtains among items of content (appearing in column 3). The two most prominent of these instances appear in the charts at t. Bek. 1:2.C-F and t. Bek. 1:3.

t. Bek. 1:2.C-F:

Scripture says:
[citation]—
that which
applies to you
in the case of
x
applies to you
in the case of
y;
[ruling]

t. Bek. 1:3:

Among all
[case a]
that which
[ruling]
[sub-case a']
only

Among all
[case b]
that which
[ruling]
[sub-case b']
only

In the former passage, Scripture supplies an authoritative basis for an analogy, which is spelled out in the remaining clauses. The relative pronoun is now embedded in a larger linguistic pattern, the force of which is not to link a further defining characteristic to some preceding circumstance. Rather "which" is now integral to the larger formal structure, which constitutes a formalized analogical argument leading to a conclusion. Here, then, we find a formal use of language resembling that of column 2 of the Bavli, that column in which I previously isolated the Talmud's dialectical formularies.

The latter passage, t. Bek. 1:3, exhibits another usage of "which" differing from the now expected use of the relative pronoun to concatenate the circumstances of a case. "Which" stands within a larger formalized linguistic structure. The structure is not, however, an argument but a statement limiting the application of a rule. Instead of a law applying to a class of objects, it applies only to one specific item of the class. In essence, from the perspective of the law in question, the item is *sui generis*. T. Bek. 1:3 is not argumentative as it stands; it does not draw conclusions from accepted premises. But surely lurking behind it is an unstated problem to which t. Bek. 1:3 is the solution. That problem for 1:3.A will certainly have been the contradiction between relevant biblical verses pertaining to the firstling of unclean animals: Numbers 18:15 specifies that the firstling of an "unclean beast" must be redeemed; Exodus 13:13 enjoins the redemption of the "firstling of an ass" with a sheep. Herein lies the problem, as well as the premises for its resolution. The verses are taken not to be contradictory but complementary, as (encoded) premises for an argument which might be formulated as follows:

	[citation of Scripture pertaining to case a]
	[citation of Scripture pertaining to sub-case a']
Among all	
	[case a]
that which	
	[ruling]
	[sub-case a']
only	

The statement has now become a formalized argument based on accepted data. (I should point out, by way of anticipation, that some of the substance, although not the form, of this argument is to be found in Sifre on Numbers 118, which I shall examine later in this chapter).

The literary-critical question is whether t. Bek. 1:3 or t. Bek. 1:3.A was originally formulated in some other context, where the limiting statement was prefaced with scriptural citations. I suspect so, for m. Bek. 1 contains no pericope which explicitly supplies an intelligible and literary antecedent for t. Bek. 1:3.A. Only the general topic of m. Bek. 1, and no specific element therein provides a context for t. Bek. 1:3.A. Why is this bit of source criticism of the Tosefta important for our immediate task, the understanding of the Bavli's use of language as highlighted by the rhetoric of earlier rabbinic materials, with which the Bavli's editors were likely familiar? First, if my analysis is correct, one finds yet again in column 2 of Tosefta a reflection of linguistic usage paralleling the Bavli's formalized dialectical language. Second, in compiling their "commentary" to Mishnah, Tosefta's editors appear to have used at times materials original to other contexts. Excised from their original settings and stripped of phrases which in that previous setting made the intent of the materials fully apparent, toseftan editors have felt free to press that now denatured material into service as Mishnah commentary. Here too one is reminded of the eclecticism of the Bavli's editors in excising materials from other contexts in the service of constructing larger analytic composites.

T. Bek. 1:5 offers a triplet comparable in many respects to the argument reconstructed from the passage at t. Bek. 1:3.A. T. Bek. 1:5 exhibits the following structure:

[citation of Scripture specifying law applies to sub-case a', sub-case a'' and sub-case a''' of larger category a]

[repeat of scriptural specification of sub-case a']
unless/until it be [the case] that (עד ש)
[both x and y (= Mishnah) are a']

[repeat of scriptural specification of sub-case a'']
unless/until it be [the case] that (עד ש)
[both x and y (= Mishnah) are a'']

[repeat of scriptural specification of sub-case a''']
unless/until it be [the case] that (עד ש)
[both x and y (= Mishnah) are a''']

The recurring formulary, "unless/until it be [the case] that (עד ש)," again provides the force of argument linking scriptural premises to a conclusion. One need only supply the still implicit assumption that something is to be drawn from the fact that Scripture took pains to specifiy three sub-cases, a', a'' and a''', when, ostensibly, reference to larger category "a" should have sufficed. This is a not an atypical early rabbinic form of argument based on Scripture. One need only peruse such legal midrashic works as Sifra, Sifre on Numbers and Sifre on Deuteronomy (and other sections of Tosefta) to find its conceptual parallels. To be sure, the logic is not syllogistic, an important fact; the conclusions are known at the outset. Otherwise one would be hardpressed to reach them from the scriptural premises and the logical operator, "unless/until it be [the case] that." The conclusion known in advance appears in Mishnah, the language of which is replicated in each unit of the triplet. This is an interesting point since, while entirely intelligible on its own with only the biblical law as its logical context, the current toseftan pericope has been formulated explicitly as a commentary and a complement to the text of the Mishnah. Again one has in Tosefta the use of formalized language which is comparable to the Bavli's dialectical formularies. Again in Tosefta the use of such language appears in passages formulated as legal exegesis of Scripture, that is halakic midrash.

Another case in point is t. Bek. 1:9.A-B(+C), which I discussed earlier in the treatment of items in column 1. This independent halakic midrash is attributed to R. Simeon and made part of a rather poorly formulated and quite artificial dispute. T. Bek. 1:9.A-B exhibits the following structure:

t. Bek. 1:9.A-B:

A. R. x

says:

Why does Scripture say:

[scriptural citation specifying species a]

and

[second scriptural citation specifying species a]

twice?

B. [It does this] in order to (ל) include

[something that looks like species a, but is species b],

just as (כ)

[species a].

The nature of the argument is by now familiar. Scripture supplies authoritative data, taken to be necessary and sufficient to draw the requisite conclusions. T. Bek. 1:9.A-B concludes that with respect to scriptural law, which here deals with clean animals permitted for consumption, animals of unclean species and their look-alikes borne by animals of clean species are to be treated equally. Again the argument is no syllogism, as a number of premises must be supplied. For example, one must assume that Scripture never actually repeats itself. So if the first verse refers to one matter, a parallel verse must be a (cryptic) reference to some related, but different matter. The conclusion, as before, is logically prior to the premises from which it is said to flow, and directly contradicts Mishnah. Hence Tosefta's redactors have refashioned this otherwise independent halakic midrash as a dispute with Mishnah's anonymous authority. Once again stock formularies ("in order to include ... just as ...") provide the force of argument in the structure.

Finally, I turn to this chapter's most elaborately structured argument from Scripture, t. Bek. 1:2.A-F. The latter's structure is as follows:

t. Bek. 1:2.A-F:

A. And

so you [must] say

in the case of
[sub-category a']
and
in the case of
[sub-category a''].
B. Because,
since
[statement: ruling applies to a' and a'']
in the case of
[sub-category b'],
one might [think]
[ruling]
in the case of
[sub-category b''].
C. Scripture [however] says:
[Scripture grouping larger category a and larger category b with respect to law at issue]—
D. that which
applies to you
in the case of
[category a]
applies to you
in the case of
[catgory b].
E. That which
does not apply to you
in the case of
[category a]
does not apply to you
in the case of
[category b].
F. [Thus]
[statement of law].

The pericope is entirely unintelligible on its own. Some local antecedent is required for "And so you must say ...." M. Bek. 1:1b supplies that context for this complement in Tosefta. Relative to the other midrashic proofs encountered thus far in t. Bek. 1, this pericope is striking, for it does not content itself with such a proof only. It begins with the scriptural citation, introduced by "Scripture, however, says ..." (at C). What precedes the citation is quite a different type of argument. It is a critique which, it seems, demonstrates the necessity of the scripturally based proof. This critique in itself makes no reference to Scripture, but in its current toseftan context, offers an analysis of the necessity for a mishnaic ruling (at m. Bek. 1:1b). T. Bek. 1:2.A-B strikes one as the rhetorical cognate of dialectical language within constituent units of the Bavli's elaborated composites. With the latter, too, we are used to seeing analyses and critiques of antecedent propositions and rulings. But something is amiss in this toseftan pericope. If one reads the critique of the first half of the pericope with m. Bek. 1:1a, the second part of t. Bek. 1:2, the argument from Scripture, does not follow at all. How so? Mishnah states that "priests and levites are exempt" from the law pertaining to the firstling of an ass. Reading t. Bek. 1:2A as referring to this ruling in Mishnah, Tosefta must be understood as arguing for the necessity of Mishnah so specifying matters. The argument states that if Mishnah had not done so, one might have concluded from the fact that priests and Levites must observe the law of the firstling with respect to clean animals (as specified in m. Bek. 2:1), that they are equally liable in the case of the firstling of an ass. Mishnah must therefore specify otherwise. This indeed is reminiscent of the type of Mishnah criticism with which b. Bek. 2a opens. But why resort in the second half to a midrashic proof? Has Tosefta not in fact already satisfactorily disposed of the issue, which, in the current context is the question, Why must Mishnah so inform us at m. Bek. 1:1b? The midrashic proof which follows constitutes a complete *non sequitur*.

I propose that one finds in this pericope a unit formulated for another context altogether and put to quite another inappropriate use, as critical analysis of Mishnah. I suspect that t. Bek. 1:2 was formulated with precisely that scriptural verse cited at C as necessary and sufficient evidence as its original opening unit and logical context. With Scripture replacing m. Bek. 1:1b's ruling, the entirety of t. Bek. 1:2.A-F logically follows nicely. That logic is as follows. Why does one need the scriptural verse in question? If it were not there one would (mistakenly) conclude that priests and Levites are liable under the law pertaining to the firstling of an ass. Scripture allegedly provides the basis for an argument from analogy that proves (correctly) that matters are otherwise. If I am correct, we have here once more an example of typical halakic midrash such as is found in Sifre on Numbers and elsewhere. As with the other examples in t. Bek. 1, we find a structured sequence of rhetorical formularies constituting the force of such midrashic argument. In this respect, t. Bek. 1:2's formularies are reminiscent of items in column 2 of my charting of the Bavli.

Column 2 of the chart of Tosefta offers only six more passages for discussion. They are:

t. Bek. 1:8 (twice):		
	since (שׁ)	
		[statement of fact]
	but only (אלא)	
		[statement of complementary contrasting fact]
t. Bek. 1:11:		
		[species a do x]
and		
		[do y]
	like (כ)	
		[species b]
t. Bek. 1:14:		
	A. Just as (כשם שׁ)	
		[citation of Mishnah's ruling]
	so (כך)	
		[complementray ruling + circumstance]
	which	
		[circumstance]
t. Bek. 1:16:		
	Lo (הרי)	
	who (שׁ)	
		[circumstance]
and		
		[circumstance]
	lo (הרי)	
		[ruling]
	unless (אלא אם כן)	
		[exceptional circumstance]
	that (שׁ)	
		[completion of exceptional circumstance]
t. Bek. 1:17:		
		[prohibition a]
and		
		[prohibition a']
and		
		[prohibition a'']
	so that (בשביל שׁ)	
		[ultimate circumstance which would result in carrying out prohibited act a'']
and		
	if (אם)	
		[prohibited act a'']
	lo (הרי)	
		[subsidiary ruling]

t. Bek. 1:18:

	While yet (ב)	
		[circumstance]
		[operative verb of ruling]
	as regards (ב)	
		[objective phrase of ruling]
and		
	as regards (ב)	
		[additional objective phrase of ruling]

We have already seen in Mishnah something similar to t. Bek. 1:8, which uses "since" in adducing a statement of fact to support a ruling; "But only" permits the contrasting of two facts which together comprise the probative observation. As noted in the discussion of Mishnah, the provision of factual evidence to support a classification with respect to the law is not in itself an argument. At best such a rationale may be seen as an argument fragment.

T. Bek. 1:11 is part of a longer list comprising a biological taxonomy from which no legal rulings flow. The use of "like" apparently draws a taxonomic analogy. In reality it permits the inclusion of the analogue in the list without repeating the relevant facts that pertain to it. That is, it is no analogy, but rather skilful editorial joining language.

T. Bek. 1:14, by contrast, does offer an argument from analogy, without scriptural premises. Rather, the citation of Mishnah's ruling provides a necessary and sufficient basis for drawing the conclusion. As in the toseftan passages of halakic midrash examined, "just as ... so ..." at t. Bek. 1:14 constitutes a structured sequence of formulae which function together to provide the force of argument. The structure is exceedingly simple and succinct, perhaps in imitation of Mishnah's own highly laconic style.

As regards the remaining toseftan passages outlined above, none of the formularies provisionally placed in column 2 function individually or together to provide arguments or analyses. These formularies link circumstances to one another to define cases and join cases to their rulings. If they appear to us at first glance to play some other, more analytic function, perhaps it is because we have become used to Mishnah's somewhat more laconic style, in which the same is often achieved using merely "and" and "which."

Let us return to the principal purpose of this analysis, the manner in which Tosefta may elucidate what I have found in the Bavli. What may I now say of the use of rhetorical or formalized language, those recurrent linguistic formularies which are distinct from the idiomatic content of Tosefta?

First and foremost, whether one speaks of Tosefta passages which are commentary upon, complementary to, or supplementary of Mishnah, Tosefta shows a propensity to imitate or to parallel Mishnah's use of conjunctions and relative pronouns to concatenate items. These toseftan passages, when organized as a more or less sustained companion-document to Mishnah, extend Mishnah's program of classifying objects and circumstances with respect to those laws which may apply to them. In this respect the redactors of Tosefta underwrite Mishnah's *listenwissenschaftliche* agenda. That is not to say that Tosefta at these junctures is simply like Mishnah. Tosefta could not be like Mishnah, if for no other reason than that it relies upon Mishnah at so many junctures for an intelligible context. Unlike Mishnah, it is not formulated as a document whole and complete in itself, a series of coherent "studies." Even when Tosefta is most mishnaic in its interests and style, readers of Tosefta must always halt their reading in order to consult Mishnah. I shall return to this important fact later when I pull together and interpret the meaning of our observations concerning the Bavli. Both Tosefta and the Bavli are organized as commentaries of a sort upon Mishnah. Yet in comparison to Tosefta, the Bavli moves from points of departure in Mishnah to elaborate composite essays which are relatively coherent and self-contained. This, Tosefta does not generally attempt—we must suppose by design. Perhaps for this reason Tosefta displays virtually no structural language in our column 1 cognate to formularies isolated in column 1 of our charts of the Bavli.

Where Tosefta is not imitative of Mishnah's taxonomic interests and of its concatenating formularies, Tosefta attempts to offer support for a mishnaic ruling. To these ends t. Bek. 1 sometimes resorts to midrashic proofs of various lengths. It is here that one sees sequences of stock formularies operating as the machine of a probative argument. Here one finds in Tosefta the use of language reminiscent of the Bavli's use of dialectical formularies. The premises of these arguments are supplied by explicitly cited verses from Scripture and by implicit propositions about the nature of Scripture. Such a proposition would be, for example, that Scripture is never repetitive; scriptural parallels are, therefore, apparent, not real. Considered apart from their current location in Tosefta as elucidating Mishnah, the primary purpose of these midrashic proofs is not the proof of some mishnaic law but the demonstration by example of certain propositions about Scripture. It is significant indeed that even our cursory literary analysis suggests that, unlike other Tosefta passages, these scriptural proofs were originally formulated with scriptural passages, not mishnaic pericopes, as their literary and logical antecedents. T. Bek. 1:2 is most suggestive in this respect. The structured sequence of formularies constitutive of argument in evidence in these toseftan halakic midrashim contrasts sharply with those several instances in Tosefta where an allegedly probative fact is joined to an antecedent ruling with "since." We have already seen this usage in Mishnah. At one instance only do we have an "argument" from analogy (using the language, "just as ... so ...") that does not proceed from Scripture.

It is on this note that I turn to a third document, the compilation of halakic midrash called Sifre on Numbers, in a third attempt to shed more light upon the Bavli through comparison of its use of language with that of several other ancient rabbinic texts.

Points of comparison in Sifre on Numbers

In Sifre on Numbers redactors have compiled or composed units of legal midrash to constitute a systematic treatment of selected sections of the book of Numbers. In this respect Korah 118a, translated and charted below, is typical of the document (see Neusner, 1986c). The units or pericopes of Korah 118a are arranged to deal in order with the constituent phrases of Numbers 18:15-18, which we have cited in full before proceeding with our presentation of Sifre.

The precise date and provenance of Sifre need not concern us much. Most scholars would agree that Sifre's redaction occurred prior to the Bavli's. It matters little for my purposes whether Sifre is mid-third, late-fourth or early fifth century CE. For us Sifre represents yet another ancient rabbinic document the language of which provides a relevant point of comparison in the effort to elucidate the Bavli's rhetorical formularies. I turn, then, to Numbers 18:15-18 and to Sifre on Numbers, Korah 118a. Once more I have applied the conventions and literary categories used in our presentation of the Bavli. Verbatim parallels to Mishnah are in boldface type, to Tosefta in italics.

Numbers 18:15-18

Every firstling of all living flesh, which shall be offered to the Lord, both of humankind and of beast, shall be yours [i.e., the priests']; but you shall surely redeem the firstling of humankind, and the firstling of the unclean beast you shall [as well] redeem. And [concerning] its redemption, from the age of one month you shall redeem [it] for your silver measure of five shekels in the shekels of the Sanctuary, that is twenty gerah. But the firstling of an ox, or the firstling of a sheep, or the firstling of a goat you shall not redeem; they are holy; their blood you shall splash on the altar; and their fatty parts you shall ignite as a fire-offering of pleasing odour to the Lord. And their flesh shall be yours [i.e., the priests']; like the chest of the waive-offering and the right shoulder, it shall be yours.

Sifre on Numbers
Korah, Pisqa 118a

I

A. "Every firstling of all living flesh"—

B. I [might] surmise [that] (שומע אני)
even
[of] the wild beast
is implied (במשמע)!

C. Scripture says (תלמוד לומר):
"which shall be offered to the Lord"—
D. to exclude
the wild beast.

E.1.. [Perhaps, rather,] the implication is (משמע)
to exclude
[both] the wild animal
E.2. and
to exclude
the blemished [animal, which also cannot be offered as a sacrifice].

H. Scripture says:
"Both of humankind and of beast"—
I. to include
the blemished.

IIa

A. "Both of humankind and of beast"—
B. that which
applies to you
in the case of
humankind,
applies to you
in the case of
an animal.
C. [Thus]

Levites
are excluded (t. Bek. 1:2; see Sifre Zutta, Korah, 18:15, ed. Horowitz, 295; see Mek. deR. Ish., Bo, 16, eds. Horowitz and Rabin, 58);
D.1. since (שׁ)
[the law of the firstling] of humankind does not apply to you in their case,
D.2. [the law of the firstling] of an [unclean] animal should not apply to you in their case.

IIb

A. "Both of humankind and of beast"—

B. [Scripture] equates (מקישׁ)
the firstling of humankind
with (ל)
the firstling of an animal.
C.1. Just as (מה)
[concerning] the firstling of an animal, aborted foeti exempt [subsequent offspring] from the law of the firstling,
C.2. so too (אף)
[concerning] the firstling of humankind, aborted foeti exempt [subsequent offspring] from the law of the firstling (see m. Bek. 8:1; t. Bek. 6:1; Mek. deR. Ish., Bo, 16, eds. Horowitz and Rabin, 58).

D.1. Just as (מה)
[concerning] the firstling of humankind, one is obligated to give [the redemption money] to the priest wherever he shall desire,
D.2. so too (אף)
[concerning] the firstling of an animal, one is obligated to give [the redemption-lamb, or the firstling itself in the case of a clean animal] to the priest wherever he shall desire (see Mek. deR. Ish., Bo, 16, eds. Horowitz and Rabin, 58).

IIc

A. Because it says (לפי שהוא אומר):
"And there you shall bring your burnt offerings and your holocaust offerings, etc.,... and the firstlings of your flock" (Deut. 12:6),
B. I [might] surmise [that] (שומע אני)
even
in the case of

the place [of the Sanctuary] being distant, it would be incumbent upon one to sustain it and bring it to the Temple.

C. Scripture says (תלמוד לומר):

"Both of humankind and of beast"—

D.1. just as (מה)

[concerning] the firstling of humankind, one is obligated to give [the redemption money] to the priest wherever he shall desire,

D.2. so too (אף)

[concerning] the firstling of an animal, one is obligated to give [the redemption-lamb, or the firstling itself in the case of a clean animal] to the priest wherever he shall desire (see Mek. deR. Ish., Bo, 16, eds. Horowitz and Rabin, 58).

E.1. And

just as (ומה)

[concerning] the firstling of humankind, one sustains it for thirty days [and then redeems it]

E.2. so too (אף)

[concerning] the firstling of an animal, one sustains it for thirty days [and then redeems it or gives it to the priest to be sacrificed] (see m. Bek. 3:1; t. Bek. 3:1; 1:14; see Mek. deR. Ish., Bo, 16, eds. Horowitz and Rabin, 58).

III

A. "But you shall surely redeem"—

B. This was a question which was asked before the sages in the Vineyard at Yavneh:

C. [Concerning] a firstling [of an ass]

which

died (see t. Bek. 1:14),

D.1. what (מהן)

of the owners [being permitted] to redeem it

D.2. and

to feed it to dogs?

E. Expounded

R. Tarfon:

F. "But you shall surely redeem"—

G.1. you redeem the living,

G.2. and [on the contrary]

you do not redeem the dead;

H.1. you redeem the unclean,

H.2. and [on the contrary]

you do not redeem the clean.

IV

A. "But you shall surely redeem"—
B. I [might] surmise [that] (שומע אני)
even
[redeeming] all other unclean animal[s]
is implied (במשמע).

C. Scripture says (תלמוד לומר):
"And the firstling of an ass you shall redeem with a sheep" (Ex. 34:20)—
D.1. you redeem the firstling of an ass,
D.2. and [on the contrary]
you do not redeem the firstling of any other unclean animal (see t. Bek. 1:3).

E.1. Or [perhaps, I may conclude from this verse that] (או)
the firstling of an ass you redeem with a sheep,
E.2. and [on the contrary]
any other unclean animal with clothing
E.3. and
utensils!?
F. Scripture says, again, elsewhere (תלמוד לומר עוד במקום אחר):
"And any firstling of an ass you shall redeem with a sheep" (Ex. 13:13) (Ex. 13:13 is the only other possible cognate verse, but reads: וכל פתר ...)—
G.1. with a sheep you redeem,
G.2. and [on the contrary]
you do not redeem with clothing
G.3. and
utensils.

H. If so (אם כן),
why does Scripture say (מה תלמוד לומר):
"But you shall surely redeem?"

I.1. If
it is not
[concerned with] the matter
that
they redeem an unclean beast,
I.2. [then]
assign it to
the matter
that
they sanctify an unclean beast for the upkeep of the Temple,
I.3. and

they subsequently redeem it from the sanctity of the upkeep of the Temple [and that with which they redeem it is donated for the Temple's upkeep] (see parallel to section IV in Mek. deR. Ish., Bo, 18, eds. Horowitz and Rabin, 71, lns. 8-14).

V

A. "Redeem"—
B. [i.e.,] immediately.
C. Do you say (אתא אומר)
"Redeem"—
[i.e.,] immediately?
D. Or (או)
is it (אינו)
after a time
only (אלא)?
E. Scripture says:
"And [concerning] its redemption, from the age of one month you shall redeem [it] for your [...] measure...."

F. "Five shekels"—
G. [i.e., only] the one redeemed with five selahs is redeemed after a time.

H. Lo,
why does Scripture say (מה תלמוד לומר):
"You shall redeem?"
I. You shall redeem immediately [the firstling of an ass with a sheep] (contrast V.A,H and t. Bek. 1:14 and sec. II above).

VI

A. "And [concerning] its redemption, from the age of one month you shall redeem [it]"—
B. a general statement (כלל).
C. "For your silver measure of five shekels"—
D. a specification (פרט).

E. A general statement and [subsequently] a specification—
included in the general statement is
that which is
in the specification
only.
F. "And all firstborn sons of humankind you shall redeem" (Ex. 13:13)—
G. [Scripture] reverted to a general statement!?
H. Or

have you [merely re-]stated
a general statement [inherent in] the first general statement [i.e., the two general statments are to be assimilated to one another and not treated as two independent sources]?

I.1. It [can] only [be taken as] (לאו אלא)
a general statement and a specification [following] and a [second] general statement—
I.2. you [must] reason
[by generalizing] on the basis of the specification
only.
J.1. [The verses, therefore, intend]
to inform you (לומר לך) [that]
J.2. just as
the specification
indicates [one redeems with something in the larger category of] movable property
J.3. [against] which
there [can be] no liability [that is, it cannot be mortgaged],
J.4. so too
the general statement [comprises the use of]
only
movable property
J.5. [against] which
there [can be] no liablity [that is, it cannot be mortgaged].

K.1. On the basis of this they said (מיכן אמרו):
K.2. With anything they redeem the firstling of humankind,
K.3.except
slaves
K.4. and
deeds
K.5. and
immovable property (see m. Bek. 8:8; t. Bek. 6:13).

L.1. Rabbi [Judah the Patriarch]
says:
L.2. Even so (אף)
with anything they redeem the firstling of humankind,
L.3. except
deeds (see parallel to section VI in Mek. deR. Ish., Bo, 18, eds. Horowitz and Rabin, 72, lns. 1-8).

VII

A.1. "That is twenty gerah"—
A.2. why is it said (למה נאמר)?

B.1. Because it says (לפי שהוא אומר):
"And [concerning] its redemption, from the age of one month you shall redeem [it] for your silver measure,"
B.2. I [might] have [understood]
only(אין לי אלא)
silver [is used].
C. Whence [do I learn] (מנין)
that equal in value to silver [may be used]?
D. Scripture says:
"That is twenty gerah."

VIII

A.1. "But the firstling of an ox"—
A.2. [i.e.,] a genuine ox.

B.1. "Or the firstling of a sheep"—
B.2. [i.e.,] a genuine sheep.

C.1. "Or the firstling of a goat"—
C.2. [i.e,] a genuine goat;

D. [Scripture thereby intends]
to exclude
mixed-kinds (see m. Bek. 1:2; t. Bek. 1:5 and 1:130).[3]

Applying to Sifre those analytic conventions used to characterize rhetorical formularies in the Bavli has this time proven relatively more successful than attempts with Mishnah or Tosefta. Trying to identify in SifN. 118a language which in the Bavli we called structural formularies has generated little material in column 1. Yet, as we shall presently see, what does so appear differs radically from what resulted from the earlier analyses of the language of Mishnah and Tosefta. The attempt to apply my conventions for locating items in column 2 has produced a wealth of materials which resemble what I have called in the Bavli dialectical for-

3. The charting and translation of SifN., Korah 118 (ed. Horowitz, 138[ln. 1] - 139[ln. 16]) are my own.

mularies. In all, our exercise for SifN. 118a differs substantially from what we have come to expect from similar analyses of m. Bek. 1 and t. Bek. 1.

I turn first to column 1 with its structural formularies. One immediately notes the relative paucity of materials in column 1 of SifN. 118a in comparison to the charting of m. Bek. 1 and of t. Bek. 1. Yet in the latter two instances, the comparative plethora of items in column 1 was more apparent than real. Our perusal of Mishnah and Tosefta did not result in finding language which accorded with the Bavli's use of structural formularies. Rather, what in Mishnah and Tosefta virtually filled column 1 was the conjunction "and" used to concatenate items into orderly lists of cases and circumstances. That usage of the conjunction "and" in the service of producing hierarchical lists (to use Neusner's term [Neusner, 1981; 1983b]) is dramatically less common in SifN. 118a. SifN. 118a, which is approximately 15 percent longer than m. Bek. 1, exhibits only 8 uses of the concatenating *vav*. T. Bek. 1, some 80 percent longer than chapter 1 of m. Bek. and 30 percent longer than SifN. 118a, shows 46 such usages—that is, somewhat less frequently than Mishnah, but still constituting the dominant mode of organization within toseftan pericopes. If in Tosefta and Mishnah the use of *vav* serves these documents' *listenwissenschaftliche* purposes, then it is precisely the latter orientation and intent which SifN. 118a appears not to share.

Overlooking now the use of "and," the following items remain in column 1.

1. *SifN. 118a I.E.1.*

[exegesis]

[Perhaps, rather,] the implication is (משמע)

[alternative exegesis]

2. *SifN. 118a III.B-D.*

[base-Scripture]

This was a question which was asked before the sages in the Vineyard at Yavneh:

[circumstances]—

what (מהן) [is the law if]

[complementary circumstances]

3. *SifN. 118a IV.E.1.*

[exegesis]

Or [perhaps, I may conclude from this verse that] (או)

[alternative exegesis]

4. *SifN. 118a IV.H.*

[exegesis]

If so (אם כן),
why does Scripture say (מה תלמוד לומר):

[seemingly redundant Scripture]

5. *SifN. 118a V.C-H.*

Do you say (אתא אומר)

[Scripture]—
[previously given interpretation]?

Or (או)
is it (אינו)

[alternative mistaken interpretation]
[exegetical proof of former]

Lo,
why does Scripture say (מה תלמוד לומר):

[now seemingly redundant Scripture]
[complementary exegesis]

6. *SifN. 118a VI.H-I.*

[Scripture]
[operative exegetical principle]?

Or

[alternative operative exegetical principle]?

It [can] only [be taken as] (לאו אלא)

[statement as to which principle applies]

7. *SifN. 118a VI.K.*

[exegesis]

On the basis of this they said (מיכן אמרו):

[statement of law extending further former exegesis]

8. *SifN. 118a VII.A.*

[citation of Scripture]

why is it said (למה נאמר)?

Of the eight items listed, two (numbers 2 and 7) constitute joining language permitting the remainder of the perciope to follow upon the citation of the scriptural base-text. The other six items, numbers 1, 3, 4, 5, 6 and, to a lesser extent, 8 appear, however, strikingly reminiscent of the Bavli's structural formularies, for these items do not simply provide joining language permitting the orderly progression from one case with its attendant ruling to another. Rather the units which they occasion *challenge* what has preceded them, in order to expedite further *analysis, argument or proof.* To be sure, that proof or analysis always takes place within strictly confined parameters. It must always emerge from Scripture, all of the phrases of which are understood to be necessary and (in combination) necessarily sufficient. The issuing of a challenge always evokes an exegetical analysis which, for the topic or verses in question, continues until the necessity and/or sufficiency of the relevant verses are demonstrated. Hence, just as the permissible parameters of analysis thereby evoked are severely limited, so too the sequence of analyses thereby produced is never open-ended. Analysis is brought to completion when one has accounted for all the scriptural verses, at which point the subsequent, autonomous pericope dealing with the next phrase of the Scripture ensues. So the pericopes follow upon one another in a sequence determined by the order of the biblical text, upon which Sifre is organized as a type of commentary.

This dependency of Sifre upon Scripture for unity and coherence of the larger construct (or "chapter") of Sifre highlights a second striking trait of these potential correlates in Sifre of the Bavli's structural formularies. The rhetorical formularies listed above play no role outside the individual, independent and disconnected exegetical pericopes of Sifre. That is to say, they do not link individual analyses and pericopes into larger, more elaborated composites that might be deemed comparable to the Bavli's *sugyot.* Nor do they provide rhetorical links between *sugyot* in order to create what in the context of the Bavli I have called larger composite essays. If, therefore, we have seen in items 1, 3, 4, 5, 6 and possibly 8 language functioning in a manner like the Bavli's structural formularies, that correspondence is, at the same time, limited, for Sifre seems intent upon two things: first, Sifre's editors appear intent to rely necessarily upon Scripture for the unity of its "chapters"; second, the document seems committed to reaching definite conclusions within any one pericope, for only by so doing, in pericope after pericope, can Sifre demonstrate the validity of the fundamental propositions its seeks to propound about the nature of Scripture in relation to law.

I turn now to those materials in SifN. 118a which I have placed in column 2, which is replete with *structured sequences of formularies* which *operate together* to constitute argument from "facts" supplied by Scripture and implicit premises about the nature of Scripture. In Mishnah such structured sequences, while extant, are rare. The analysis of Tosefta leads one to suspect that sequences of logical operators functioning together may be relatively more common in Tosefta; yet in our perusal of t. Bek. 1, all such instances were in fact arguments from Scripture reminiscent of the pericopes of Sifre. In this regard, one notes that t. Bek. 1:2, which required a scriptural citation as its opening unit, here appears with just such a heading at SifN. 118a II.

While column 2 of SifN. 118a is replete with structured sequences of formulaic logical operators, the variety of argumentative forms is limited. The most frequently recurring formalized sequence produces an argument from analogy. Six times over four pericopes SifN. 118a incorporates these stock analogical operators into what seems larger, recurrent forms or structures. They are:

1. *SifN. 118a IIb* (twice):

A. [citation of base Scripture]—

B. [Scripture] equates (מקיש)
[category a]
with (ל)
[category b].
C.1. Just as (מה)
[category b]
[law]
C.2. so too (אף)
[category a]
[law] (see m. Bek. 8:1; t. Bek. 6:1; Mek. deR. Ish., Bo)

D.1. Just as (מה)
[category a]
[law],
D.2. so too (אף)
[category b]
[law] (see Mek. deR. Ish., Bo, 16)

2. *SifN. 118a IIc* (twice):

A. Because it says (לפי שהוא אומר):
[citation of Scripture from elsewhere]
B. I [might] surmise [that] (שומע אני)
even
in the case of
[circumstance]
[law]
C. Scripture says (תלמוד לומר):
[citation of base Scripture]"—
D.1. just as (מה)
[category a]
[law]
D.2. so too (אף)
[category b]
[law] (Mek. deR. Ish., Bo, 16)

E.1. And

just as (ומה)

[category a]
[law]
E.2. so too (אף)
[category b]
[law] (see m. Bek. 3:1; t. Bek. 3:1; 1:14; Mek. deR. Ish., Bo, 16)

3. *SifN. 118a VI*:

A. [citation of base Scripture]"—
B. a general statement (כלל).
C. [citation of base Scripture]—
D. a specification (פרט).

E. A general statement and [susequently] a specification—
included in the general statement is
that which is
in the specification
only.
F. [citation of Scripture from elsewhere]—
G. [Scripture] reverted to a general statement!?
H. Or
have you [merely re-]stated
a general statement [inherent in] the first general statement [i.e., the two general statements are to be assimilated to one another and not treated as two independent sources]?
I.1. It [can] only [be taken as] (לאו אלא)
a general statement and a specification [following] and a [second] general statement—
I.2. you [must] reason
[by generalizing] on the basis of the specification
only.
J.1. [The verses, therefore, intend]
to inform you (לומר לך) [that]
J.2. just as
the specification
[category a]
J.3. [against] which
[additional circumstances]
J.4. so too
the general statement [comprises the use of]
only
[category a]
J.5. [against] which
[additional circumstances]

4. *SifN. 118a IIa*:

A. [citation of base Scripture]—
B. that which
applies to you

in the case of
[category a],
applies to you
in the case of
[category b]
C. *[Thus]*
[class c]
are excluded (t. Bek. 1:2; Sifre Zutta 18:15; Mek. deR. Ish., Bo, 16);
D.1. since (ש)
[law for class c vis-a-vis category a],
D.2. [law for class c vis-a-vis category b].

In three of the four pericopes schematized above, the formulary, "just as (מה) ... so too (אף) ...," constitutes the analogical argument, five times in all given the doublets at items 1 and 2. In these same three pericopes the analogical arguments are preceded by sections which explicate the problematic addressed by the subsequent analogical arguments. At items 1 and 3, these prefaces are relatively elaborate affairs constituting mini-analyses defining the problematic. One is left in these two cases with a sense of an underlying polemic or implicitly communicated assertions about the nature of Scripture and its relationship to rabbinic law. They recall the assertions and principles which generated the language of column 1: all of Scripture's data are necessary to derive correct legal opinions; nothing in Scripture is superfluous. At item 2 the prefatory section differs; it takes the form of a simple assertion about Scripture's intent. The language in column 2 of all three prefatory sections is stock.

Item 4 differs from the first three. Other than the citation of Scripture, no preface sharpens or defines the issue. The logical operators "that which applies to you ... applies to you ...," constituting the argument from analogy, differs. Further explication is required to translate the analogy into specific legal views. "Since," then, joins the two parts of the analogical argument. While most of the content of SifN. 118a has its counterpart in t. Bek. 1, only in item 4 (SifN. 118a IIa) is the language of Tosefta reflected. On the basis of the evidence at hand I will not venture an account of the literary relationship between Tosefta and SifN. 118a IIa, but it is clear that SifN. 118a exhibits modal stock formularies for casting analogical arguments; these modal formularies are not reflected at IIa, the only section of SifN. 118a which directly parallels the language of a perciope in Tosefta.

Another dominant form of exegetical argument found in SifN. 118a are assertions that apparent redundancies or seemingly unnecessary specificity either includes items under, or excludes items from, the force of a law. SifN. 118a I and VIII use the formularies, "to include" (להביא) and "to exclude/excluding(להוציא/מוציא)," to gloss directly scriptural citations with the items or class of items to be retained or discarded. The legal injunctions themselves are not given; the reference to the relevant Scripture suffices to give the legal context, as follows:

1. *SifN. 118a I* (four times):

A. [citation of base Scripture]—
B. I [might] surmise [that] (שומע אני)
even
[category a]
is implied (במשמע)!

C. Scripture says (תלמוד לומר):
[citation of base Scripture]"—
D. to exclude
[category a].

E.1. [Perhaps, rather,] the implication is (משמע)
to exclude
[category a]
E.2. and
to exclude
[category b]!?

F. Scripture says:
[citation of base Scripture]—
G. to include
[category b]

2. *SifN. 118a VIII*:

A.1. [citation of base Scripture]—
A.2. [species a']

B.1. [citation of base Scripture]—
B.2. [species a'']

C.1. [citation of base Scripture]—
C.2. [species a''']

D. to exclude
[category b] [See m. Bek. 1:2; t. Bek. 1:5 and 1:13]

Again SifN.'s implicitly communicated assertions about the nature of Scripture, discussed earlier, inform the "analytic" section which prefaces the pericope at SifN. 118a I.A-B as well as the subsequent, equally analytic section at E engendering further exegeses at F-G. The language in column 2 of the preface at A-B is identical to similar prefatory sections commented upon above.

In several pericopes, schematized below, "and" is not used to concatenate items, as is the case in Mishnah and Tosefta, but carries the force of argument and is, therefore, located in column 2 of the chart of SifN. 118a. These arguments recall the use of "to exclude" in that one infers from Scripture's apparent redundancies a more limited application of the scriptural law than one might otherwise suppose. "And [on the contrary]" limits an enjoined action by asserting a related prohibition or more restricted injunction.

1. *SifN. 118a III*:

A. [citation of base Scripture]—

B. This was a question which was asked before the sages in the Vineyard at Yavneh:

C. [circumstance]

which

[complementary circumstance] (see t. Bek. 1:14),

D.1. what (מהן)

[proposed action]

D.2. and

[proposed action]?

E. Expounded

R. x:

F. [citation of base Scripture]—

G.1. [enjoined action a],

G.2. and [on the contrary]

[prohibited action b];

H.1. [enjoined action c],

H.2. and [on the contrary]

[prohibited action d].

2. *SifN. 118a IV*:

A. [citation of base Scripture]—

B. I [might] surmise [that] (שומע אני)

even

[category a]

is implied (במשמע).

C. Scripture says (תלמוד לומר):

[citation from Scripture from elsewhere]—

D.1.[law + sub-category a'],

D.2. and [on the contrary]
[not law + category a] (see t. Bek. 1:3).

E.1. Or [perhaps, I may conclude from this verse that] (או)
[sub-category a' + law b]
E.2. and [on the contrary]
[category a + law c]
E.3. and
[law d]!?
F. Scripture says, again, elsewhere (תלמוד לומר עוד במקום אחר):
[citation of Scripture from elsewhere]—
G.1. [law b]
G.2. and [on the contrary]
[not law c]
G.3. and
[not law d]

In addition to the use of "and" with argumentative force, one should note at A-B in item 2 the appearance of the now familiar sequence of formularies constituting the tendentious preface to the exegesis. The structuring, joining language at E.1 (column 1) permits the positing of an alternative and false interpretation, which facilitates the introduction of the "necessary," complementary verse and the presentation of the final contrastive argument (x and [on the contrary] not y). In item 1 a single contrastive argument using "and" as the logical operator is attributed to a named rabbinic authority. The language of the opening section provides an intelligible protasis for the attributed exegesis, on the one hand, and (somewhat inelegantly perhaps) links the whole to the scriptural citation of the base-text. The effect of the whole does not, to my mind, directly serve Sifre's apparent agenda, to propound by example after example its propositions about the necessity and sufficiency of all phrases of Scripture in the proper derivation of the law.

The final instance in which the character of Scripture is seen implicitly to limit the range of items in a set is to be found at SifN. 118a VI.K-L, which may be schematized as follows:

SifN. 118a VI.K-L:
K.1. On the basis of this they said (מיכן אמרו):
K.2. [law]
K.3.except (חוץ מ/מן)
[category b']
K.4. and
[category b'']

K.5. and

[category b'''] (m. Bek. 8:8; see t. Bek. 6:13).

L.1. R. x

says:

L.2. Even so (אף)

[law]

L.3. except (חוץ מ/מן)

[category b']. [Mek. deR. Ish., Bo, 18]

The operative word "except" differs from what we have seen. I submit that we have no argument here all, and certainly no exegetical argument, constituted in whole or in part through the use of "except" (חוץ מ/מן). Rather, K.2-L.3 stands as an independent non-exegetical pericope of a type that would be typical of a toseftan or (were it not for the attribution to Rabbi [Judah the Patriarch]) of a mishnaic passage. The redactional language at K.1. joins the quite independent and non-exegetical pericope to the remainder of SifN. 118a VI, giving this pericope the semblance of being both exegetical and argumentative.

Three items remain to complete our survey of language in column 2 of our chart of SifN. 118a.

1. *SifN. 118a IV*:

H. If so (אם כן),

why does Scripture say (מה תלמוד לומר):

[citation of base Scripture]

I.1. If

it is not

[concerned with] the matter

that

[action a + category a]

I.2. [then]

assign it to

the matter

that

[action b + category a],

I.3. and

[action a] (see Mek. deR. Ish., Bo, 18)

2. *SifN. 118a V*:

A. [citation of base Scripture]—

B. [i.e.,] immediately.

C. Do you say (אתא אומר)

[citation of base Scripture]—

[action a]?

D. Or (או)

is it (אינו)

[action b]

only (אלא)?

E. Scripture says:

[citation of base Scripture]

F. [citation of base Scripture]—

G. [circumstance c + action b].

H. Lo,

why does Scripture say (מה תלמוד לומר):

[citation of base Scripture]

I. [action a + implied circumstance d] [contradicts earlier sections and t. Bek. 1:14]

3. *SifN. 118a VII*:

A.1. [citation of base Scripture]—

A.2. why is it said (למה נאמר)?

B.1. Because it says (לפי שהוא אומר):

[citation of base Scripture]

B.2. I [might] have [understood]

only(אין לי אלא)

[category a']

C. Whence [do I learn] (מנין)

[category a]?

D. Scripture says:

[citation of base Scripture]

In the final item, SifN. 118a VII, formularies in column 2 together with language in column 1 constitute an analysis defining a problematic. In other other pericopes such a feature was prefatory to an exegetical argument. Here the mere citation of Scripture at D suffices without further exegesis. The analysis, with its implied (familiar) polemic, remains the dominant note of the pericope as a whole. The same holds true for the second item, SifN. 118a V, which commences with just such an analysis, the weight of which is carried by the combination of rhetorical formularies in columns 1 and 2. Here the exegeses of the relevant verses are presented, but as assertions. The first item, SifN. 118a IV, does not fall far from the mark of the subsequent two. The analysis and statement of the problematic remains paramount, except that in item 1 we find explicitly enunciated in language in column 2 the theory of Scripture which is only implicit elsewhere: if Scripture seems redundant when understood to pronounce in a certain legal domain, then it must be understood to apply to something else. The something else follows without further exegesis or argument.

Let us review the results of the study of the rhetorical language in SifN. 118a as it sheds light upon the Bavli's formalized rhetorical operators. First, in column 1 of the chart of SifN. 118a I have placed language which appears to function like the structuring formularies of the Bavli. By setting an analytic agenda, by posing hypothetical questions or by offering challenges, these formularies facilitate further exegetical proofs and arguments. On the other hand, this posing of problems appears not to be open-ended in its intent. Indeed, the evidence points to the contrary. The use of interrogative, joining language serves the specific polemic of SifN. 118a, namely, to demonstrate the necessity and sufficiency of all scriptural data pertaining to a legal problem. So the character of the interrogatives in column 1 is doubly narrow: it is limited (in SifN. 118a at least) to two principal issues: (1) Given the immediately foregoing exegetical analysis, what is our need of some second, seemingly redundant piece of scriptural data? (2) Given the aforementioned scriptural data, as interpreted above, might one (mistakenly) understand that something else is the case? The former invokes an exegesis demonstrating that the second, apparently redundant verse is required to teach us something else. The latter allows the introduction of further scriptural evidence which in conjunction with already adduced data limits one to the first (appropriate) legal interpretation of matters.

Because of this limited and limiting rhetorical plan, SifN. 118a effectively demonstrates its polemical assertions about the nature of Scripture in the derivation of the law. In addition, the narrow focus of the interrogative, formulaic, joining language permits an analytical exegetical exercise always to reach a probative conclusion within the confines of a single pericope, a single composition with a beginning, middle and end. In Bavli, by contrast, what we have called structuring formularies often achieve precisely the opposite; language in column 1 of Bavli usually serves to undermine the probative claims of a foregoing unit or pericope so that analysis may continue without regard to reaching any conclusive end.

In examining column 2 of the chart of SifN. 118a, we have found recurrent formalized language used for two purposes. First, they define the exegetical problem at hand; in function these rhetorical operators may be likened to interrogative joining language of the prefaces and serve the same agenda. Second, they provide logical operators in exegetical argument; here SifN. 118a is replete with a use of language of which t. Bek. 1 furnished just a few examples. Three types of exegetical argument are constituted by this language:

1) analogical arguments derived from Scripture;
2) the inclusion or exclusion of items based upon scriptural evidence;
3) simple exegetical assertions following a scriptural citation.

This narrowly defined array of linguistic usages strikingly correlates with Sifre's limited agenda, at least as evident in SifN. 118a.

Finally, one should note that the use of concatenating language to build lists of cases, laws and circumstances—so dominant in m. Bek. 1 and t. Bek. 1—is all but absent in SifN. 118a. This is all the more noteworthy given the fact that, as documented in the square brackets of the chart, almost the entirety of the legal content of SifN. 118a parallels t. Bek. 1 and, therefore by one remove, m. Bek. 1. But if SifN. 118a's pericopes are literarily dependent upon our texts of Mishnah and Tosefta, that cannot be demonstrated from the evidence at hand, much as I suspect it to be the case. Only one perciope replicates language of a Toseftan passage. The paucity of verbatim parallels among SifN. 118a, on the one hand, and Mishnah and Tosefta, on the other, underscores the degree to which the formulators of SifN. 118a's pericopes (who are perhaps also the document's penultimate redactors) have imposed their stock rhetorical formularies on almost all that they had at hand before them. And what they had before them, I maintain, would likely have included Mishnah and Tosefta or, at the very least, some version of the materials contained therein. Because of this penchant totally to recast antecedent materials in the service of its own agenda, Sifre may be likened to Mishnah (see Neusner, 1981; 1983b), from which Sifre's polemical propositions so radically differ.

Having completed this whirlwind analysis of formalized linguistic operators in m. Bek. 1, t. Bek. 1 and SifN. 118a, I turn to one final point of reference, the use in the Yerushalmi of what one might call dialectical formularies. Only then shall I return (in chap. 6) to consider further the Bavli's formalized rhetorical language and its meaning—understood against a somewhat larger backdrop of early rabbinic literature.

Points of comparison in the Yerushalmi

The Palestinian Talmud was redacted, by most accounts, in the land of Israel *ca.* 400 CE (Neusner, 1983c), or some one-and-a-half to two-and-a-half centuries before the editing of the Bavli. One would expect this other and earlier Talmud to have been an important, even authoritative reference point or model for the Bavli's redactors and, therefore, to be particularly eludicating of the Bavli's rhetoric.

Despite their use of quite disparate methodological perspectives and foundational assumptions, recent scholars seem almost unanimous in asserting that the Bavli, as we have it, does not depend upon the Yerushalmi in its penultimate or final form (see, e.g., Neusner, 1986b; Kraemer, 1990; see also Jaffee, 1989). The Bavli and Yerushalmi may share a number of common pools of tradition of both Babylonian and Palestinian provenance, but beyond that, maintains the scholarly consensus, the two talmuds are independent creations. Indeed the comparisons in chapter 3 of structural language and its role in fashioning elaborated composites in the Bavli and Yerushalmi, respectively, bear out this consensus. Our earlier comparisons showed that Yerushalmi offered relatively little in the manner of a rich vocabulary of structural formularies with which to develop larger analytic composites and to combine these into encompassing composite essays.

I return now to the Yerushalmi in order to gain purchase upon the nature and function of the Bavli's dialectical formularies, as documented in the previous chapter for b. Bek. 2a-3b and 3b-5b. Since there is no talmudic tractate of Bekorot in the Yerushlami and since, in the course of reading chapter 3, readers will already be acquainted with y. AZ 1:6, the latter will serve in this last attempt to put into context Bavli's rhetoric at the "micro-level." Below is a schematized charting of the same text of the Yerushalmi presented earlier in full. In the schematized version which follows I have eliminated the idiomatic substance of column 3, leaving ellipsis points to show the placement of rhetorical formulae among content items and to permit the formulae in column 2 with their immediate contextual language in column 1 to stand out better. All previous conventions concerning indentation and the use of italics still hold (see p. 26).

Talmud Yerushalmi, Avodah Zarah 1:6

I

1. What?

  And ...!?

 2. Said

  R. a:

As is the case of

....

II

1. They should have said:

2. ...,

3. and

....

4. [Said]

R. b:

[Said]

R. c

in the name of

d:

And even

...,

[it would be]

....

5. And what distinguishes

...

from

...?

6. ....

7. ...,

8. and ....

III

1. [citation of m. *ad locum*]

1. Why?

2. Because

...

3. Consider (הגע עצמך)

....

5. Because

....

6. Consider

that it was a male.

7. Because

....

9. Henceforth [if this were the reason]

...,

10. because

...;

11. ...,

12. because

13. ....

IV

1. [Citation of m. *ad locum*]

2. Why?

3. …,

4. but

.

5. But

…!?

6. *One [can] say:*

7. *there [in the former case],*

….

8. Verily, here

….

9. Since [i.e., from the moment]

…

is it not

…!?

10. Said

R. e

in the name of

f:

that there [in the former case]

….

11. Henceforth [if this were the reason]

…!

12. ….

V

1. ….

2. Just as

…,

so [too]

….

3. And whence (ומניין) [do we learn]

…?

5. *A certain …*

….

6. *The case came before*

R. g,

7. *and*

…,

8. *so that (בגין ש)*

….

9. *Said*

R. h:

10. …,

11. and

....

12. [Said]

R. g:

[the foregoing] accords with [the view of]

R. i,

13. as it is taught (דתני) (cf. t. Bek. 2:1)

in the name of

R. i:

15. ...

16. ...,

17. and

....

18. ...,

19. ...,

20. and

....

21. And

sages

say:

22. Since

...,

23. [then]

... (cf. m. Bek. 1:1).

24. [Of] greater [legal weight] than

[the law according to] R. g

is

[the law according to] R. i.

25. That which said (מה דמר)

R. i

[was said] on account of (משום)

...

26. That which said

R. g

[was said] for (ל)

....

VI

1. [Citation of m. *ad locum*]

2. R. a

stated [his view] only (2.1.- 2.3. parallels t. AZ 2:3)

2.1. IN THE CASE OF

...[= m.]]

which

....

2.2. They said to him:

and is it not [the case] that

...?

3. He said to them:

moreover I stated [my view] only
....
which
....
4. They said to him:
and is it not [the case] that
...?
5. [Said]
R. b.
in the name of
R. c.
that there (דתמן)
that is to say that (זאת אומרת ש׳)
....

6. *There* (תמן)
we have learned (תנינן) [in m. Bek. 1:1]:
7.1. ...
7.2. ...,
7.3. ...,
7.4. ...,
7.5. ...,
7.6. ...
7.7. ....
8. R. d.
inquired before (בעא קומי)
R. e:
Does this not state that
....
9. He said to him:
R. b
[speaking] in the name of
R. c
has already anticipated you:
10. that there (דתמן)
that is to say that (זאת אומרת ש׳)
....

VII

1. [citation of m. *ad locum*]
2. R. a
stated [his view] only
IN THE CASE OF
... [see m.],
3. which
.... [compare 2-3 to t. AZ 2:3]
4. And there are those who say:
which
....

5. And there are those who say:
which
....
6. What [cases account for] the differences among them?
7. A gelding.

8. [With respect to] the one who says:
which
...
9. ....
10. But [with respect to] the one who says:
...
11. even so this one
....
12. R. b.
[said]:
....
13. [Said]
R. c
in the name of
R. d:
R. a and R. e
have both said [essentially] the same thing.
14. *As it has taught* (דתני) [in t. Shab. 8(9):34]:
14.1. ...
14.2. ...
14.3. ...
14.4. R. e
says:
...;
14.5. ...

15. And
Our Rabbis—
they are [of the view that]
....
16. *But*
[would] they have responded to him [R. a] (ואינון מיתיבין ליה) *thusly?*
17. In accordance with his approach they responded to him—
18. In accordance with your approach,
19. when you say:
because of
...,
20. then I [would] be [of the view that]
when
....
....
21. R. f.
says (see t. AZ 2:3):

21.1. Say I
that
…
21.2. on account of
…
21.3. on account of
…,
21.4. and on account of
….

VIII

1. And it has taught (דתני) (see t. AZ 2:2):
so [too] is
…
like
….
2. Who taught it (מאן תניתה)?
R a.
3. [However] the words of
the sages [are]
4.[as]
R. b
[said:]
R. c
[said] in the name of
R. d:
…
is like
….

As we previously found in chapter 3, Yerushalmi at first glance resembles the Bavli: it takes Mishnah as a point of departure, defines questions or problems occasioned by the mishnaic text and undertakes an analysis of those questions by offering answers, providing supportive arguments and, at times, challenging the latter. But in chapter 3 we found that the range of questions and problems defined with the aid of structural formularies was quite limited in scope. Beyond formulae used to preface citations of some extra Mishnaic source, y. AZ 1:6 displays a remarkably limited vocabulary of structuring formularies. The following list is an exhaustive accounting of these formulae in y. AZ 1:6:

1. What? (once);
2. Why? (twice);
3. And whence? (once);
4. Who taught it? (once);
5. They should have said… (once);

6. And what distinguishes ... from .../what are the differences among them? (once each);
7. [Would] they have responded to him thusly[?] (once).

Previously we noted that this relative paucity of structuring language is combined in Yerushalmi with relative disinterest to sustain coherent elaborated composites and to bind these together in some fashion to form more encompassing composite essays. But the differences in the nature and use of structural formularies in Yerushalmi and the Bavli, as we may now see, relates not merely to the sustained creation and linking of elaborated *sugyot*. Our examination of dialectical language in the Bavli has demonstrated the degree to which the structured sequences of formulaic "logical operators" are well integrated with, and often engendered by, structural formularies in the immediate literary context. That is to say, the richness of structural language in the Bavli closely correlates with the frequent appearance and variety in the Bavli of complex argument-statements whose syntax is provided by these structured sequences of dialectical operators.

A study of dialectical formularies in y. AZ 1:6 forcefully underscores this situation in the Bavli. Yerushalmi's paucity of language in column 1 combines with a quite different use of language in column 2. Even a quick scan of items in column 2 shows that beyond attributional and citation formulae (e.g., "said [in the name of]/he said to him," "we have learned," etc.), most of the formulaes in column 2 merely stand alone and preface a statement. They do not, with other stock language in column 2, structure an argument or analytic statement as much as they simply ascribe the appropriate valence to the claim which follows. For example, "because" (at III.2,5,7), "on account of" (at V.25 and within a passage at VII.21 paralleling Tosefta) and "so that" (at V.8) mark subsequent words as a reason for some antecedent opinion. In one case (at V.13) and within a passage designated as a cited tannaitic source, "since" precedes an adverbial clause, followed by a complete statement of the ruling in the main clause. "Even/even so" (III.4; VII.11) opens a phrase which glosses and extends in some fashion an earlier statement or ruling. "Only" (at identically formulated passages at VI.2 and VII.2) marks a gloss which will limit the application of an antecedent law or view. "As in the case of" (I.2) precedes a statement and specifies that at hand is a comparable and therefore corroborating state of affairs. "There that is to say" (VI.5,10) prefaces a remark which explicates an antecedent ruling. In all of these cases, were one to ignore the literary context which by other literary means evokes a sense of debate, one would construe all of these prefatory formulae and their subsequent statements to be glosses which comment upon or complement antecedent rulings or remarks by explication, justification, limitation or extension of the latter's substance.

Even where Yerushalmi appears most analytic or most engaged in argument, stand-alone prefatory formulae still prevail. "Consider" (III.3,6) marks new, perhaps extenuating circumstances. "Henceforth" (III.9; IV.11) precedes a statement which we are to understand as false and or patently absurd.

Such stand-alone prefatory formularies, unlike structured sequences of logical operators, do not engender complex, lengthy argument-statements. Rather, they facilitate the enunciation of concise statements, or mere phrases and sentence fragments. They cannot bind clauses into grammatically complex argument-sentences. Even where y. AZ 1:6 tends to what we might call more open analytic interests, the text is relatively laconic in style, using a sequence of juxtaposed, simple statements to carry the valence and weight of more extended analysis. Y. AZ 1:6.III provides an apt example. The citation of Mishnah is followed by the question "Why?" Alternative simple statements prefaced by "because" are interspersed with equally pithy statements of circumstances introduced by "consider." When the redactor has run out of such derailing circumstances, the text offers a counterfactual statement with the aid of "henceforth." Often in y. AZ 1:6 juxtaposed glosslike phrases and clauses are further given an air of extended debate and analysis by the use of attributional language ("[said] R. x/[said] R. x in the name of R. y/that which said R. x"), debate formulae ("he/they said to him/them;" "say I") or, where no named protagonists are at hand, impersonal uses of the verb, "to say" ("that which said/the one who said/there are those who say/one can say/they should have said").

Beside stand-alone prefatory formulae which introduce glosslike remarks and various formulaic uses of the verb, "to say," little else appears in column 2 of the chart of y. AZ 1:6. "And" and "which" function much as they did in Mishnah and Tosefta. The conjunction "but" appears at times to aid in the juxtaposition of contrasting statements. Indeed, at only a few junctures in y. AZ 1:6 do we find any language in column 2 which reminds one of the Bavli's complex structured sequences of argument-building formulae. At V.1-2 "just as ... so too ... " effects an associative statement. At IV.7-8 "there ... verily here ..." contrasts evidence. Interestingly, "there" represents the only formulaic term in column 2 (other than attributional language and other uses of the verb, "to say") which is consistently in Aramaic. And its usage at IV.7-8 in conjunction with "here" (in Hebrew) is unique in y. AZ 1:6. In all other instances "there" functions together with a stand-alone prefatory formulary and helps designate the antecedent statement or ruling to which the subsequent gloss applies.

Finally, we note in y. AZ 1:6 the use of (Aramaic) formularies, similar to those seen in the Bavli, which create an air of narrative in which the behaviour or remarks of a rabbinic authority in some allegedly historical situation constitute an authoritative precedent.

Overall, this analysis of language in column 2 of the chart of y. AZ 1:6 leaves one with an impression of the closeness of the Yerushalmi's language not to the Bavli, but to Tosefta. Most of the formulaic use of language in column 2 is similar to Tosefta. Indeed, were one now to compare in detail y. AZ 1:6 to t. AZ 2, a task which would take us too far afield from our main endeavour, that likeness would be immediately and boldly apparent. Not only is the language of the two extended sections in Tosefta and Yerushalmi close, the length of several complementary and supplementary toseftan pericopes would, in the aftermath of our examination of Yerushalmi, begin to look like proto-*sugyot* by Yerushalmi's (although not the Bavli's) standards.

Whence, then, the initial (and not entirely invalid) sense of Yerushalmi's similarity to the Bavli, if it is not in the former's use of dialectical formularies? First, we have seen in chapter three that Yerushalmi has an (admittedly highly limited) array of structural formularies (in column 1) which may be seen to be a constricted subset of those found in the Bavli. Second, with the help of attributional formulae and other forms of the verb, "to say," y. AZ 1:6 juxtaposes statements to a degree which goes far beyond what one normally expects of a toseftan passage. Yet in the final analysis, what y. AZ 1:6 accomplishes is not terribly far from Tosefta. For y. AZ 1:6, like Tosefta, tends to use glosses and complementary statements to explicate antecedent rulings culled from both Mishnah and extra-mishnaic sources (and among them materials which parallel Tosefta itself).

Against the backdrop provided by analyses of passages from Mishnah, Tosefta, Sifre on Numbers and the Yerushalmi, the Bavli's use of stock rhetorical terminology stands out in sharp relief, even when viewed in relation to that other Talmud. It is with these comparisons and contrasts in mind that I turn in the next chapter to the meaning and significance of the Bavli's use of rhetorical language.

6

Summary and Conclusions: The Social Meaning and Context of Bavli's Rhetoric

Rehearsing the initial problematic and agenda

With the evidence in hand concerning the Babylonian Talmud's use of rhetorical formularies and with those data set in relief against a backdrop provided by other types of early rabbinic literature, I may interpret that evidence. First, let me briefly rehearse the questions and concerns with which this volume commenced and summarize what we have found so far.

This book emerged from an interest in the relationship between the editing of the sacred, canonical texts of early rabbinic Judaism and concommitant (not necessarily concurrent) social transformations within the communities which produced, and which imbued with authority, those texts. Specifically, we wished to understand something of the social meaning of the Babylonian Talmud within the social context which produced and received it. I proposed at the outset that the editing and promotion *ca.* 550-650 CE of the Babylonian Talmud might profitably be viewed in relation to (1) changes in social definitions of religious authority, and (2) the emergence and ascendancy of the *yeshiva* (the academy) and its presidency (eventually entitled, "Excellency," גאון) as the principal institutions of the rabbinic movement in late Persian (and subsequently Muslim) Babylonia of the sixth and early seventh centuries. One major and key route to exploring the social meaning of the Bavli lay, in my view, in exploring the Bavli's use of language, particularly the Talmud's pervasive use of stock rhetorical formularies.

Both my initial interests and hypotheses, and the method by which I proposed to pursue them, were derived from some basic theoretical and methodological perspectives. The production of a text is a social act of political significance and communicative of shared meanings of a normative, or would-be-normative, nature. This political behaviour, in conjunction with other activities, helps to reflect and bolster existing or emergent social roles or to facilitate political and institutional transformations (Goody, 1986). What was the relationship between the redaction of the Babylonian Talmud and new social definitions or institutional transformations that revamped the organizational structure and locus of authority of sixth- and seventh-century Babylonian Rabbinism? My analysis has been founded upon a particular methodological perspective: that perceptions or meanings conveyed by highly redacted and stylized documents are to be sought not simply in what is communicated in its constituent passages, but notably in the pervasive, recurrent, rhetorical patterns or formal structures which the editors have used to create the final, unified product (Lightstone, 1983; 1988; 1994b). Such communication remains of course implicit only, and the perceptions thereby conveyed are non-discursive in nature. When these recurrent linguistic patterns replicate, or are replicated by, other patterns such as organizational structure, the implicit meanings communicated in each highly patterned domain reinforces those perceptions conveyed elsewhere. The overall effect lends an air of "self-evident truth," to the resulting "system" of meanings (Douglas, 1975a; 1975b; 1978).

An additional proposition underlying my analyses derives from the fact that highly redacted, sylized and formulaic texts, and the meanings implicitly communicated by their rhetoric, are the products of, and are received by, social environments which imbue these documents with authority. Their expression of matters in set ways of saying things reflects and reinforces, or disposes toward certain normative social definitions. Let me spell out this proposition, informed by the sociolinguists Gumperz (1985) and Goody (1986). In Bavli and other earlier rabbinic documents not only is content item "a" regularly brought into relationship "x" with item "b," giving us a form or structure, but also these texts often use a specialized formulaic vocabulary or a stylized rhetoric to create individual units evincing a given structure. The mastery of that rhetoric in itself constitutes a requisite for reading the text, quite apart from the mastery of a document's subject matter. Where that rhetoric is divorced from the everyday use of language, its mastery implies training within a particular group for whom such rhetoric is common coin. Hence highly stylized rhetoric reflects and helps reinforce distinctive sub-units within a larger community, Gumperz's "speech community."

Extrapolating from Gumperz (1985), I further suggested that a community's authoritative texts, particularly those exhibiting a pronounced rhetorical style and specialized formulaic vocabulary, provide within a given social setting an *authoritative* model for speech. Speaking in a style reminiscent of the text may attest to the interpreter's learning, representing years of study of the canonical documents. Such a correspondence between literary style and human speech would lend the authority of the canon to the speaker. The existence of a shared pattern of discourse, mimicking that of the canonical literature, among those learned in the texts may serve to define and set apart these people as a distinctive and authoritative class of religious virtuosi.

Command of an officially endorsed stylized rhetoric not only helps define and perpetuate an authoritative sub-group for whom command of that rhetoric constitutes a hallmark. Specialized language and rhetoric also models authoritative modes of communication and reasoning. That is, special, elite modes of speech play an important role in the social construction of normative, institutionalized authoritative roles. With respect to rabbinic documents accepted as canonical within rabbinic circles, specialized rhetoric encodes information germane to the social role, "rabbi" (literally, "my master"). The title itself conveys nothing of the socially defined *content* of the role in question, other than its self-serving claim to an elite and authoritative position. Some important aspects of that content may be sought in the recurrent stylized rhetoric of these documents. The subject matter of the documents represents, of course, another major constitutent element defining the role. Together rhetoric and subject matter prescribe what one is to talk about and how one is to talk about these data in a manner marking one (at least among one's would-be peers) as a member of the rabbinic elite, as a "master."

In Goody's view, the production of written authoritative texts produces organizational transformations in the community in question (Goody, 1986). He argues that the promulgation of a written canon contributes to the increasing emergence and differentiation of religion as a distinctive entity within culture and society. Because of this differentiation and as a direct result of the production of sacred documents, institutions of learning dedicated to the preservation of the documents and the production of those schooled in them emerge. In other words, the production of canonical texts is closely tied to the institutionalization of schools as well as to the allocation of specialized roles and elevated status to its students and teachers.

These propositions derived from Gumperz and Goody, in conjunction with claims about the communicative power of recurrent rhetorical patterns and their contribution to constructing a self-evidently appropriate "universe of shared perceptions," provide particularly fruitful avenues for interpreting the evidence now at hand. For, as we shall discuss at length in this chapter, soon after its redaction in about the sixth century of our era, the Bavli displaced virtually all other rabbinic works at the top of the pyramid of authoritative and sacred texts revered and studied within rabbinic circles. To be sure, the rest of the Hebrew Bible and Mishnah, the first magnum opus of the rabbinic movement (*ca.* 200 CE), remained for the rabbis the highest formal authorities. The

Talmud, however, came to provide the window upon all earlier holy texts. During the sixth to tenth centuries, study and mastery of the Talmud became the most important act and achievement which marked one as a rabbi, a "master." It is, moreover, now apparent from the preceding chapters that reading the Talmud required any ancient disciple of the rabbinic sages to master a pervasive, consistent and highly laconic code of formalized linguistic terms by means of which the analyses of the Talmud proceed. Gaining and imparting to others an intimate familiarity with such a laconic code of formularies implies, I hypothesize, a social context in which such rhetoric is common coin. To control that rhetoric would have marked one as a member of a group (Gumperz, 1985). Hence, just as the rhetorical formularies of the Talmud are constitutive of the text, so too is that rhetorical linguistic code, sanctified by the revered text, capable of constituting a decidedly elitist form of social organization and identity.

Before developing further these propositions and hypotheses regarding the social meaning and context of the Bavli's rhetoric, I will quickly summarize what we have discovered thus far about that rhetoric.

The Bavli's rhetorical language: A summary

Analyses of passages of the Babylonian Talmud both in AZ and elsewhere led me to differentiate between two "types" of rhetorical formulae and formularies, both of which permeate the Talmud. One comprises a group of "logical operators" by means of which the argumentation within an individual, small or primary unit of discourse develops. In chapter 1 I offered a simple (contrived) example:

> *If* circumstances, *since* operative principle, *then* conclusion.

"If," "since" and "then" create, along with the substantive material which follows each, a small virtually indivisible unit of argument. The Babylonian Talmud is replete with these units of argument formed by a rich but limited and specialized vocabulary of linguistic formulae and formularies that function as logical operators. Since these formulaic logical operators are the very building blocks of individual argumentational units of thought—producing an argument-sentence—their removal from such "sentences" leaves behind virtually nothing intelligible as an organized thought or statement. These formularies are part and parcel, then, of the grammar and syntax of individual units of thought in the Talmud. These recurrent and pervasive formulae and formularies I dubbed "dialectical."

Dialectical formulae and formularies tend overwhelmingly to be in Aramaic. They tend to encompass both attributed and unattributed argument/analytic statements, which these formulaic operators serve to constitute. Individual formulaic operators can be "stand-alone" formulae. One notes, however, a decided tendency to stock structured sequences of such formulae, constituting formularies as I defined them in chapter 1 (n.9). Statements created by their agency are generally complex, in the formal grammatical sense.

Dialectical formularies may be distinguished from, but do not necessarily operate independently of, "structural formulae and formularies" which pervade the Babylonian Talmud. This second type, again overwhelmingly in Aramaic, invites argument of a particular type (and hence predisposes toward the use of one or another structured sequence of dialectical operators), for example,

What is the reasoning?

As with dialectical formularies, the Babylonian Talmud exhibits a rich but still relatively limited number of this second class of formularies. While inviting argument or answers of a particular type, these formularies are not as grammatically integral to the argumentation which follows them. Nor are they part and parcel of any argument or statement which preceded them. Those statements and arguments stand on their own, grammatically intelligible, quite apart from this second class of formularies, which structure and order preceding and subsequent statements and arguments into a more extensive and broader analysis. They join individual parts and provide direction in the creation of larger literary compositions. These roughly correspond to what traditional talmudic exegetes refer to by the Aramaic term, *sugya*. Such formularies aid as well in linking a number of *sugyot* together to form larger composites, extended "essays." Despite the relative grammatical "independence" of structural formularies from individual argument-statements, we noted a decided tendency for the precise choice of dialectical formularies to be influenced or determined by structural rhetoric. This suggests that much of the language in the Talmud in its present form derives from its penultimate redactors, notwithstanding the redactors' use of antecedent sources.

These formularies, both structural and dialectical, so pervasive in the Bavli, stand out in stark relief against the use of language in evidence in those passages from Mishnah, Tosefta and Sifre on Numbers analyzed in chapter 5. Even our sample passage from the Yerushalmi, that other "talmud," falls far from the Bavli's mark.

The Babylonian Talmud's "data" are those citations and statements which remain after both structural and dialectical formularies have been removed. These "data," a significant proportion of which are culled from Mishnah and from other antecedent rabbinic documents or collections, reveal two more pervasive traits of the Talmud. Although the Bavli is ordered as a commentary on Mishnah, neither Mishnah nor any other document plays an exclusive role in structuring Bavli's elaborated composite units (*sugyot*) or their combination into larger composite essays. The Bavli effectively deconstructs Mishnah and excises from it phrases and words often considered outside of the context of the pericopes and intermediate units of Mishnah which give these fragments their meaning. The Bavli effects the same for other "sources" it has at hand.

To stand this on its head, meaning, order and purpose in the Bavli derive only in part from Mishnah, and rarely if ever from other authoritative data. In large measure order and purpose emanate from the Bavli's structural and dialectical formularies. What the Talmud undertakes with its argument-statements, elaborated composites (*sugyot*) and larger composite essays is more open-ended analysis, seemingly for its own sake. The dialectical, scholastic-like process of analysis to no particular end is a central purpose of the Bavli. Just as the Bavli may be said not to be exclusively (or even primarily) interested in Mishnah's meaning—a trait highlighted by our comparative examination of toseftan and Yerushalmi passages—so too it is not particularly interested in legal adjudication based upon Mishnah alone, or in combination with any other data. The Bavli deconstructs in order to create its own characteristic structures of open-ended questioning based upon diverse and discrete snippets of holy-text material. These claims I shall discuss at greater length toward the end of this chapter. First, what may be made of the significance of the Bavli's rhetoric in the context of the situation obtaining in Late Persian, Babylonian Rabbinism?

The social meaning of the Bavli's rhetoric in context

Earlier in this work and elsewhere (Lightstone, 1988:1-21) I argued that the cogency of a community's perceptions and mapping of the world is enhanced by the mutually reinforcing character of the various structured systems comprising the group's socially constructed universe. The rhetorical structures of a community's texts, especially those enjoying canonical status, constitute one such patterned realm. The formal traits of these documents reflect the culture of the text's framers and are replete with social knowledge, even though implicitly communicated.

In order to explore the issue of the implicitly communicated social meaning of the Bavli's recurrent rhetorical patterns of language, I proceed by a somewhat indirect route. First, I will consider the implicit meaning encoded in the Bavli's recurrent rhetoric, especially social meanings related to definitions of religious virtuosity and authority. This requires a return to comparison, in particular with Mishnah, for, at the very least, the framers of the Bavli's rhetoric had before them the Mishnah, with its own implicitly communicated meanings, as an authoritative model. Mishnah is a constraining social fact in the world of the Bavli's redactors; we need to consider the Bavli's rhetorical character and language, and any social meaning therein encoded, as change relative to Mishnah's. Second, I shall consider the immediate organizational context, the rabbinic academy, within which the study of the Bavli took root. Third, I turn to the larger social world of Late Persian Babylonia. Finally, this chapter takes up once more the social meaning in the context of the Bavli's rhetoric.

From Mishnah's priestly scribe to Bavli's scholastic philosopher

Talmud, which became paradigmatic for rabbinic intellectual activity for over a millennium, imposing its formulaically driven operations upon all antecedent sources, differs greatly from Mishnah, even while organized as a commentary upon Mishnah. So too, the mapping of the social universe implicit in Mishnah's formal traits is transformed by the Talmud's rhetorical structures. We turn, then, briefly to Mishnah itself (see Neusner, 1981; 1983b; Green, 1983; Lightstone, 1988; 1990; 1994b).

Mishnah provides a study of an ideal, self-contained world—that of a Temple state. Mishnah's tractates each represent a study of a set of legal issues, largely related to the workings of the Jerusalem Temple cult and its associated Temple state, both of which ceased to function about a century and a quarter before the editing of Mishnah. Indeed it is in the aftermath of, and perhaps due to, the demise of that state and the disastrous attempt under Bar Kochba to re-establish it that earliest Rabbinism developed after 70 in Judea and after 135 in the Galilee. But Mishnah is not a study, and certainly not a reconstruction, of the world of the Temple as it had existed on the eve of its destruction. Rather, the Temple and Temple-centred polity as defined in Scripture forms the basis of Mishnah's treatment of the law (see Neusner, 1981; 1983b;

Lightstone, 1988). So in the aftermath of 70 and 135 the framers of Mishnah retreated to the Pentateuch's Temple state, only sketched out in the laws of Scripture. Scripture's narrative which, after all, is a principal literary genre of Scripture, appears removed from early Rabbinism's visual field.

With Scripture reduced to law, Mishnah's editors, then, explored a scripturally based utopian world (see Neusner, 1981; 1983b; Green, 1983). This utopia, defined by a taxonomy of the items constituting that world, is dealt with in highly formalized language, a language as stylized and listlike as the taxonomic structure therein conveyed. To be sure, Mishnah is replete with the names of early rabbinic masters, to whom personal views are attributed and whose authority is recognized. But in reality personality and individuality have been assimilated to Mishnah's *listenwissenschaftliche* agenda and means; what all named masters "say" is generally couched in the same stylized, laconic language of Mishnah's unattributed phrases. By means of these laconic, formalized lemmas, which account for the majority of attributed data, masters are made to offer differing classificatory schemata of an imagined world based upon a different, implicit rationale (see Neusner, 1981; 1983b; 1987c; Green, 1983). If an item belongs to one *taxis* and not another, then a rule applies to it appropriate to that *taxis* and not to others.

The effects of Mishnah's laconic, list-building style and of its reducing the rabbinic master's persona to attributions for alternative classifications of items in Mishnah's utopian Temple-centred world are multifold. First, the focus remains the system of classification, its cogency, reality and rationality; the rational system, not the rabbinic masters' personal qualities, effect a meaningful, intelligible order in the universe. Second, what Mishnah's framers value about the masters is nothing more or less than their ability, through reason, to tighten this system. Since in Mishnah all masters "talk" and reason alike (even if different conclusions are sometimes reached) there is no place for personal charisma or highly individual traits as a locus for authority. True, those who can so reason may be elite, but there seems to be no first among equals, at least as Mishnah portrays matters. Here are persons who are utterly separate from the everyday, the mundane, whether the world of personal speech, action, emotion, history or biography (Lightstone, 1990; 1994b). What social definitions of religious virtuosity and authority are reflected in Mishnah's distinctive rhetorical character, constituting an inherited "social fact" for Bavli's editors?

Mishnah's rhetorical language serves overwhelmingly to set forth hierarchically organized lists of cases requiring classification with respect to whether one rule or another applies. Bavli tends to offer extended analytic argument and critique. These enterprises overshadow other concerns—including the determination of which ruling is appropriate. I suggest that distinctive "types" of religious authority and virtuosity correlate with different shared perceptions of what is enduringly the case or real, reflected in Bavli's and Mishnah's pervasive rhetorical characters respectively.

Mishnah, with its focus on an enduring underlying taxonomy of the "objects" of this world (both physical and social), sees "the world" and its inherent order as that which constitutes the enduringly real. To be an expert in Mishnah, that is, to study and know its lists and to comprehend its underlying taxonomy and the principles which inform it, is to be a living, breathing text of Mishnah's mapping of reality. Virtuosity and authority derive from knowing how the world really is. Since the study and comprehension of Mishnah plays a significant part in becoming a rabbi, a "master," in the land of Israel in the early third century, then the rabbi is in large part master because the rabbi is the comprehensive and comprehending repository of the knowledge of "the world order" expressed in Mishnah's lists.

In Greco-Roman and Late Antiquity in the Near East, temples and their officials (priests, scribes and, sometimes, prophets) were the repositories and guardians of such knowledge. In Egypt the "sacred books" resided in temples under the aegis of its "priests, scribes and prophets" (see J.Z. Smith, 1978; Breasted, 1962; 1964; Harris, 1971; Fishbane, 1985:21-37). II Kings portrays Josiah's reform as having been sparked by "finding" "the Torah of Moses" in its repository in the Jerusalem Temple. Mishnah itself assumes there to have been an official copy of the Torah in the Temple (m. Kelim 15:6). When in Sassanid Persia the Zend-Avesta was first committed to writing a limited number of copies were deposited in several major temples in different districts of the Empire. In these temples the official versions could be consulted to resolve all doubt about "how things really were." This transpired even as Zoroastrian tradition and "literature" endured on a day-to-day basis in its oral form among the priests of local Zoroastrian shrines (see Boyce, 1986:132-44). Indeed it is remarkable and highly instructive that with respect to basic rhetorical features late-Sassanid Zoroastrian literature provides such close literary comparisons to Mishnah and its particular *Listenwissenschaft*. The *Bundahis* (*ca.* sixth or seventh century), like much of the earlier Zend-Avestan literature of which the *Bundahis* is a partial epitome, is overwhelmingly preoccupied with classification and list-making. In Zoroastrian ritual and legal texts from the end of the Sassanid era the likeness to Mishnah's use of language emerges more starkly still. Anyone who has analyzed the literary form of Mishnah and who has dealt with the content of its Division of Purities would be in familiar territory when reading the *Shayast La-Shayast*. In all, the *Shayast La-Shayast* exhibits the preoccupation with classificatory list-making, already evident in the *Bundahis*, but translated into a legal framework. In the case of the *Bundahis* and the *Shayast La-Shayast*, however, actual cultic centres continue to function even after the Muslim conquest and provide the context for the preservation and application of these documents (Boyce, 1986). Indeed, literary activity generally both in the Sassanid and Muslim periods remained the principal prerogative of members of the priestly class.

In light of the above it is significant that the "world" constructed by Mishnah in its lists is one in which the Temple and its related institutions of the cult, national governance, adminstration and judiciary (destroyed over a century earlier) constitute the centre (see Neusner, 1981; 1983b). With the perspective provided by Zoroastrian texts dating from around the Muslim conquest of Persia, one may better appreciate that with the demise of the Jerusalem cult, Mishnah presented rabbis as priestlike and the direct inheritors of priestly knowledge and authority. Clearly establishing that claim and implicitly asserting in Mishnah that the "world" has not fundamentally changed with the destruction of the Jerusalem cult (see Neusner, 1981; 1983b) appears for nascent Rabbinism the first, most important order of business.

Mishnah, then, chooses to describe in hierarchical lists and related rules this "classical" Temple-centred world and thereby to imply that its model enduringly holds. The text does this rather than focus on the institutions which by 200 CE must already have emerged to replace that Temple. This fact represents clearly the "type" of authority to which Mishnah's editors wished to lay claim. The rabbis and their disciples, who produced and received the Mishnah, were a "type" of priest, even while in reality they were not. Perhaps it would be more appropriate to say that they thereby portrayed themselves as the direct successors of the Jerusalem priests, possessing their knowledge of "the world" and exercising the attendant authority of the now defunct priesthood. Among the skills which one would expect such a "type" of elite class to value would be the accurate retention and transmission of knowledge and its full comprehension. The opening chapters of m. Avot, perhaps the first apology for the authority of early rabbinic traditions and masters, unequivocally expresses just these sentiments.

The Mishnah, in sum, portrays its masters as the guardians of the old, perfect order and the inheritors of its power and authority. Indeed, that order exists nowhere other than in the intellectual pursuits which define the early circles of rabbinic masters and disciples. The message is clear. The rabbinic circle is the Temple state; its bounded, closed topography lives on in the rabbinic circle, and the rabbinic master and disciples are the priestly scribes. Here are neither itinerant, charismatic missionaries of a new cult which transcends ethnic and national boundaries, as in the emergent, Roman church universal, nor local holy men who provide the focus of loyalty for a distinct subcommunity in a larger society.

In what context at the turn of the third century, the era of Mishnah's redaction, might Mishnah's *Listenwissenschaft* and stylized, reduced portrayal of rabbinic masters seem intelligible or "self-evidently appropriate" to its framers and intended readers (see Douglas, 1975a; 1975b)? In posing this question with regard to Judean-Galilean Rabbinism of the late second and early third century I am conscious of what I earlier maintained about sixth-century Babylonian Rabbinism. The evidence is severely limited, as sources do not slavishly mimic the social worlds which produced them. This being said, one may note that named persons, in particular, named rabbinic figures from the several generations preceding Mishnah's redactors, figure so importantly at the turn of the third century that attributions to them must be preserved, on the one hand, and that they must be neutralized or homogenized within some unified system which effaces all personal traits, on the other. These persons matter a great deal, but their mattering at all is a situation to be overcome. That appears to me to be part of the meaning communicated by Mishnah's literary and formal characteristics. Briefly put, there is a turning point from individual item to overarching system, as Mishnah takes each item of its ideal world and integrates it into an all-inclusive taxonomy.

Mishnah offers both a precise homology for the social and political transformation of the rabbinic movement occurring from approximately 165 CE to 220 CE, and an effective means of appropriating the normative ethos of the nascent period of Rabbinism from 70 to 135 CE. Of this transformation we have only the vaguest echos, which I shall attempt briefly to present.[1]

1. Given the problematic nature of the evidence that exists, any attempts to describe the events in question must not be mistaken by the reader as anything other than statements bordering on speculation. Elsewhere (Lightstone, 1994b) I have attempted systematically to present, analyze and to tie together these threads of evidence. I present in what follows a synopsis of the results of that exercise.

First, emerging in the aftermath of the disastrous war with Rome (ending in 74 CE), the earliest rabbinic groups would have had no established norms for defining rabbinic roles, institutions or authority. Second, the immediate social context of early Rabbinism appears limited to the close circle of master and disciples. This view of matters is consistent with the pervasive impetus to preserve the names, and putative traditions, of different masters with apparently diverse views. M. Avot preserves along with the notion of the chain of tradition an exceedingly strong ethos of discipleship, in which individual masters were "served" by and taught a limited number of closely associated disciples. Of particular interest is the toseftan passage that provides an account of the origin of disputes, which ascribes the divergence of views among the early rabbis to the erosion of Torah in the process of its transmission. Tosefta offers the failure of "disciples to serve their masters" as the explanation (see t. Hagigah 2:4; t. Sukkah 14:1). Service to the master, depictions of a fractious rabbinate and diversity of tradition in late first- and second-century Rabbinism, and especially the negative value assigned to that diversity, is consonant with the hypothesis that earliest Rabbinism was chiefly organized as small circles of masters and their disciples, and that by the end of the second century a movement toward supplanting that earlier state of affairs with some other had begun. Third, the wars of 70 and especially 135 brought about significant dissolution of the fabric of Judean society, sparking migration of much of the Jewish populace. The circle of master and disciples will have provided an island of order in this sea of chaos. In this insular structure the early rabbis adumbrated in the realm of the mind a Temple state that, in their view, had once stood in the earthly Jerusalem. Defining this "ideal" Temple state created in the intellectual sphere an order that the rabbinic circles strove to achieve in their lives together in the face of the chaos about them.

The Mishnah, with its stylized, laconic and listlike form, emerged at the turn of the third century. Its redaction was roughly concurrent with the emergence of a new form of rabbinic organization, in which the rabbinic movement found its unified institutionalization in a "college" of rabbis, of which the Patriarch was the president. The Patriarch is portrayed at times as *primus inter pares*, and at times as simply *primus* outright. The college is depicted as having legislative and judicial authority and an instructional role. This state of affairs replaced over the final decades of the second century the earlier form of organization, in which Rabbinism consisted of autonomous circles of masters and disciples. The normative character and authority of the latter had to be overcome and then transferred to the newer organization. And a balance of power between the Patriarchate and the united College of Sages had to be defined. How might Mishnah have served in this transformational process? Mishnah, which came to be attributed to Judah the Patriarch's personal editorial activity, preserves the identity of the earlier rabbinic sages, each of whom constituted the centre of a circle of master and disciples. At the same time their individuality is largely effaced, and subsumed within a new literary whole that imposed its peculiar style on everything and everyone. The individual and the individual's inherent authority is preserved only in the new whole, soon to become the chief object of study of would-be sages. So Mishnah represents, preserves, builds upon, and borrows the authority of the old social form in order to supplant it with another. All this transpires via implicitly communicated, non-discursive "knowledge" of "how things really are," communicated by the pervasive literary and rhetorical traits of Mishnah itself.

The Bavli's rhetorical traits differ blatantly from those of the document upon which the Bavli is organized as a commentary. The formalized rhetoric of the Talmud breaks Mishnah's carefully unfolding taxonomy, which systematically permutates lists of circumstances in order to locate each newly generated datum in its classificatory structure. First, Talmud fragments the mishnaic text, eclipsing its system (Lightstone, 1988:71-94). Second, the talmudic editors freely examine excised pieces of Mishnah in relation to other sources, equally deconstructed, such as an homiletical, scriptural exegesis (aggadic midrash) or more often a datum from an extra-mishnaic legal pericope. This shifts one's focus from Mishnah's ideal world to the Talmud's own process of query and relational analysis. That process is the principal sustained trait of the Talmud, overshadowing any structured definition of the world contained in Mishnah, the Pentateuch or any other authoritative document or tradition. Thus the authority of the documents, everywhere cited in fragmented form, lies behind the talmudic authorship, yet the Talmud effectively borrows that authority for its own scholastic critique. In relativizing Mishnah, the process of critique remains enduringly holy and authoritative. If there is sacred power in the documents, only the Talmud's rhetorical endeavours make manifest that force in this world, just as the early medieval Roman bishops claimed that the saints' relics work their miracles subject to episcopal authority (Brown, 1981). In so far as persons engaged in Talmud-like activity, the rabbis' authority both subsumed and displaced that of Mishnah.

What specific "type" of rabbi is modelled in the Talmud's rhetoric? Mishnah's lists of the "things of this world" and their classification with respect to the rules appropriate to them depict a "type" of religious virtuosity which I called "priestly scribal." In Bavli, questioning, argument, analysis and critique for its own sake overshadows any attempt to portray an overarching and enduring order of things. As I stated earlier, Bavli's formulaically driven rhetoric of analysis eclipses even the taxonomy of Mishnah itself, the "base-text" upon which Bavli is organized as a type of commentary. Bavli's stock dialectical language shows a decided penchant toward the use of structured sequences of logical operators which probe the *relations* that *might* entail between objects in the world, as in the following:

> item or case A,
> which has characteristic B,
> and to which rule C applies,
> is or is not like item A',
> which has characteristic B',
> and to which, therefore, rule C does or does not also apply.

In this type of exercise, Bavli attempts to uncover the reasons for classifying together A and A'. Such modes of thought may underlie Mishnah's list-making but remain implicit. In Bavli, however, such formulaically driven argument-statements do not tend to stand alone as an explication of Mishnah's or any other document's taxonomy. My documentation of Bavli's rhetoric leads one to expect the argument-statement schematized above to be followed immediately by structural terminology, such as:

> No!
> How are they [,A and A', to be considered] the same?!

Structural rhetoric of this sort invites further argument-statements offering rationales for the opposing stances.

In what does reality and authority inhere according to Bavli with its particular sort of pervasive rhetoric? Not in the taxonomy of the items of the world; not even in the reasons underlying such a classificatory order. Rather, Bavli's rhetoric represents the value of an ongoing, open-ended process of reasoning (admittedly, about certain things and on the basis of data provided by authoritative sources). Such an open-ended process is a basic trait of analysis and critique, valued for their own sake. In the social realm, the authoritative virtuoso is the one who has the capacity to engage effectively in this process. It is not the possession of knowledge of some enduring reality that underwrites the authority of the sage. Rather, that reality evaporates before an enduring rational critique, itself viewed as ultimately authoritative (see Kraemer, 1989). For lack of a better term, I have dubbed this "type" of religious virtuosity scholastic and contrast it with the priestly scribal mode discussed earlier.

Again, an appeal to the gross literary traits of non-Judaic evidence from Late Antiquity will prove helpful to illustrate this association between a distinctive mode of language and rhetoric, on the one hand, and a "type" of elitist virtuosity, on the other. The *Discourses* of the second-century Roman stoic, Epictetus, provide one of the longest extant examples of stoic dialectical rhetoric, or "diatribe" (see Stowers, 1988:71-84; Malherbe, 1986:129-34). A brief look at the literary style of Epictetus's *Discourses* will shed some light on the rhetoric of Bavli. The dialectical style of the *Discourses* radically differs from Platonic dialogues, in which one of the "protagonists" merely punctuates the otherwise unbroken presentation of Socrates or some other principal. Nor do the *Discourses* resemble the treatises of Aristotle, which take the form of coherent unified essays. Rather, in the *Discourses* one enounters a single voice, that of the author, in constant argument with itself. Sections or chapters open with some stated stance and end with a restatement of the defended thesis. What lies in between is of particular interest in that it leads the intended hearer or reader through the issues at hand by continuously raising and addressing questions and problems, including possible objections to earlier stated positions and arguments. Throughout, the voice remains that of the document's author. In these respects, the dialectical rhetoric of the *Discourses* appears reminiscent of the combined effects of structural and dialectical formularies in Bavli. One of the several blatant differences between the Bavli and the *Discourses*, lies, however, in the fact that Bavli uses as data earlier rabbinic traditions and documents and creates open-ended analytical "essays" in which arriving at a probative solution is not the chief aim. The chapters of the *Discourses* do not as a rule cite earlier authors as authorities in order to convince the reader of the validity of a proposition. It is by means of the give and take of contrived argument that the author has with himself that the author intends to lend weight to his enterprise.

Given the *Discourses'* purpose to present and defend propositions, one striking feature of the dialectical rhetorical style of Epictetus's *Discourses* is its apparent superfluity. Book II, chapter 1, for example, argues for the proposition that real freedom derives from a state of mind which one might call educated equanimity. To paraphrase an aphorism, one must learn to accept what one cannot change, exercise one's judgement and will upon things which can and should be changed, and know the difference. This, argues the *Discourses* is dependent upon education. One could readily compose a straightforward, clear and cogent syllogistic and propositional argument in defence of these claims, a treatise-like essay "On the True Freedom." One must suppose, therefore, that something more is gained by approaching matters by means of dialectical rhetoric, beyond offering a convincing argument leading inexorably to a given conclusion. That "something more" is the modelling of a pervasive self-critical, analytic way of being, an academic ethos. The processes of arguing with oneself more properly reflect such an enterprise than does syllogistic propositional treatises, since the latter is the distilled, reworked, almost *ex post facto* recasting of anterior processes of analysis and critique. In modeling such an an ethos, dialectical rhetoric seems, moreover, to recall a real or imagined social context in which debate and discussion take place. In contrast, the use of language in a treatise has a socially disembodied character, functioning in part to veil or direct attention away from institutional and social provenances, of ways of being in the world.

In modelling implicitly an ethos characterized by challenge, critique and analysis, the *Discourses* parallel Bavli. The authoritative figure reflected in the *Discourses*' rhetoric is the critical, analytical, scholastic academic, a figure which in the *Discourses* is part of a community of like-minded, challenging and challenged philosophers (see Saldarini, 1982:79-82; Stowers, 1988:73). Not only is this implicit in the rhetoric of the body of the *Discourses*. The editor of Epictetus's *Discourses*, Arrianus, also makes this claim in stating that he has recorded in the *Discourses* Epictetus's lectures in his school in Rome. For our purposes, it does not matter whether his claim stands up to critical historical scrutiny. Of importance is the understanding of the editor that such language recalls the academic context of critical scholastic philosophers. Bavli's rhetorical style appeals to a similar model of authority and virtuosity and therefore represents a major modulation of the image of the rabbi implicit in Mishnah's principal modes of rhetoric.

Above we briefly described what may be said of the social universe in relation to which the perceptions encoded in Mishnah's substantive and formal traits evoked a sense of "self-evident appropriateness" (see Lightstone, 1988; 1994b; Douglas, 1975a; 1975b). The universe of Babylonian Rabbinism was as distant from the social world in the land of Israel during the 150 years following the events of 70 CE as the Talmud's character is from the Mishnah's. Before discussing in detail the particular states of affairs obtaining within Babylonian Rabbinism and Persian society toward the end of the Sassanid era, we need to consider first the situation of Jews and rabbis throughout the "talmudic" era in Babylonia. Their world was typical of the Diaspora (see Lightstone, 1984); Jews had seriously to intermingle and do commerce with non-Jews. A Judaic universe with socially homogeneous insularity and protection from encroachment was an impossibility. Their situation required as well traversing non-Jewish territory (a mixed and ambiguous space) in order to effect commercial and ethnic links with neighbouring or more distant Jewish communities. So boundary-crossing, whether to do business with non-Jews or to maintain ties with other Jews, characterized the situation in which these talmudic rabbis found themselves.

For these Jews, and their soon-to-be rabbinic "masters," access to the sacred could not be imagined as dependent upon maintaining a unique, Temple-state-like, ethnically homogeneous island in a sea of amorphous chaos. The sacred for these Diaspora Jews had its loci on earth at the many sites and in the diverse persons where conduits from heaven above broke into this earthly realm (Lightstone, 1984; 1988). Benefit from the benevolent and lifegiving power of heaven could be had only where, at numerous loci, the boundary between heaven and earth was crossed, just as was the case across the boundaries of the social world. Hence, sacred space on earth, like social space, lacked homogeneity and contiguity; the map of the sacred, to put matters differently, had the same topographical features as the social map of Jewry.

The Talmud (and to some extent early rabbinic midrash) implicitly conveys a similar perception of reality in its treatment of its most sacred documents and traditions—Mishnah, Scripture and other post-mishnaic rabbinic traditions and corpora. Mishnah and Scripture are not permitted to remain closed, self-sufficient, and self-contained worlds, a literary counterpart to the Temple. Rather, Talmud fragments Scripture and Mishnah; it sees in these latter documents numerous, discrete, disjointed and non-contiguous holy items that feed the talmudic literary constructions. Talmud reaches into the sacred spheres of Scripture, Mishnah, and extra-mishnaic traditions and pulls out morsels for use outside the context of their original spheres, indeed for insertion into quite another literary realm. That realm values the sustained exploration of (all) possible relations among items as well as those persons who pursue that exploration according to a model given by the Talmud's rhetoric. Rabbinic holy men do with God's divine words, Mishnah, Scripture and other traditions, what the Jewish communities and their would-be rabbinic masters must achieve in the larger social world. In sum, not only do the sacred topography on earth and social topography replicate the same basic pattern, they both find their complement in the literary topography of Talmud in the manner in which the latter treats antecedent sources. The similar structures of all of these mappings makes each more plausible, establishing the cultural and social context of shared knowledge about the shape of world for post-mishnaic rabbinic communities.

The Talmud emerged not only in a typical Diaspora context but also in the particular situation obtaining for Babylonian Rabbinism during the final century or so of the Persian era. To that particular context I now turn.

The organization and structure of rabbinic academies in Saboraic and early Geonic Babylonia

Literary endeavours such as those in Talmud reflect an organized, decidedly elitist sphere of activity, where rabbis and would-be rabbis developed intellectual skills that set them apart from the general population over whom they claimed to have authority. More to the point, the production of the Talmud with its pervasive rhetorical traits and formularies represents in part the standardization of, or the attempt to impose, some normative form of scholastic critique. In this respect, too, the emergence of some institutionalized setting having influence over Babylonian Rabbinism would seem to be reflected in the rhetorical traits of the Bavli. To determine whether that setting is the rabbinic academy (the *yeshiva*) or its precursors requires that we take up at this point the problem of the evidence for the institutional structures and social settings of Rabbinism in late Amoraic and Saboraic times (*ca.* 450-650 CE).

Evidence permits but a skeletal and somewhat speculative account of the situation in talmudic Babylonia from the end of the fifth through the first half of the seventh centuries CE. To anticipate, the rabbis of late Amoraic and Saboraic times represented a locus of power which significantly displaced that of the exilarch, the "traditional" ruler of what had in the preceding centuries been the largely autonomous Jewish government of the Persian Jewish community (Neusner, 1969-70). By the eve of the Islamic conquest, the rabbis may have already removed the lines of power to the offices of the several large *yeshivot*, an institution which, evidence suggests, emerged in Babylonia only toward the end of the Persian and beginning of the Islamic periods (Goodblatt, 1975). The Talmud reflected in its rhetorical patterns the ideal rabbinic activity, ultimately based in the *yeshiva*. In part, the Talmud reinforces the triumph of the *yeshiva*'s ruling hierarchy, the *gaon* (president or "excellency"), *dayana debaba* ("judge at the gate" or head of the academy's court) and the *rabbanan demetivta* ("the rabbis of the academy" or faculty college), and bolsters the emergent social autonomy of Rabbinism, of which the institutionalization and differentiation of an autonomous locus of rabbinic learning, the *yeshiva*, is an expression (see Goody, 1986).

On the other hand, the redaction of the Talmud and the eventual emergence of the large *yeshivot* may be seen to be social transformations within the context of changes in the administrative structures and policies of the Persian Empire from the late fifth to the mid-seventh centuries (Neusner, 1969-70). Rabbis had to cope too with the new Islamic hegemony and may have harboured the reasonable expectation that the non-rabbinic aristocracy might renew its bid for control of the Jewish community. In any case, the power of the Babylonian academies, which came to be married to the supremacy of their Talmud, remained ascendant as long as Baghdad enjoyed pre-eminence in the Middle East, North Africa, and Iberia.

In order to explore these claims, let me first consider the evidence for the institutional development of Rabbinism (in particular, of the *yeshivot*) in the final century or so of the Persian era. I begin with a negative hypothesis. D. Goodblatt (1975) asserts that it is incorrect to attribute the emergence of *yeshiva*-like rabbinic institutions to the period preceding the Talmud's penultimate redaction. Goodblatt concludes that "results [of a survey of all relevant evidence within the Bavli] agree in suggesting that the organization of rabbinic instruction in Sasanian Babylonia was rather different from the way it had been described in medieval and modern accounts. The large Talmudic academies (*yeshivot* or *metivata*) known from the Islamic era did not exist in Amoraic times. Instead disciple circles and apprenticeships appear to have dominated academic activity" (Goodblatt, 1975:7).

Limiting his study to evidence from the Amoraic period, Goodblatt is unable to pinpoint when "large talmudic academies" displaced that form of rabbinic elitist organization based upon "disciple circles and apprenticeships." Similarly, he cannot spell out what major institutions, offices and social relationships were constitutive of the organization of rabbinic activity in large academies. He correctly maintains that he has no talmudic evidence pertinent to these matters, a fact of immediate importance. From this I conclude that, in all probability, the large Babylonian rabbinic academies which dominated Rabbinism in the Islamic period were unknown in the times of the Talmud's penultimate redactors or, if known, were of such recent vintage and uncertain legitimacy as not to warrant (or, perhaps, permit) their *explicit* reflection in the redactors' literary endeavours.

Large, well-structured academies of rabbinic learning did not emerge in Babylonia, therefore, until sometime after the close of the fifth century. To retrace their emergence and to elucidate their internal organization requires that one begin with later (not entirely unproblematic) evidence.

The academy's principal constituent offices and structures as they existed by the end of the tenth century are aptly reflected in the preface to the Epistle of Sherira Gaon.

> [The following] was that which our Master (מרנא) and our Rabbi (ורבנא) Jacob b. R. Nissim b. R. Josiah inquired of our Lord (אדוננו) and our Excellency (גאוננו), our Master (מרנו) and our Rabbi (ורבנו) Sherira, Head of the Academy of the Diaspora (ראש הישיבה של גולה) in the name of that holy community, the community [of Jews] in Kairuwan, and he [Sherira] commanded and they wrote the answers to those [very questions] in the year 1299 [Sel. = 4748 A.M. = 988 CE].
>
> These questions ... came before us, to the Gate of the Academy (בבא דמתיבתא), to the Court (לבי דינא) of our Master and our Rabbi Sherira, Head of the Academy (ריש מתיבתא) , son of our Master and our Rabbi Hanina, Head of the Academy, son of our Master and our Rabbi Judah, Head of the Academy, and to the Court (לבי דינא) of our Master and our Rabbi Hai, the Judge at the Gate (דיינא דבאבא), son of our Master and our Rabbi Sherira, Head of the Academy. And we took [the inquiries] in charge and had them read before us and before our Rabbis of the Academy (רבנן דמתיבתא) and they wrote answers to those [very questions] in accordance with that which occurred to us from Heaven (אחוו לנא מן שמיא). [*Iggeret Rav Sherira*, Damascus ms., ed. B. Levin, p.4, my translation.]

The Epistle, widely known among scholars for its apologetic and tendentious account of the history of Rabbinism and its canonical documents, offers in this preface excellent evidence about the organization of the rabbinic elite of tenth-century Babylonia. Jacob b. Nissim of Kairuwan bears two titles, "our Master" (מרנא) and "our Rabbi" (ורבנא). Sherira, the authority in whose name the response is officially promulgated, shares these titles with Jacob b. Nissim. In addition, Sherira commands three other titles. He is referred to as "our Lord" (אדוננו) and "our Excellency" (גאוננו). The latter is well known as the honorific salutation owed to those who hold the office of Head of one of the two principal Babylonian academies (ריש מתיבתא). The preface clearly attests to the dynastic character of the office in question. Both Sherira's father and grandfather held the office which he discharged[2] at the time of the Epistle's composition. One may suppose that during the

2. Although the terms of office of father and son are not always (or usually) contiguous.

reign of Sherira's father, Sherira held the auxiliary office of Judge at the Gate (דיינא דבבא), held in 988 by Sherira's son, Hai. (Later evidence informs us that Hai in turn succeeded Sherira.) It appears from the text before us that the honorific salutations of "Lord" and "Excellency" are owed to the currently reigning Head of the Academy only.

Sherira's superior authority as Head of the Academy is in some sense limited or derivative, for the response is attributed to the considered opinion not only of Sherira but also of Hai and of a group within the academy called, "our Rabbis of the Academy" (רבנן דמתיבתא).[3] Sherira is the official source of the response; he orders its production and refers the question to that formal body of the Academy with the requisite mandate and expertise to prepare the answer. It is difficult to say whether the reference to divine inspiration at the end of the section is merely a formulaic expression of humility, or whether it carries in addition a claim that the combined voices of Sherira, Hai and "our Rabbis of the Academy" speak with divine authority. We cannot derive from the passage precise information regarding the mandate, powers and functions of the offices referred to in the preface to Sherira's Epistle. We can, nevertheless, assert from this and other such passages that the rabbinic academy of tenth-century Babylonia had a highly developed, stable and differentiated internal structure.

When and at what pace rabbinic academies of this nature arose cannot be established with certainty. Relevant sources are notorious for anachronisms with underlying apologetic designs. In any case, we do not have a wealth of sources. The principal pieces of evidence do not precede Sherira's Epistle by much more than a century. Yet the sources, anachronisms aside, agree upon the ascendancy of two large rabbinic academies and of their "Heads" to the leadership of Rabbinism in Babylonia, a notion entirely absent in the Babylonian Talmud itself.[4]

3. I note with appreciation a cautionary remark made to me by Professor Harry Fox (University of Toronto) that whatever else may be reflected in the term "Our Rabbis of the Academy," both as used in Sherira's preface and throughout the Epistle, something of Sherira's institutional chauvinism should be seen in the language.

4. In this regard I continue to rely upon the findings of D. Goodblatt's thorough study of the evidence of the Babylonian Talmud (Goodblatt, 1975:39-41). He summarizes his findings as follows: "For BT knows nothing of 'the two *yeshivot/metivata*.' The words *yeshiva* and *metivta* are rarely, if ever, used in the sense of 'school' or 'academy.' In the entire BT, only six instances of the word *yeshiva*, in 5 pericopae, and only eleven instances of the word *metivta*, in 9 pericopae, are susceptible to the meaning 'school.' For none of these occurrences is the latter meaning the only possible interpretation. By contrast, there are 159 instances, in 108 pericopae, of the word *bet hamidrash*; 98 instances in 85 pericopae of the Aramaic cognate *be midrasha*; and 59 pericopae in which the

Midrash Tanhuma Noah, 3, dated by Goodblatt and others to the ninth century, offers one such passage. The anachronisms are so blatant as to dramatically impress upon the student of religion the central role played by deliberate anachronisms in religion.

> Therefore the Holy One, blessed be He, established two *yeshivot* for Israel, so that they would be discussing Torah day and night, and would come together from all their localities twice a year—in Adar and Elul and engage in the "wars of Torah" until they determine the correct law, bringing proof from Scripture, Mishnah and Talmud....
>
> Those two *yeshivot* have seen neither captivity nor persecution nor despoilment. Neither Greece nor Edom [Rome] have ruled over them. For twelve years before the destruction of Jerusalem [by the Babylonians] the Holy One blessed be He removed them from Jerusalem with their Torah and learning ....
>
> Rather the Holy One, blessed be He, acted righteously with Israel in that he had the exile of Yekhonyah precede the exile of Sidqiyah—in order that the Oral Torah not be forgotten by them. And they [the *yeshivot*] have dwelt in Babylonia with their Torah from that time until now; neither Greece nor Edom has ruled over them, nor have they been persecuted. And they will not even suffer the "pangs of the Messiah" ...[trans. Goodblatt, 1975:14].

Semah b. Hayyim, Head of Suran rabbinic academy in the 880s, makes similar assertions (Goodblatt, 1975:15).

It is noteworthy that the chronicle of Natan HaBavli (dated to the mid-tenth century) while sharing the anachronizing *Tendenz* of other contemporary works, nevertheless explicitly links the editing of the

term *be rav* meant advanced school. Moreover there is not a single instance of the association of any of these words with a specific town. ... The evidence does not show that the institutions called *yeshivot* in Geonic literature were called by different names in Amoraic sources. ... Undoubtedly there were rabbinic schools in towns like Nehardea, Sura and Pumbedita during the Sassanian period. But they were not called *yeshivot* or *metivata*. And more importantly, they were not organized like the institutions of the Islamic era which did bear the latter names." Goodblatt (1975:63-76) argues that tannaitic sources use the term *yeshiva* to connote: (1) the act of sitting and learning; (2) by derivation, being ordained as a sage and sitting as a colleague of the sages; (3) by derivation, an official seating of sages, especially in a court or legislative assembly. The Bavli's passages overwhelmingly adopt 2 and 3 and also use *yeshiva* as (4) a term denoting a study session. Palestinian names predominate in these sources in the Bavli. The term *metivata* shares meanings 2, 3 and 4 above, but in addition takes on two more, again by derivation: (5) a lesson, or a subject of study; (6) a specific unit of text of fixed or prescribed amount, to be the object of study (Goodblatt, 1976:76-79, following E.S. Rosenthal).

Babylonian Talmud and the establishment of large-scale rabbinic academies.

> And after him his son Tavyomi, who is Mar b. R. Ashi, presided. After him Rabbah Yosi presided, in whose days the Talmud was closed [nistam]. And when Rabbana Yosi died the two *yeshivot* remained without a gaon until the Saboraic rabbis—who were after the sages of the Talmud—agreed that they should make two *yeshivot* as there were in the days of R. Huna. For although they neither added nor subtracted from the Talmud, the Saboraic rabbis were *rashe yeshivot* [Heads of the Academies], and they were the Geonim [Excellencies] who used to sit and expound. And instruction *(hora'ah)* went forth from them to all Israel. And they conducted their *yeshivot* until this day. [Cited in Goodblatt, 1975:34 from A. Neubauer, *Medieval Jewish Chronicles*, II:78. Interpolations in square brackets are my own.]

Both the editing of the Talmud and the (re)organization of Rabbinism by centralizing authority in two main academies are clearly attributed by Natan to the activities in the sixth or early seventh century of the Saboraim. Natan appears to anticipate the charge that these institutions are, by his own admission, recent innovations by asserting that the Saboraim have only resuscitated an earlier institution. That Natan, or his detractors, view an admission of sixth- or early seventh-century origins as undermining the legitimacy of these academies increases, to my mind, the probability that Natan has accurately placed the emergence of these academies in Saboraic times.[5]

In view of the fact that Natan must seemingly apologize for what to Rabbinism's detractors appears to be the innovative activity of the

5. The notion that the Talmud was edited at the end or after the fifth century is based on several, classic sources. In addition to Natan HaBavli's chronicle, see *Seder Tannaim VeAmoraim* (890s CE): "And in the year 742 [Sel. = 431 CE], R. Yemar died, and a pillar of fire was seen in the sky—and it remained for thirty days. In the year 753 [Sel. = 442 CE], R. Huna the Exilarch died. In the year 762 [Sel. = 451 CE] R. Nahman b. R. Huna died and Yazdagird, king of the Persians, decreed that our ancestors desecrate the Sabbath. In the year 779 [Sel. = 468 CE], R. Yavyomi b. R. Ashi dies. In the year 782 [Sel. = 471 CE] R. Sama b. Rava died, and Huna b. Mar Zuttra the Exilarch was killed, and Jews were delivered over to the government. In the year 788 [Sel. = 477 CE], they destroyed the schools {batei midrashot} and decreed that the Jews must follow Persian laws, and R. Tosfa'ah died. In the year 793 [Sel. = 482 CE], the earth trembled, and Peroz, king of the Persians, was killed. In the year 811 [Sel. = 500 CE], Ravina, the end of hora'ah, died, and the Talmud was closed [nistam]" [ed. Kahan, pp. 4-6, trans. by Goodblatt, 1975]. Compare the above to *Iggeret Rav Sherira*, ed. Lewin p. 97.

Saboraim in founding the *yeshivot*, the manner in which Sherira's Epistle treats Saboraic and post-Saboraic figures deserves attention. It is only with regard to the first Saboraim that Sherira begins to use the titles, "Excellency" (גאון), Judge at the Gate (דיינא דבאבא) and "Our Rabbi" (as opposed to Rabbi or Rav). Like Natan, the transition to the Saboraim is correlated by Sherira with the completion of the Talmud.

> And after him [i.e., Rav Sama' b. Rava'] Rav Yose ruled. And in his era instruction [—usually taken to mean the production of new talmudic dicta or dialectica—] ceased, and the Talmud was completed. And the majority of our Rabbis, the Saboraim, passed away after [ruling] a few short years, as our Excellencies explained in their Books of Memoires [and] their Chronicles. [To wit:] in the year 815 [SE = 504 CE] Our Rabbi Sama' b. Our Rabbi Yehudai passed away in [the month of] Sivan. And it is said that he was Judge at the Gate [*Iggeret Rav Sherira*, ed. Levin, pp. 97-98, my translation]....
>
> And Rabbah Joseph remained the Excellency in the academies a few years. And after that Rav 'Eyna' in Sura and Rav Simunayah in Pumbedita. And after that Rav Rava'i Merov. And he was from our academy, and it is said he was the [or an] Excellency.
>
> And there were years of destruction and troubles at the end of the reign of the Persians. And they were not able to schedule sessions or seat the academies, or proceed with the leadership of the Excellencies, until after a few years [had passed], when Our Rabbis of our own [academy] came from Pumbedita to the district of Nehardea to the province of Peroz-Shappur.
>
> And these [are] the Excellencies which were in our province of Pumbedita after these matters, at the end of Persian rule, from 900 [SE = 589 CE]: Master (ms. Tzarfat adds: Rav) Hannan from Aqshaya; and after him ruled Master Rav Miri, Our Elder, b. Master Rav Dimi, Our Instructor; and his House of Study is known in Peroz-Shappur until today [and] is called the House of Rav Miri; and in his day there ruled in Sura Master Rav Mar b. Master Rav Huna, in the year 902 [SE = 591 CE]; and after Mar Rav Miri, Our Instructor, there ruled in Nehardea Mar Rav Hinnanai (or Hanninai) from the House of Gihara, and in his days Muhammad emerged upon the world['s stage].
>
> And it is said that there were in Sura at that time Rav Hanninai, and Rav Hanna, Excellency at Pumbedita, and Master Rav Isaac, Excellency. And he was at Peroz-Shappur when Ali ibn Abu-Talib conquered it ... [*Iggeret Rav Sherira*, ed. Levin, pp. 99-101, my translation].

Sherira is by no means consistent in his terminology in these several dozen lines dealing with the history of Babylonian Rabbinism from the beginning of the sixth century through the first quarter of the seventh century. Nevertheless, it is only at this point in the Epistle, when dealing with the last 125 years of Sassanid rule, that Master, Excellency, Judge at the Gate and Our Rabbi (in the Aramaic form) begin to be used as titles associated with the names of certain individual figures.[6] It is also in this section of the Epistle that Sherira begins using the term, "Excellencies" (in the plural), as a descriptive noun designating collectively the leaders of rabbinic academies. The appearance in this same section of the term "Our Rabbis" (again in the Aramaic plural, with the first-person, plural, possessive suffix) may constitute yet another significant indicator. Again, commencing with the Saboraic period only, Sherira talks of a *body* (or *college*) of Rabbis having their locus of operation in, or having a close association with, a particular educational institution in a specific locale.[7]

In the absence of better data, and in light of the Epistle's overall *Tendenz*, I attribute some significance to these terminological usages in divining information about the character and development of rabbinic institutions in the sixth and early seventh centuries. Sherira, like other Geonic chroniclers, such as Natan HaBavli, the editor of Seder Tannaim VeAmoraim, or, later, Abraham Ibn Daud (in his Sefer HaKabbalah), must demonstrate the antiquity both of rabbinic tradition and of those institutions which preserved and transmitted that tradition. This overarching purpose affects Sherira's account throughout, from his rendering of Rabbi Judah the Prince's editorial policy in the production of his Mishnah to Sherira's depiction of forms of rabbinic organization in tannaitic Judea and Galilee and amoraic Babylonia. Sherira's placement of the founding of the "academies" of Pumbedita and Sura in the period of Rav and Samuel is entirely at one with this apologetic *Tendenz*. The Epistle's overall position, therefore, is that no significant institutional or organizational revolution occurred in the Saboraic or early Geonic periods. Nevertheless, much of the institutional terminology regarding titles and offices, which in Geonic times is the hallmark of large, hierarchically organized rabbinic academies, appears for the first time in the

6. Interestingly, the title "Excellency" appears almost exclusively with named authorities associated with Pumbedita during the 150 or so years under discussion. Master, as a title rather than as part of a personal name, is used in association with heads of *all* rabbinic institutions which operated, according to Sherira, during the Saboraic period.

7. Once more, I point to the curious fact that at this point in the Epistle Sherira uses the term, "Our Rabbis," with respect to Pumbedita only. I do not know what significance may be attached to this fact. It may reflect something of Sherira's institutional chauvinism (see n.3 above). On the other hand, his records, by his own admission, are more complete for Pumbedita for the Saboraic period than for Sura (Mata Mehasia) or for elsewhere.

Epistle in association with the activities of the Saboraim. To be sure, there is no reason why this terminology may not be anachronistic. Yet our terminological data at this point belies Sherira's overall *Tendenz*. There appears, therefore, some warrant for the view that Sherira at this juncture provides evidence of a significant organizational overhaul of Rabbinism which took place over the sixth and early seventh centuries. None of this is to say, of course, that the full complement of organizational terms appearing in this section of the Epistle was in fact in use by the middle of the seventh century, or that the formal positions for which these terms came to be titles existed in Saboraic times. I claim only that the discord between the Epistle's overall tendentiousness and the account of the Saboraic period permits us to see in the latter account some reflection of important change in the organization and institutionalization of Babylonian rabbinic learning.[8] This conclusion is further borne out by the fact that Natan HaBavli provides, as we have seen, a parallel clue, when he states that the Saboraic rabbis "re-established" the academies which had previously existed.[9]

The larger social and political context of Babylonian Rabbinism: 475-652 CE

Based upon Goodblatt's assessment of the Talmudic evidence and my appraisal of the principal surviving Geonic chronicles, I have argued that sometime during the years 475-652 CE larger talmudic academies emerged in Babylonia. This places the emergence of the academies within the same period as the (final or penultimate) editing of the Talmud. We will return to the relationship between the editing and promulgation of the Talmud and the emergence of the Babylonian academies as the central institution of Rabbinism below. In the interim we should do well to review what we know of the larger social and political context of these transformational developments within Babylonian Rabbinism.

8. I do not claim and need not posit that the Pumbeditan academy of the tenth century preserved an organizational structure already present in its counterpart in Saboraic times.

9. One might well ask, Why leave such a clue at all? Our answer can be speculative at best. Perhaps detractors of Rabbinism in the ninth and tenth centuries pointed to the sixth- or seventh-century origins of the academies as part of their anti-rabbinic polemic. If so, it is significant that neither Natan nor Sherira were capable or felt free to efface totally that putative fact and, in the case of Natan, chose explicitly to finesse the issue in the manner in which we have seen.

It is facile and methodologically naive to point to a number of tumultuous events in the latter several centuries of Sassanian rule in Babylonia, and then maintain that these in some manner facilitated or engendered the formation of Rabbinic academies or the editing of the Talmud. First, we cannot comparatively measure the potential trauma for Jews of events in this period against developments in the first half of Sassanian rule, or in the convulsive period of Parthian hegemony at the end of the second and beginning of the third centuries. Second, even were some comparative measure available and were its results to focus our attention upon the sixth and early seventh centuries as particularly disruptive, we could do no more than point to a correlation between social and political context and social, organizational and literary transformative events in Rabbinism. Such correlations are not in themselves cogent arguments. Third, underlying such an approach remains a persecution theory of writing and of attendant social change. For such a theory there is no adequate empirical evidence. From a methodological standpoint, one would do better to identify particular changes in Sassanian Babylonia which would have required some attendant social and organizational adjustments among Jews.[10]

10. In any case, war was a commonplace state of affairs for inhabitants of Sassanid Persia. Whether the latter centuries of the Sassanid Period were particularly hard on the inhabitants in this regard is difficult to say, but let me document the wars of these centuries.

From its commencement in the third century CE, the Sassanid Empire was threatened by Byzantine Rome in the northeast, rebellious elements in Persian Armenia in the north and in more distant provinces of the east. In the latter half of Sassanid hegemony, the Huns and various other central Asian tribes presented ongoing threats. The heartland of Jewish population in upper Babylonia and lower Mesopotamea often proved dangerously close to the Roman-Persian lines. The fortress city of Dara changed hands with monotonous regularity. Nisibis, an important centre of rabbinic activity, was within a day's travel from Dara.

Yezdigird II, who commenced his reign in 440 CE (Sykes, 1969; Frye, 1966), inaugurated his reign with a war on Rome. But the Byzantine Emperor Theodosius proved willing to pay tribute rather than fight a war on his eastern frontier. Yezdigird's attempts to consolidate the Persian hold upon Armenia ended in hostilities and a major persecution of Christians, first in Armenia and subsequently in Mesopotamia. One hears nothing in extra-rabbinic sources of the persecution of Babylonian Jewry in this era, as reported by Sherira. After the short reign of Hormisdas (457-459), Firuz (459-483) coped with the White Huns in the northeast and with a revolt in Armenia (481-483). His death in a campaign against the White Huns brought Volagases to power in 485. Volagases eventually achieved a negotiated settlement with Armenia.

It is with Kobad (498-501 and 501-531) that all peoples of the Babylonian and Mesopotamian regions may have experienced particularly unsettling times. Kobad reopened hostilities with Rome after almost a century of relative peace on the western and northwestern frontiers. He fought a ten-year war with the White

The entire Amoraic and Saboraic periods parallel the period of Sassanid rule in Babylonia. With the Sassanids, control of the empire returned to the Aryans, whose culture and tradition differed considerably from that of the Parthian Arsacids. The Parthians instituted a model of indirect, quasi-feudal rule (Frye, 1966; Sykes, 1969). Provincial chiefs were recognized as local kings. Vassal monarchs ruled the border states. Cities of primarily Greek culture, such as Babylonian Seleucia, were permitted something like autonomous city-state status. Tribal minorities

Huns. During his reign, the Mazdakites, a Zoroastrian sect advocating what is often described as a form of communism, grew to considerable power and strength. So radical was their religiously legitimated economic and social policy and their zeal for proselytism that it is hard to imagine that they were not experienced as a convulsive element by traditional authorities and the aristocracy among Persians, Christians and Jews. Yet neither Sherira nor other rabbinic sources register their presence.

We shall discuss Noshirwan (531-578) in particular in our treatment of the administrative policies of the Sassanid era. Noshirwan, we may state here, put an end to virulent Mazdikite activity and to the wars with Rome. During Noshirwan's reign several campaigns were fought on the far Northern frontier. But hostilities nearer at home with Rome did not recommence until 572. Before Norshirwan successfully drove off the Roman forces, the Romans actually laid seige to Nisibis. The relatively short reign of Hormisdas IV (578-590) saw the continuation of battles with Rome in the Mesopotamian plain and an invasion of the Turks, who were in the end driven off.

Chosroes II (Khusru Parviz) (590-628) ushered in a last great period of Persian hegemony. Persia drove Rome almost entirely out of Asia Minor and the Levant. During this period Jerusalem itself was captured; it is reported that 26,000 Persian Jews joined with the Persian forces to liberate their ancient capital. We can but imagine the Messianic fervor which these events would have unleashed among Babylonian Jewry. So too, one may conjecture the brutal disappointment when, beginning in 623, the new Emperor of Byzantium, Heraclius, commmenced a brilliant campaign to restore Rome's holdings in the East. Heraclius drove far into Persia, through the heartland of Mesopotamia and upper Babylonia, the principal area of Jewish settlement in Persia, to sack Ctesiphon itself before withdrawing to sensible frontiers. The succession of weak Persian monarchs ruling for a few short years each marked the demise of Sassanid Persia. The last "Great King," Yezdigird III, saw the progressive fall of the Empire to Muslim Arab forces between 633 and 652, the year of the last Great King's death. While no war or persecution seems to have been aimed at the Jews or at the Persian populace generally, the general destruction brought on by the successive Arab campaigns and the resulting dissolution of social, economic and political order must have severely affected all. Only after the consolidation not only of Muslim power but also of Muslim administration in Persia would life for Jews as well as for others attain a reasonable level of stable order.

were largely autonomous as well. One may cite as an example the Arabs of Mesopotamia.

The Sassanid monarchs, by contrast, followed a policy of increased centralization throughout their hegemony. Princes of the Court were sent to govern the imperial provinces directly. While this remained the policy throughout the four centuries of Sassanid rule, it is with Noshirwan (Khusro I, 531-579) that the administrative policies of the Sassanids reached their fullest expression. The many provinces were collapsed into four large satrapies (Sykes, 1969, following Tabiri and A. Christensen), each under the rule of a powerful governor directly accountable to Noshirwan. Noshirwan completely reorganized the system of taxation and the army (which increasingly used heavy cavalry and siege engines), and instituted major infrastructural improvements to roads, water supply and irrigation systems, among others.

Sassanid administrative policy in general and Noshirwan's reorganization in particular would have considerably affected client kings or ethnarchs of various minorities. The period as a whole would have seen a whittling away of local autonomy, and, with Noshirwan, its utter disappearance in anything other than vestigial or honorific form. The effects upon Jewish polity and society may have been somewhat akin to the disappearance of the power of the Kehilla, the local autonomous Jewish governments, in early modern Europe. The blessings of Noshirwan "the Just's" rule may have been mixed blessings for many, particularly traditional artistocratic elements of the Babylonian Jewish community.

The Sassanid period also inaugurated a renaissance of Persian culture following the centuries of Parthian rule (Frye, 1966; Sykes, 1969). Writing was more in evidence than in the previous era. Pahlavi inscriptions, and Pahlavi commentaries and paraphrases (Zend) of Avestan texts survive as the concrete expression of this renaissance. The archaic Avestan language was no doubt comprehended by few people. A number of scholars over the last 80 years have voiced the view that the Avesta was first committed to writing sometime in the last century and a half of the Sassanid period. If this is so, then the writing down of the Avesta and the compilation of Pahlavi exegeses took place at a time roughly contemporary with the editing of the Babylonian Talmud.

It would be a stunning parallel were one to discover that the same century and a half saw the development within Zoroastrianism of well-organized academies for the study of Avestan and Pahlavi religious literature. Though I know of no evidence to this effect, it is important to note that this period of Sassanid rule, particularly under Noshirwan, saw the transplantation of the academies dedicated to the study of Hellenistic philosophy, science and medicine from the Roman west to Upper Babylonia and Persia in the wake of increasing intolerance in Christian Byzantium for "pagan" learning (Frye, 1966; Sykes, 1969).

In short, the production of Persian religious literature in written form, the introduction of the model of the academy by the last surviving Hellenistic philosophers, coupled with the degrading of traditional Jewish government and administration, first as a result of the centralizing policies of the Sassanids, and later as a result of the invasions by Heraclius and the Muslims—all this may have had a major effect upon the organizational structure of the Babylonian Jewish community and might offer some insight into developments which, we have argued, took place within Babylonian Rabbinism in the last century or so of Sassanid rule.

Talmud rhetoric and redaction in their larger social, political and cultural context

We have seen that what is characteristic and pervasive about the Talmud at its penultimate redactional level are its structural formularies as well as structured sequences of dialectical logical operators, which, to a significant degree, are engendered by the Bavli's structuring terminology. Dialectical formularies in use throughout the Babylonian Talmud tend to be grammatically integral parts of the materials and individual analytic/argument-statements which the Talmud has woven into its larger structures (its *sugyot*).[11] Structural formularies differ from the dialectical

11. This very fact accounts for the presence as well in Bavli of dialectical formularies representing the rhetorical patterns of the redactors' sources. To a large degree, these dialectical formularies replicate those which are characteristic of rabbinic documents which historically stand between Mishnah and the Babylonian Talmud, such as Tosefta and the several Halakic Midrashim. Another stratum of dialectical argumentation appears within materials attributed to Amoraim. In large measure, our research and the research of others has demonstrated clear similarities in form and function between the dialectics bearing Amoraic attributions and those which pervade Sifra, Sifre on Deuteronomy, Sifre on Numbers, Tosefta, or the numerous *baraitot* in the Bavli which have no parallel in these pre-talmudic sources but which may be shown to mimic to a "t" their characteristic linguistic patterns (Kraemer, 1989, 1990; see also Weiss-Halivni, 1986). The fact that the Bavli contains as well the rhetoric of the sources it cites is an unremarkable finding. That redactors of the Bavli can, as we have seen, mimic this rhetoric in toseftan-like *baraitot* or in passages imitative of, or expanding upon, pericopae of halakic midrash is more interesting. For it highlights the fact that while quite capable of simply copying the literary style of its authoritative

not only in terms of the grammatical relationship obtaining between these formularies and the surrounding words, phrases and passages, but also, and because of that relationship, in function. By using their established assortment of structural formularies, redactors order sometimes disjointed and unrelated materials into more developed units of inquiry. But such units of inquiry go nowhere, to use a colloquialism entirely suitable to our evidence. To be sure, much of the material exhibiting dialectic formularies serves to argue for a particular conclusion based on evidence and premises. A (supposedly) probative argument will be given for a position, based on Scripture, or upon an analogy, or some other basis. But, by their use of structural formularies to bring into relationship with one another these otherwise discrete materials, the Talmud's editors tend to undermine the probative nature of the argument contained in any one unit. Sometimes these larger structures conclude with a constituent element wherein is contained an argument declared to be probative (for example, *sugyot* concluding with the formulary, "learn from this [שמע מיניה]"). In other instances, in a larger structure the final item is left as the implicit winner of the contrived debate or extended analysis. But more often it would overreach the bounds of the evidence to maintain that the final element of a *sugya* remains the victor. More to the point, finding the answer is not the principal point of structures we have seen. And this is so whether or not an obviously probative pericope terminates a longer construct linked by structural formularies; otherwise the editors' interests would have been better served by presenting only the conclusive argument or source. By not so doing, the redactors imply that the process of inquiry is of as great or greater importance than reaching any conclusive end, even where such an end is at hand. Inquiry, then, is an open-ended process of the highest intrinsic value in and of itself, quite apart from any probative stance which may thereby be attained.[12]

sources, the Bavli exhibits a tendency to use structured sequences of dialectical operators which show a preoccupation to explore complex relationships.

12. I believe that in not distinguishing dialectic from structural formularies and the quite different literary constructions which each serves to produce, David Weiss-Halivni (1986) was led to his conclusion that the generative ethic or ideology which informed the Talmud's redactors was the desire to attain "justified law" through argument. In fact, the redactors of the Bavli communicate a profound ambivalence for the generation of justified law. For they have everywhere included pericopes and Amoraic sayings, excised from their contexts, which indeed appear interested in the production of justified law, while, at the same time, constructing from those sources larger structures which value open-ended inquiry for its own sake. David Kraemer (1990) appears closer to the mark.

It is a tantalizing contradiction that this fundamental valuing of open-ended inquiry and argument for its own sake, and to no particular end, becomes the fulcrum for the redaction of a closed document that quickly attains canonical status within the community of scholars which produced it. Are we not caught between two contradictory sets of implicitly communicated meanings about what is ultimately of value?

I propose that in so representing this fundamental contradiction, the Babylonian Talmud in fact offers an affectively, if not intellectually, satisfying resolution to a fundamental, problematic situation facing Rabbinism toward the end of Sassanid rule. In order to explore this hypothesis, let us examine further some aspects of Talmudic rhetoric and redaction.

As noted by Kraemer (1989), it has long been recognized that *sugyot* appearing at the beginning of tractates or of chapters appear much more fully developed than *sugyot* dealing with the latter sections of a mishnaic tractate or intermediate division. Scholars have for the last century offered various explanations for this phenomenon. Their accounts have often exhibited a naive historicist positivism; many have been unable to escape a sentiment that predisposes them to view these *sugyot* as nearly stenographic records of actual sessions in academies. They have surmised, therefore, from the length of *sugyot* opening tractates or chapters that these *sugyot* emerge from special celebratory sessions—somewhat in the vein of commencement exercises—for which a highly elaborate and skillfully constructed lesson (perhaps by some distinguished person) was appropriate academic fare.

The redactional studies of Kraemer (1989; 1990) and Hauptman (1988) render preposterous the view that *sugyot* in their currently structured form represent actual lessons. From their work as well as from our analyses of talmudic rhetoric, one must conclude that the structure of *sugyot* are entirely the work of relatively late or penultimate redactors.

Sugyot, then, are artifacts. And redactors have so structured matters to suit their own interests and thereby implicitly communicate their own perceptions and, one may suspect, the perceptions of whatever guild, group or class they represent in their enterprise.[13] What, then, may be concluded from the rather consistent evidence that opening *sugyot* are longer, while the further one progresses in a chapter or trac-

13. Of course one may cling to the view that they composed the opening *sugyot* to serve as appropriate lessons for commencement exercises. But that is now a total conjecture and speculation. Since without the assumption that records of actual sessions are the immediate origins of *sugyot*, it no longer follows from the length of a *sugya* that a special academic event took place.

tate the shorter (and at times almost perfunctory) *sugyot* become? First, one must take note that there seems no relative lack of source material of relevance to the latter sections of chapters and tractates. Tosefta, Sifra, Sifre on Deuteronomy, Sifre on Numbers, Mekilta deRabbi Ishmael and Mekilta deRabbi Simeon all preserve sources which one must suppose were in the main available in some form or another to the Bavli's editors and of relevance to these latter sections.[14] I am therefore inclined to conclude that editors seem not to have deemed it necessary to sustain the production of elaborate *sugyot* from the beginning to the end of a tractate. Furthermore, if comprehensiveness is not a sustained editorial goal, then all *sugyot*, especially the longer ones, may well be intended to be exemplary. Longer structures, suitably located at the opening of tractates, constitute examples of *the lengths* to which an inquiry may, or should, be taken. Shorter *sugyot* are simply examples of points of departure for lengthier analyses modelled on the efforts at the commencement of tractates.

If talmudic literary structures are both open-ended and exemplary, then Talmud stands, in this regard too, in sharp contrast to Mishnah, the document which supposedly sets Talmud's agenda. Mishnah, in literary terms, purports to be a complete and entirely sufficient universe unto itself (see Lightstone, 1988, 1990, 1994b). In this respect it provided the literary homology of the crystalization at the end of the second century of individual circles of Judean-Galilean rabbis and their disciples into an organized movement in which the College of rabbis and the Patriarch constituted necessary and complementary parts and powers. How may the Talmud, with its particular rhetorical traits, have served in the literary realm as a homology and collective representation of the institutional transformations from which it emerged or which it facilitated?

To answer the queston, let us review what we have concluded thus far. First, the Talmud deconstructs those sacred authoritative sources from which it draws its materials. Each of these documents, even Mishnah, in some sense disappears as an objective, externally constraining and integral whole. Second, the process of critical analysis to no particular end displaces these sources as the locus of that which is authoritative. The rhetorical patterns by which this process takes place constitute a sustained and pervasive characteristic of the Babylonian Talmud. Third, the open-ended "debates" which characterize the structure of the Talmud are products of the work of the penultimate redactors. It is they who by

14. In so stating matters, I do not intend to beg the question of whether all of these documents were edited prior to the work of the Bavli's redactors.

artifice bring into open-ended, inconclusive deliberations any antecedent "parties" to the analysis of rabbinic tradition. Fourth, not only is this analysis often incomplete and without concrete results, the Talmud's analyses are intended to be exemplary; they invite the continuation of a process of inquiry on the basis of the models provided in the text. Fifth, the text appears to its recipients to be a closed document—in some sense brought to completion by redactors at a certain moment in time. We may now more precisely articulate the paradox referred to earlier; a text which invites completion, addition and extension of its analysis nevertheless is experienced by the group which received and promulgated it as an autonomous, fixed and enduring "object in the world."

Precisely by representing, albeit implicitly, this paradox to members of the community, Talmud can have provided an homology for those institutional transformations undergone by Rabbinism over the last several centuries of the Sassanid period. Toward the latter part of this period, individual rabbinic circles comprising masters and disciples gave way to the emergence of autonomous, more complex and well structured institutions of learning, the rabbinic academies. Within this newly emerged autonomous realm, rabbinic scholastic philosophers and their students engaged in the study of the Talmud. The Talmud became both the object of, and the model for, analysis. What is implicitly communicated in the Talmud was clearly heard. So just as the Talmud "emerged into the world" as an objective, autonomous realm of discourse deconstructing so as to incorporate and supplant the objective texts and traditions which preceded it, so too the academy emerged as an autonomous institutution characterized by the pursuit of talmudic discourse (as invited by the exemplary nature of the Talmud's passages).

Prior to the emergence of such academies, the rabbinic movement had assiduously avoided, were dissuaded from, or considered imprudent the establishment of such *yeshivot*, in spite of the fact that Judean-Galilean Rabbinism offered from the mid-third century on a model and point of departure in the form of their "houses of study" (Lightstone, 1994b; Goodblatt, 1975). As J. Neusner has shown (Neusner, 1969-70), Babylonian rabbis of this same period were visible in the public realm as officers of various administrative entities in the semi-autonomous Jewish government ruled by the Exilarch. In this public sphere, no autonomous, organized rabbinic institution existed. But Sassanid rulers systematically disempowered such autonomous forms of ethnic governance as the Exilarch's administration. By the end of the reign of Noshirwan, Jewish self-government had all but disappeared. The Exilarch may have retained extensive prestige, but little more. If Rabbinism had earlier "hitched its wagon" by design or by necessity to the Exilarch's administration, such a locus for the exercise of rabbinic power and authority no longer remained a viable one by the sixth century. From this period of structural turmoil for the rabbis and the Exilarchate emerged a document, the Talmud (modelling a "type" of "scholastic rabbi"), and a new autonomous, objective realm of rabbinic activity, the rabbinic academy. The text, the type of religious virtuosity reflected in its rhetoric, and the institution subtended and superseded that which preceded them.

Which, the Talmud or the academy, first emerged and facilitated the emergence of the other, I cannot say. But each finds in the other an implicitly communicated representation of its own foundational norms and dispositions. Together, near the time of the Islamic conquest of Persian Babylonia, they aided the continued emergence of Rabbinism as an autonomous and important social realm in the Jewish community.

APPENDIX A

A Comparative Analysis of the Distribution of Selected Structural Formulae in Nine Tractates of the Bavli

As stated in chapter 1 (n.5), I have undertaken an additional analysis to check that the rhetorical language of the passages analyzed in this book (and of b. Bek. chaps. 2-3 and b. Ta'an. chap. 4) are not atypical or eccentric features of the Bavli. This appendix documents the frequency and distribution in b. Bek., b. Ta'an. and seven other tractates of a selection of those structural formulae which emerged in my analyses as key items of Bavli's rhetorical vocabulary. The five structural formulae selected challenge antecedent propositions, invite further inquiry or introduce alternative hypotheses for analysis. In serving these functions the selected items are central to the Bavli's rhetorical character as described in this book. By examining their frequency and distribution in nine tractates I am therefore probing the claim that that rhetorical character is a feature of all nine tractates. This does not mean that what follows is intended to be a definitive and comprehensive test of that claim. My purpose here is limited: to support further the assertion that in terms of their rhetorical character the passages analyzed in this book, b. Bek. chapters 2-3 and b. Ta'an. chapter 4 do not constitute a body of evidence so skewed as to misrepresent the rhetorical character of the Bavli.

The five structural formulae selected are: (1) "if you were to question [my response], I would say ..." (איבעית אימא); (2) "it was asked of them ..."(איבעיא להו); (3) "[Rabbi x] challenged it ..." (מתקיף לה/ליה); (4) "how are they/is it similar?" (היכי/הכי דמי); (5) "and they rebuffed it ..." (ורמינהו). Using software by *Otzar HaTorah HaMemuhshevet* (Bnai Brak, Israel) I counted the total number of times each formula appears in the Bavli as a whole. The same software permitted me to examine all instances of each formula's use in the following nine tractates: b. Berakot; b. Shabbat; b. Eruvin; b. Ta'anit; b. Megilah; b. Ketuvot; b. Baba Qama; b. Baba Mesia; b. Bekorot. Together these nine tractates constitute a significant and extensive sample of the Bavli.

Chart 1 summarizes the results of a number calculations performed on the information retrieved. Column 1 of the chart gives in percentages the proportion of the entire Bavli accounted for by each tractate. For example, all of b. Berakot represents 3.7 percent of the Bavli. For these calculations, the number of folio pages in the Munich manuscript was used, since in the standard Vilna edition of the Bavli the amount of text appearing on each folio page varies greatly. In columns 2 through 6 the number of occurrences in a tractate of each of the five formulae is given as a percentage of the total number of occurrences in the Bavli; hence, the number of times "f1" (i.e., "if you should question [my response], I would say ...") appears in b. Berakot represents 2.6 percent of occurrences of that formula in all of Bavli. Column 7 provides the total count of all five formulae ("f1" through "f5") in any one tractate as a percentage of the appearance of all five formulae in the entire Bavli. Thus b. Berakot contains 2.5 percent of the total number of instances in the Bavli of the five formulae taken together. The rationale for giving this cumulative statistic derives from the fact that the rhetorical character of the Bavli is not so much the product of each of its formulae operating in isolation as the result of their cumulative effects over successive sustained composite "essays." The figures, again in percent, in the final column of the chart ("dev.") respond to the question, Do the percentages appearing in column 7 for any one tractate vary wildly from what one would expect, given the proportion of the Bavli accounted for by that tractate? For example, b. Berakot, which constitutes 3.7 percent of the Bavli, contains 2.5 percent of the total count in the Bavli of all five formulae; this amounts to 1.2 percent less than what one would expect if the use of these formulae were completely evenly distributed across Bavli's tractates.

CHART 1: Distribution of selected structural formulae in nine tractates of the Bavli

	% Munich	% occurrences in b. f1	f2	f3	f4	f5	% in b. (f1-f5)	% dev. (f1-f5)
Berakot	3.7	2.6	2.6	2.8	1.6	4.7	2.5	-1.2
Shabbat	5.5	3.3	11.0	7.7	5.0	9.4	6.6	+1.1
Eruvin	3.4	5.4	2.8	3.2	4.4	1.7	3.8	+0.4
Ta'anit	1.5	0.3	1.2	0.7	0.5	1.2	0.7	-0.8
Megilah	1.7	0.9	0.6	0.7	1.0	1.2	0.8	-0.9
Ketuvot	4.0	5.2	5.7	6.7	4.2	2.9	5.2	+1.2
Baba Qama	4.4	5.0	3.8	5.6	11.0	2.9	5.9	+1.5
Baba Mesia	4.0	6.7	4.0	1.9	8.4	7.0	5.8	+1.8
Bekorot	2.6	3.5	3.2	2.3	1.0	3.5	2.6	+0.0

The results of this exercise bear out my assertion that there is nothing significantly eccentric about the data of this study. Taken as a whole, the type of structural formulae that help give Bavli its particular rhetorical character appear well represented throughout the nine tractates in question. A specific formula may appear more often than one would expect for a particular tractate, were *individual* formulae completely evenly distributed across the Bavli. But I would have been surprised to find an even distribution at the level of single formulae. We have seen in analyses in this book that once Bavli's editors have used a formula, they often will repeat its use several times in sequence before turning to some other. This tendency was confirmed in the computer searches of other tractates. In addition, particular subject matter does lend itself to certain types of analysis; this predisposes toward the use of some formulae and not others in a given composite. For my purposes the cumulative effect of the use of the range of available rhetorical terms is significant. At this level the data in the chart does not show that there is anything significantly atypical or eccentric about the materials analyzed in detail in our research.[1]

1. I thank once more Dr. Michael Broyde, whose gadfly questions led me to conceive and undertake the investigations reported in this appendix.

APPENDIX B

The Hebrew-Aramaic Texts of b. Avodah Zarah 14b-16a and b. Bekorot 2a-5b

Printed below are the Hebrew-Aramaic Texts of b. Avodah Zarah 14b-16a and b. Bekorot 2a-5b. I have reproduced the text of the standard Vilna edition as reissued in computer-retrievable form by *Otzar HaTorah HaMemuhshevet* (Bnai Brak, Israel).

Babylonian Talmud, Avodah Zarah 14b-16a

-עבודה זרה דף יד/ב-

מתני'. מקום שנהגו למכור בהמה דקה לעובדי כוכבים מוכרין, מקום שנהגו שלא למכור אין מוכרין. ובכל מקום אין מוכרין להם בהמה גסה, עגלים וסייחים, שלמין ושבורין, ר' יהודה מתיר בשבורה, ובן בתירא מתיר בסוס.

גמ'. למימרא, דאיסורא ליכא, מנהגא הוא דאיכא, היכא דנהיג איסור נהוג, היכא דנהיג היתר נהוג, ורמינהי אין מעמידין בהמה בפונדקאות של עובדי כוכבים, מפני שחשודין על הרביעה אמר רב מקום שהתירו למכור התירו לייחד, מקום שאסרו לייחד אסרו למכור.

-עבודה זרה דף טו/א-

ור"א אומר אף במקום שאסרו לייחד מותר למכור, מאי טעמא עובד כוכבים חס על בהמתו שלא תעקר. ואף רב הדר ביה דאמר רב תחליפא א"ר שילא בר אבימי משמיה דרב עובד כוכבים חס על בהמתו שלא תעקר. ובכל מקום אין מוכרין בהמה גסה כו'. מ"ט נהי דלרביעה לא חיישינן, מעביד ביה מלאכה חיישינן. וניעביד, כיון דזבנה קנייה גזירה משום שאלה ומשום שכירות. שאלה קנייה, ואגרא קנייה אלא אמר רמי בריה דר' ייבא גזירה משום נסיוני, דזמנין דזבנה לה ניהליה סמוך לשקיע' החמה דמעלי שבתא, וא"ל תא נסייה ניהליה, ושמעה ליה לקליה ואזלא מחמתיה וניחא ליה דתיזל, והוה ליה מחמר אחר בהמתו בשבת, והמחמר אחר בהמתו בשבת חייב חטאת. מתקיף לה רב שישא בריה דרב אידי ושכירות מי קניא והתנן אף במקום שאמרו להשכיר, לא לבית דירה אמרו, מפני שמכניס לתוכו עבודת כוכבים, ואי ס"ד שכירות קניא, האי כי קא מעייל לביתי' קא מעייל שאני עבודת כוכבים דחמירא, דכתיב (דברים ז) ולא תביא תועבה אל ביתך. מתקיף לה רב יצחק ברי' דרב משרשיא ושכירות מי קניא והא תנן ישראל ששכר פרה מכהן יאכילנה כרשיני תרומה, וכהן ששכר פרה מישראל, אע"פ שמזונותיה עליו לא יאכילנה כרשיני תרומה ואי ס"ד שכירות קניא, אמאי לא יאכילנה פרה דידיה היא אלא ש"מ, שכירות לא

קניא. והשתא דאמרת שכירו׳ לא קניא, גזירה משום שכירות, וגזירה משום שאלה, וגזירה משום נסיוני. רב אדא שרא לזבוני חמרא אידא דספסירא, אי משום נסיוני הא לא ידעה לקליה דאזלא מחמתיה, ואי משום שאלה ושכירות כיון דלא דידיה היא לא מושיל ולא מוגר, ועוד, משום דלא ניגלי ביה מומא. רב הונא זבין ההיא פרה לעובד כוכבים, אמר ליה רב חסדא מ״ט עבד מר הכי אמר ליה אימור לשחיטה זבנה.

-עבודה זרה דף טו/ב-

ומנא תימרא דאמרינן כי האי גוונא דתנן, בש״א לא ימכור אדם פרה החורשת בשביעית, וב״ה מתירין, מפני שיכול לשוחטה. אמר רבה מי דמי התם אין אדם מצווה על שביתת בהמתו בשביעית, הכא אדם מצווה על שביתת בהמתו בשבת א״ל אביי וכל היכא דאדם מצווה אסור והרי שדה, דאדם מצווה על שביתת שדהו בשביעית, ותנן, בש״א לא ימכור אדם שדה ניר בשביעית, וב״ה מתירין, מפני שיכול להובירה מתקיף לה רב אשי וכל היכא דאין אדם מצווה שרי והרי כלים, דאין אדם מצווה על שביתת כלים בשביעית, ותנן, אלו הן כלים שאין אדם רשאי למוכרן בשביעית המחרישה וכל כליה, העול והמזרה והדקר אלא אמר רב אשי כל היכא דאיכא למיתלא תלינן ואע״ג דמצווה, וכל היכא דליכא למיתלי לא תלינן אע״ג דאינו מצווה. רבה זבין ההוא חמרא לישראל החשיד למכור לעובד כוכבים, א״ל אביי מ״ט עבד מר הכי א״ל אנא לישראל זביני. א״ל והא אזיל ומזבין ליה לעובד כוכבים לעובד כוכבים קא מזבין, לישראל לא קא מזבין איתיביה מקום שנהגו למכור בהמה דקה לכותים מוכרין, שלא למכור אין מוכרין, מ״ט אילימא משום דחשידי ארביעה, ומי חשידי והתניא אין מעמידין בהמה בפונדקאות שלעובדי כוכבים, זכרים אצל זכרים ונקבות אצל נקבות, ואין צ״ל נקבות אצל זכרים וזכרים אצל נקבות, ואין מוסרין בהמה לרועה שלהן, ואין מייחדין עמהם, ואין מוסרין להם תינוק ללמדו ספר וללמדו אומנות, אבל מעמידין בהמה בפונדקאות של כותים, זכרים אצל נקבות ונקבות אצל זכרים, ואין צ״ל זכרים אצל זכרים ונקבות אצל נקבות, ומוסרין בהמה לרועה שלהן, ומייחדין עמהם, ומוסרין להם תינוק ללמדו ספר וללמדו אומנות, אלמא לא חשידי ועוד תניא אין מוכרין להם לא זיין ולא כלי זיין, ואין משחיזין להן את הזיין, ואין מוכרין להן לא סדן ולא קולרין, ולא כבלים ולא שלשלאות של ברזל, אחד עובד כוכבים ואחד כותי, מ״ט אי נימא דחשידי אשפיכות דמים, ומי חשידי האמרת ומייחדין עמהן, אלא משום דאתי לזבונה לעובד כוכבים וכי תימא כותי לא עביד תשובה, ישראל עביד תשובה, והאמר רב נחמן אמר רבה בר אבוה כדרך שאמרו אסור למכור לעובד כוכבים, כך אסור למכור לישראל החשוד למכור לעובד כוכבים רהיט בתריה תלתא פרסי, וא״ד פרסא בחלא, ולא אדרכיה. א״ר דימי בר אבא כדרך שאסור למכור לעובד כוכבים, אסור למכור ללסטים ישראל. ה״ד אי דחשיד דקטיל, פשיטא, היינו עובד כוכבים ואי דלא קטיל, אמאי לא לעולם דלא קטיל, והב״ע במשמוטא, דזימנין דעביד לאצולי נפשיה. תנו רבנן אין מוכרין להן תריסין, וי״א מוכרין להן תריסין. מ״ט אילימא משום דמגנו עלייהו, אי הכי, אפילו חיטי ושערי נמי לא אמר רב

-עבודה זרה דף טז/א-

אי אפשר ה״נ. איכא דאמרי תריסין היינו טעמא דלא, דכי שלים זינייהו קטלי

בגוייהו. ויש אומרים מוכרים להם תריסין, דכי שלים זינייהו מערק ערקי. אמר רב נחמן אמר רבה בר אבוה הלכה כיש אומרים. אמר רב אדא בר אהבה אין מוכרין להן עששיות של ברזל, מ"ט משום דחלשי מינייהו כלי זיין. אי הכי, אפילו מרי וחציני נמי אמר רב זביד בפרזלא הינדואה. והאידנא דקא מזבנינן, א"ר אשי לפרסאי דמגנו עילוון. עגלים וסייחים. תניא רבי יהודה מתיר בשבורה, מפני שאינה יכולה להתרפאות ולחיות. אמרו לו והלא מרביעין עליה ויולדת, וכיון דמרביעין עליה ויולדת אתו לשהויה אמר להן לכשתלד. אלמא, לא מקבלת זכר. בן בתירא מתיר בסוס. תניא בן בתירא מתיר בסוס, מפני שהוא עושה בו מלאכה שאין חייבין עליה חטאת, ורבי אוסר מפני ב' דברים, אחד משום תורת כלי זיין,ואחד משום תורת בהמה גסה. בשלמא תורת כלי זיין איכא, דקטיל בסחופיה, אלא תורת בהמה גסה מאי היא אמר רבי יוחנן לכשיזקין מטחינו ברחיים בשבת. א"ר יוחנן הלכה כבן בתירא. איבעיא להו שור של פטם, מהו תיבעי לרבי יהודה, תיבעי לרבנן, תיבעי לרבי יהודה, עד כאן לא קא שרי רבי יהודה אלא בשבורה דלא אתי לכלל מלאכה, אבל האי דכי משהי ליה אתי לכלל מלאכה אסור, או דלמא אפילו לרבנן לא קא אסרי התם אלא דסתמיה לאו לשחיטה קאי, אבל האי דסתמיה לשחיטה קאי, אפילו רבנן שרו ת"ש, דאמר רב יהודה אמר שמואל של בית רבי היו מקריבין שור של פטם ביום אידם, חסר ד' ריבבן שאין מקריבין אותו היום אלא למחר, חסר ד' ריבבן שאין מקריבין אותו חי אלא שחוט, חסר ד' ריבבן שאין מקריבין אותו כל עיקר, מ"ט לאו משום דלמא אתי לשהויי. וליטעמיך, שאין מקריבין אותו היום אלא למחר מאי טעמא אלא, רבי מיעקר מילתא בעי, וסבר יעקר ואתי פורתא פורתא. וכי משהי ליה, בריא ועביד מלאכה אמר רב אשי, אמר לי זבידא בר תורא משהינן ליה ועביד על חד תרין.

Babylonian Talmud,
Bekorot 2a-5b

-בכורות דף ב/א-

מתני'. הלוקח עובר חמורו של עובד כוכבים, והמוכר לו אע"פ שאינו רשאי, המשתתף לו, והמקבל הימנו, והנותן לו בקבלה פטור מן הבכורה, שנאמר בישראל אבל לא באחרים

גמ'. כל הני למה לי צריכי, דאי תנא לוקח, ה"א משום דקא מייתי לה לקדושה, אבל מוכר דקא מפקע לה מקדושה, אימא ליקנסיה, קמ"ל. והמשתתף לו למה לי לאפוקי מדרבי יהודה, דאמר שותפות עובד כוכבים חייבת בבכורה, קמשמע לן דפטורה מן הבכורה. והמקבל ל"ל משום דקא בעי למיתני והנותן לו בקבלה. והנותן לו בקבלה למה לי איצטריך, סד"א הואיל ועיקר בהמה דישראל היא, ליקנסיה, דלמא אתי לאיחלופי בבהמה אחריתי, קמשמע לן. תנן התם ר' יהודה מתיר בשבורה, בן בתירא מתיר בסוס. איבעיא להו עובר מה לי א"ר יהודה טעמא דר' יהודה התם דשרי משום דשבורה, עובר נמי שבור הוא,

או דלמא, שבורה לאו היינו אורחיה. אבל עובר, כיון דהיינו אורחיה לאו שבור הוא ת״ש והמוכר לו אף על פי שאינו רשאי ולא פליג ר׳ יהודה, וליטעמיך המשתתף לו, והמקבל ממנו, והנותן לו בקבלה דלא קתני, הכי נמי דלא פליג אלא פליג ולא קתני, ה״נ פליג ולא קתני. ת״ש, ר׳ יהודה אומר המקבל בהמה מן העובד כוכבים וילדה מעלין אותו בשוויו, ונותן חצי דמיו לכהן. והנותן לו בקבלה, אף על פי שאינו רשאי קונסים אותו עד עשרה בדמיו, ונותן כל דמיו לכהן,

–בכורות דף ב/ב–

מאי לאו אעובר לא, אבהמה, והא דמיו קתני תני דמיה, והא נותן כל דמיו לכהן קתני ואי בהמה, כהן מאי עבידתיה הכא במאי עסקינן כגון דיהיב ליה בהמה מעברתא לפטומה, דמיגו דקנסינן ליה אבהמה, קנסינן ליה אעובר. אמר רב אשי, ת״ש רבי יהודה מתיר בשבורה, מפני שאינה יכולה להתרפאות, הא יכולה להתרפאות אסר, והא עובר נמי כיכול להתרפאות דמי שמע מינה. ואיכא דמתני לה אמתני׳ והמוכר לו, אע״פ שאינו רשאי לימא מתני׳ דלא כרבי יהודה, דתנן רבי יהודה מתיר בשבורה אפילו תימא רבי יהודה, שבורה לאו היינו אורחיה, עובר היינו אורחיה ת״ש, רבי יהודה אומר המקבל בהמה מן העובד כוכבים וילדה מעלין אותו בשויו, ונותן חצי דמיו לכהן. והנותן לו בקבלה, אע״פ שאינו רשאי קונסין אותו עד עשרה בדמיו, ונותן כל דמיו לכהן, מאי לאו אעובר לא, אבהמה, והא דמיו קתני תני דמיה, והא נותן כל דמיו לכהן קתני ואי בהמה, כהן מאי עבידתיה הכא במאי עסקינן, כגון דיהיב בהמה מעברתא לפטומה, דמיגו דקנסינן ליה אבהמה, קנסינן ליה אעובר. אמר רב אשי, ת״ש ר׳ יהודה מתיר בשבורה, מפני שאינה יכולה להתרפאות, הא יכולה להתרפאות אסור, והאי נמי כיכול להתרפאות דמי שמע מינה. איבעיא להו מכר בהמה לעובריה. מאי תיבעי לר׳ יהודה, תיבעי לרבנן, תיבעי לרבי יהודה, עד כאן לא קא שרי ר׳ יהודה אלא בשבורה, דלא אתיא לאיחלופי, אבל שלמה דאתיא לאיחלופי אסר, או דלמא, ומה שבורה דפסקה מיניה, וכל שכן שלמה דלא פסקה מיניה תיבעי לרבנן, עד כאן לא קאסרי רבנן, אלא בשבורה דפסקה מיניה, אבל שלמה דלא פסקה מיניה, שרו, או דלמא, ומה שבורה דלא אתיא לאיחלופי אסרי, וכל שכן שלמה דאתיא לאיחלופי. וטעמא דרבנן משום הכי הוא והתניא אמרו לו לרבי יהודה, והלא מרביעין עליה ויולדת אלמא משום עובריה הוא הכי קא״ל, טעמא דידן משום דאתיא לאיחלופי בבהמה, אלא את, מ״ט שרית משום דאין יכולה להתרפאות, כמאן דזבנה לשחיטה דמי, והלא מרביעין עליה ויולדת, וכיון דמרביעין עליה ויולדת, משהא לה ואמר להו לכשתלד, דלא מקבלת זכר. תא שמע והנותן לו בקבלה, ולא קתני אע״פ שאינו רשאי וליטעמיך, המשתתף לו, דלא קתני, הכי נמי דרשאי והא אמר אבוה דשמואל אסור לאדם שיעשה שותפות עם העובד כוכבים, שמא יתחייב לו שבועה, ונשבע לו בשם עבודת כוכבים שלו, והתורה אמרה (שמות כג) לא ישמע על פיך אלא, תנא מכירה והוא הדין לשותפות, ה״נ תנא מכירה, והוא הדין לקבלנות, ומאי שנא מכירה דנקט דעיקר מכירה היא. תא שמע, רבי יהודה אומר המקבל בהמה מן העובד כוכבים וילדה מעלין אותו בשוויו, ונותן חצי דמיו לכהן. והנותן בקבלה, אע״פ שאינו רשאי קונסין אותו עד עשרה בדמיו, ונותן כל דמיו לכהן. וחכמים

אומרים כל זמן שיד עובד כוכבים באמצע פטורה מן הבכורה.
-בכורות דף ג/א-
מאי לאו אבהמה לא, אעובר, דיקא נמי דקתני קונסין אותו עד עשרה בדמיו, שמע מינה. מסייעא (ליה) לריש לקיש, דאמר ריש לקיש המוכר בהמה גסה לעובד כוכבים קונסין אותו עד עשרה בדמיה. דוקא או לאו דוקא תא שמע, דאמר רבי יהושע בן לוי המוכר עבדו לעובד כוכבים קונסין אותו עד מאה בדמיו שאני עבד, דכל יומא ויומא מפקע ליה ממצות, ואיכא דאמרי אמר ריש לקיש המוכר בהמה גסה לעובד כוכבים קונסין אותו עד מאה בדמיה, תנן והנותן לו בקבלה, אף על פי שאינו רשאי, קונסין אותו עד עשרה בדמיה מכירה פסקה מיניה, קבלנות לא פסקה מיניה. דוקא או לאו דוקא תא שמע, דאמר ר׳ יהושע בן לוי המוכר עבדו לעובד כוכבים קונסין אותו עד עשרה בדמיו שאני עבד דלא הדר ליה, בהמה מאי טעמא משום דקא הדרא ליה ניקנסיה טפי חד אלא, עבד מילתא דלא שכיחא היא, וכל מילתא דלא שכיחא לא גזרו ביה רבנן. וחכמים אומרים כל זמן שיד העובד כוכבים כו׳. אמר רבי יהושע ושניהם מקרא אחד דרשו, (שמות י״ג) כל בכור, רבנן סברי בכור מקצת בכור משמע, כתב רחמנא כל עד דאיכא כוליה, ורבי יהודה סבר בכור, כוליה בכור משמע, כתב רחמנא כל דאפילו כל דהוא. איבעית אימא דכולי עלמא בכור רובא משמע, מר סבר כל משמע למלויי אתא, ומר סבר לגרועי אתא. וכמה תהא שותפות של עובד כוכבים, ותהא פטורה מן הבכורה אמר רב הונא אפילו אזנו, מתקיף לה רב נחמן ולימא ליה שקיל אזנך וזיל איתמר, רב חסדא אמר דבר שעושה אותו נבלה, ורבא אמר דבר שעושה אותו טריפה. מאי קמיפלגי בטריפה חיה, למאן דאמר דבר שעושה אותו טריפה, קסבר טריפה אינה חיה, ולמאן דאמר דבר שעושה אותו נבלה, אבל טריפה חיה, אמרוה רבנן קמיה דרב פפא הא דרב הונא, ורב חסדא ורבא לא פליגי, הא בו, הא באמו, אמר להו רב פפא מאי שנא בו דבעינן כל בכור וליכא, אמו נמי, בעינן (שמות ל״ד) כל מקנך תזכר, וליכא אלא, לא שנא. מתקיף לה מר בר רב אשי מאי שנא מנפלים דאף על גב דלאו בני חיותא נינהו קדשי, דאמר מר (שמות י״ג) פטר שגר בהמה שגר בבהמה התם, כיון דלא עריבו בהו חולין, קרינא בהו בבהמה כל בכור, הכא כיון דעריבו בהו חולין, לא קרינא בהו כל בכור. ר׳ אלעזר לא על לבי מדרשא, אשכחיה לרבי אסי, א״ל מאי אמור רבנן בי מדרשא א״ל
-בכורות דף ג/ב-
הכי אמר רבי יוחנן אפי׳ מום קל. והדתנן רחל שילדה מין עז, ועז שילדה מין רחל פטורה מן הבכורה, ואם יש בו מקצת סימנין חייב מום קבוע הוי לשחוט עליו, בשלמא מום קל, קא משמע לן כדרב הונא, ולאפוקי מדרב חסדא ורבא, אלא מום קבוע, מאי קא משמע לן דכיון דאישתני הוה ליה מומא תנינא ופיו דומה כשל חזיר הרי זה מום וכי תימא, התם נשתנה בדבר שאין במינו קדוש בבכורה. הכא נשתנה, בדבר שבמינו קדוש בבכורה, הא נמי תנינא עינו אחת גדולה ואחת קטנה, ותנא גדולה גדולה כשל עגל, וקטנה קטנה כשל אווז, בשלמא קטנה כשל אווז אין במינו קדוש בבכורה, אלא גדולה כשל עגל, יש במינו קדוש בבכורה אלא לאו משום דאמרינן כיון דאישתני הוה ליה מומא לא, משום דהוה ליה שרוע, הכי נמי מסתברא, דתנן מומין אלו, בין קבועין בין

עוברין פוסלין, יתר עליהן, אדם, עיניו שתיהן גדולות, שתיהן קטנות, גבי אדם הוא דכתיב (ויקרא כ״ב) איש איש מזרע אהרן, דבעינן, איש שוה בזרעו של אהרן, אבל בהמה שתיהן גדולות שתיהן קטנות נמי לא הוי מומא, אחת גדולה ואחת קטנה מאי טעמא אי משום שינוי אפילו שתיהן גדולות שתיהן קטנות נמי אלא לאו משום דהוה ליה שרוע, לא, לעולם אימא לך משום שינוי, שינוי הוי מומא, ודקא קשיא לך, אפילו שתיהן גדולות שתיהן קטנות, התם, אי מחמת בריותא יתירא תרווייהו בעי למיברא אי מחמת כחישותא יתירא, תרווייהו בעי מיכחש ההיא גיורתא, דהוו מסרין לה אחי, חיותא לפטומה, אתאי לקמיה דרבא, אמר לה לית דחש לה להא דרבי יהודה, דאמר שותפות עובד כוכבים חייבת בבכורה. רב מרי בר רחל הויא ליה ההיא חיותא, הוה מקנה לאודנייהו לעובד כוכבים, ואסר להו בגיזה ועבודה, ויהיב להו לכהנים, וכלאי חיותא דרב מרי בר רחל. וכי מאחר דאסר להו בגיזה ועבודה, ויהיב להו לכהנים, אמאי מקנה להו לאודנייהו לעובד כוכבים דלמא אתי בהו לידי תקלה, אי הכי, מאי טעמא כלו חיותא דרב מרי משום דמפקע להו מקדושתייהו, והאמר רב יהודה מותר לאדם להטיל מום בבכור קודם שיצא לאויר העולם התם מקדושת מזבח קא מפקע ליה, מקדושת כהן לא מפקע ליה, הכא אפי׳ מקדושת כהן קא מפקע ליה. ואיבעית אימא רב מרי בר רחל ידע לאקנויי קנין גמור, וחזי ליה איניש אחרינא ואזיל ועביד, וסבר רב מרי מילתא הוא דעבד, ואתי בה לידי תקלה.

מתני׳. כהנים ולוים פטורין, מק״ו, אם פטרו את של ישראל במדבר דין הוא שיפטרו את של עצמן.

גמ׳.

–בכורות דף ד/א–

אינהו פטרי אדם אדם פטר, בהמה בהמה פטרה, דכתיב (במדבר ג׳) קח את הלוים תחת בכור בבני ישראל ואת בהמת הלוים תחת בהמתם. אמר אביי, הכי קאמר כהנים ולוים פטורין בהמתם מקל וחומר, אם הפקיעה בהמתם של לוים בהמה של ישראל במדבר, דין הוא שתפקיע את של עצמן, א״ל רבא והא פטרו אינהו קתני ועוד, אם איתא, אפילו מבכור בהמה טהורה נפטרו, אלמה תנן לא נפטרו מבכור בהמה טהורה, אלא מפדיון הבן ופטר חמור אלא אמר רבא, הכי קתני כהנים ולוים פטרו הן עצמן מקל וחומר, אם הפקיעה קדושתן של לוים קדושת של ישראל במדבר, לא יפקיע את של עצמן אשכחן אדם בהמה טמאה מנלן אמר קרא (במדבר י״ח) אך פדה תפדה את בכור האדם ואת בכור הבהמה הטמאה תפדה, כל שישנו בבכור אדם ישנו בבכור בהמה טמאה, וכל שאינו בבכור אדם אינו בבכור בהמה טמאה. אמר ליה רב ספרא לאביי לדידך דאמרת בהמתם, בן לוי דהוה ליה שה דאפקע ליפקע, דלא הוה ליה שה דליפקע לא ליפקע בין לדידך בין לרבא, בן חדש דאפקע ליפקע פחות מבן חדש דלא אפקע לא ליפקע לויה לא תיפקע, אלמה אמר רב אדא בר אהבה, לויה שילדה בנה פטור מחמש סלעים הא לא קשיא, כדמר בריה דרב יוסף משמיה דרבא, דאמר פטר רחם בפטר רחם תלה רחמנא. ואהרן שלא היה באותו מנין לא ליפקע דתניא למה נקוד על אהרן שבחומש הפקודים שלא היה באותו מנין, אמר קרא

הלוים הוקשו כל הלוים זה לזה, כהנים מנלן כדרבי יהושע בן לוי, דאמר ר׳ יהושע בן לוי בעשרים וארבעה מקומות נקראו כהנים לוים, וזה אחד מהן (יחזקאל מ״ד) והכהנים הלוים בני צדוק,

-בכורות דף ד/ב-

ולדורות מנלן אמר קרא (במדבר ג׳) והיו לי הלוים והיו בהווייתן יהו. וממאי דבשה אמר רב חסדא נאמר כסף לדורות, ונאמר שה לדורות, מה כסף האמור לדורות בו פדו לדורות, בו פדו לאותה שעה, אף שה האמור לדורות בו פדו לדורות, בו פדו באותה שעה, מה לכסף שכן פודין בו הקדשות ומעשר שני אלא אמר קרא (במדבר י״ח) אך פדה תפדה את בכור האדם ואת בכור הבהמה הטמאה תפדה מה בכור אדם לא חלקת בין לדורות בין לאותה שעה בכסף, אף בהמה טמאה לא תחלוק בו בין לדורות בין לאותה שעה בשה. אמר ר׳ חנינא שה אחד של בן לוי פטר כמה פטרי חמורים מישראל, אמר אביי תדע, שהרי מנה הכתוב עודפים באדם, ולא מנה עודפין בבהמה. ממאי דילמא לא הוי נפישי להו בהמות טובא לא ס״ד דכתיב (במדבר ל״ב) ומקנה רב היה לבני ראובן ולבני גד, דילמא אפילו הכי, פשוטים דלוים הוו קיימי לבהדי בכורי ישראל אמר קרא (במדבר ג׳) ואת בהמת הלוים תחת בהמתם בהמה אחת תחת, בהמות הרבה, ואימא, (יונה ד׳) בהמה רבה א״כ, ליכתוב קרא או בהמה תחת בהמה או בהמתם תחת בהמתם, מאי בהמת תחת בהמתם ש״מ חד פטר טובא, אמר רבא, אף אנן נמי תנינא ופודה בו פעמים הרבה, ור׳ חנינא טעמא דמתני׳ מפרש, והכי קאמר מאי טעמא פודה בו פעמים הרבה משום דשה אחד של בן לוי פוטר כמה פטרי חמורים של ישראל. איתמר, ר׳ יוחנן אמר קדשו בכורות במדבר, וריש לקיש אמר לא קדשו בכורות במדבר, ר׳ יוחנן אמר קדשו בכורות במדבר דרחמנא אמר ליקדשו, כדכתיב (שמות י״ג) קדש לי כל בכור, וריש לקיש אמר לא קדשו בכורות במדבר מדכתיב (שמות י״ג) והיה כי יביאך וכתיב בתריה והעברת, מכלל דמעיקרא לא קדוש, איתיביה רבי יוחנן לריש לקיש עד שלא הוקם המשכן היו במות מותרות ועבודה בבכורות אמר ליה באותן שיצאו ממצרים, הכי נמי מסתברא, דאי לא תימא הכי, בן שנה בר מיעבד עבודה הוא ודקארי לה, מאי קארי לה הכי קא קשיא ליה אי אמרת בשלמא דלא פסיק קדושתייהו הנך דמעיקרא נמי לא פקעא קדושתייהו, אלא אי אמרת דפסק קדושתייהו הנך דמעיקרא נמי פקעא ליה קדושתייהו ואידך דקדוש קדוש דלא קדוש לא קדוש. איתיביה אותו היום שהוקם המשכן קרבו להם בישראל נדרים ונדבות חטאות ואשמות בכורות ומעשרות הכי נמי באותן שיצאו ממצרים ומינה אותו היום הוא דקרוב, מיכן ואילך לא קרוב איכא דאמרי איתיביה ריש לקיש לר׳ יוחנן אותו היום שהוקם המשכן קרבו להם ישראל נדרים ונדבות חטאות ואשמות בכורות ומעשרות אותו היום אין, מיכן ואילך לא אימא מאותו היום ואילך, ומאי קמשמע לן מאותו היום אין, מעיקרא לא, אלמא חובות בבמה לא קרוב, תא שמע נמצאת אתה אומר, בשלשה מקומות קדשו בכורות לישראל, במצרים ובמדבר ובכניסתן ישראל לארץ, במצרים מהו אומר (שמות י״ג) קדש לי כל בכור, במדבר הוא אומר (במדבר ח׳) כי לי כל בכור בבני ישראל, בכניסתם לארץ הוא אומר והיה כי יביאך והעברת אמר רב נחמן בר יצחק בשלשה מקומות הוזהרו על הבכורות ליקדש ולא קדשו, ובמצרים נמי לא

קדוש הא קאמרי׳ דקדוש ה״ק מהן קדשו ומהן לא קדשו, מתקיף לה רב פפא ובמדבר לא קדשו והכתיב (במדבר ג׳) פקוד כל בכור זכר לבני ישראל אלא, אי איתמר הכי איתמר רבי יוחנן אמר קדשו ולא פסקו, וריש לקיש אמר קדשו

-בכורות דף ה/א-

ופסקו, בשלמא ריש לקיש כדאמר טעם אלא לר׳ יוחנן מאי טעמא אמר ר׳ אלעזר ר׳ יוחנן חזאי בחילמא, דמילתא מעליתא אמינא אמר קרא לי יהיו בהוייתן יהו. ורבי יוחנן והיה כי יביאך והעברת מאי עביד ליה ההוא מיבעי ליה לכדתנא דבי רבי ישמעאל עשה מצוה זו שבשבילה תיכנס לארץ. אמר ליה רב מרדכי לרב אשי אתון הכי מתניתו לה, אנן איפכא מתנינן לה רבי יוחנן אמר לא קדשו בכורות במדבר, וריש לקיש אמר קדשו בכורות במדבר אמר ליה ואפכית נמי תיובתא, ואפכיתו לה להא דרבי אלעזר א״ל לא קדשו (להו) לא הוצרכו ליקדש, אי הכי, היינו דידן קמ״ל חייב אדם לומר בלשון רבו. שאל קונטרוקוס השר את רבן יוחנן בן זכאי בפרטן של לוים אתה מוצא עשרים ושנים אלף ושלש מאות, בכללן אתה מוצא עשרים ושנים אלף, ושלש מאות להיכן הלכו א״ל אותן שלש מאות בכורות היו, ואין בכור מפקיע בכור. מאי טעמא אמר אביי דיו לבכור שיפקיע קדושת עצמו. ועוד שאלו בגיבוי כסף אתה מוצא מאתים ואחת ככר ואחת עשרה מנה, דכתיב (שמות ל״ח) בקע לגלגלת מחצית השקל בשקל הקדש וגו׳, ובנתינת הכסף אתה מוצא מאת ככר, דכתיב (שמות ל״ח) ויהי מאת ככר הכסף לצקת וגו׳. משה רבכם גנב היה, או קוביוסטוס היה, או אינו בקי בחשבונות נתן מחצה ונטל מחצה, ומחצה שלם לא החזיר אמר לו משה רבינו גיזבר נאמן היה, ובקי בחשבונות היה, ומנה של קודש כפול היה. הוי בה רב אחאי מאי קא קשיא ליה ויהי מאת ככר הכסף לצקת וגו׳, הנך לצקת, ואינך בי גזא כתב קרא אחרינא (שמות ל״ח) וכסף פקודי העדה מאת ככר וגו׳, ודקא״ל מנה של קודש כפול היה מנא ליה אילימא מיניה, שהרי כאן, שבעים ואחד מנה (שמות ל״ח) ואת האלף ושבע מאות וחמשה ושבעים עשה ווים לעמודים ולא מנאן הכתוב אלא בפרוטרוט, ואם איתא, מאה ואחד ככר ואחת עשרה מנה מיבעי ליה אלא, מדלא מנאן הכתוב אלא בפרוטרוט, ש״מ מנה של קודש כפול היה, ודילמא כללי קחשיב בככרי, פרטי לא קא חשיב בככרי אלא מהכא (שמות ל״ח) ונחושת התנופה שבעים ככר ואלפים וארבע מאות שקל שהרי כאן תשעים וששה מנה, ולא מנאן הכתוב אלא בפרוטרוט, שמע מינה מנה של קודש כפול היה, ודילמא פרטא רבה קא חשיב בככרי, פרטא זוטא לא קחשיב בככרי אלא אמר רב חסדא, מהכא (יחזקאל מ״ה) והשקל עשרים גרה עשרים שקלים חמשה ועשרים שקלים עשרה וחמשה שקל המנה יהיה לכם,

-בכורות דף ה/ב-

והא מאתן וארבעין הויין אלא ש״מ מנה של קודש מנה כפול היה ושמע מינה מוסיפין על המדות, ואין מוסיפין יתר על שתות, ושמע מינה שתותא מלבר. אמר ר׳ חנינא, שאלתי את ר׳ אליעזר בבית מותבא רבא מה נשתנו פטרי חמורים מפטרי סוסים וגמלים א״ל גזירת הכתוב היא, ועוד, שסייעו ישראל בשעת יציאתם ממצרים שאין לך כל אחד ואחד מישראל שלא היו עמו תשעים חמורים לובים טעונים מכספה וזהבה של מצרים. ועוד שאלתיו מאי לשון

רפידים ואמר לי רפידים שמה. כתנאי, ר׳ אליעזר אומר רפידים שמה, ר׳ יהושע אומר שריפו עצמן מדברי תורה, וכן הוא אומר (ירמיהו מ״ז) לא הפנו אבות אל בנים מרפיון ידים. ועוד שאלתיו מאי לשון שטים ואמר לי שטים שמה. כתנאי, ר׳ אליעזר אומר שטים שמה, רבי יהושע אומר שנתעסקו בדברי שטות, (במדבר כ״ה) ותקראן לעם לזבחי אלהיהן רבי אליעזר אומר ערומות פגעו בהן, ר׳ יהושע אומר שנעשו כולן בעלי קריין.

References and Selected Bibliography

Alon, G.

1967-70 מחקרים בתולדות ישׂראל. 2 vols. Tel Aviv: HaKibbutz HaMeuhad.

1977 *Jews and Judaism in the Classical World*. Jerusalem: Magnes Press.

Amir, A.S.

1977 מוסדות ותארים בספרות התלמוד. Jerusalem: Mosad HaRav Kook

Baras, Z., S. Safrai, M. Stern, and Y. Tsafrir

1984 ארץ ישׂראל מחורבן בית שׁני ועד הכיבוש המוסלמי. 2 vols. Jerusalem: Yad Izhak Ben Zvi.

Beer, M.

1976 ראשׁות הגולה בבבל בימי המשׁנה והתלמוד. Tel Aviv: Dvir.

Berger, P.

1967 *The Sacred Canopy: Elements of a Sociological Theory of Religion*. Garden City, New York: Doubleday

Berger, P., and T. Luckmann

1966 *The Social Construction of Reality: A Treatise in the Sociology of Knowledge*. Garden City, New York: Doubleday.

Boyce, M.

1986 *Zoroastrians, Their Religious Beliefs and Practices*. London and New York: Routledge and Kegan Paul.

Breasted, J.H.

1962 *Ancient Records of Egypt*. 5 vols. New York: Russell and Russell.

1964 *A History of Egypt*. New York: Bantam Books. Reprint of the 1909 edition.

Brown, P.

1981 *The Cult of the Saints*. Chicago: University of Chicago Press.

Chernick, M.L.

1989 "Contemporary Talmudic Studies: The Continuing Agenda." In *New Perspectives of Ancient Judaism*. vol. 4, *The Literature of Early Rabbinic*

Judaism: Issues in Talmudic Redaction and Interpretation, ed. A.J. Avery-Peck. New York: University Press of America.

Christensen, A.

1939 "Sassanid Persia." In *Cambridge Ancient History*. 12. London: Cambridge University Press.

1944 *L'Iran sous les Sassanides*. 2nd ed. Copenhagen.

Cohen, J.D., and E.L. Greenstein, eds.

1990 *The State of Jewish Studies. The Jewish Theological Seminary of America*. Detroit: Wayne State University Press.

Crossan, J.D.

1975 *The Dark Interval*. Niles, IL: Argus.

Da-Paris, B.

1965 "המינוח בתלמוד בבלי." לשוננו. 29.

Dhalla, M.N.

1963 *History of Zoroastrianism*. Bombay: Cama Oriental Institute.

Douglas, M.

1973 *Natural Symbols*. 2nd ed. London: Barrie and Jenkins.

1975a "Self-Evidence." In *Implicit Meanings*. London: RKP.

1975b "In the Nature of Things." In *Implicit Meanings*. London: RKP.

1978 *Cultural Bias*. London: Royal Anthropological Society.

Durkheim, E.

1976 *The Elementary Forms of Religious Life*. 2nd ed. London: Allen and Unwin.

1980 *Emile Durkheim, Contributions to L'Année sociologique*, ed. Y. Nandan. New York: Free Press.

1982 *The Rules of Sociological Method*. New York: Free Press

Durkheim, E., and M. Mauss

1970 *Primitive Classification*. London: RKP Press.

Epstein, Y.N.

1962 מבואות לספרות האמוראים: בבלי וירושלמי. Tel Aviv: Dvir and Magnes Press.

1983 מחקרים בספרות התלמוד ובלשונות שמיות, ed. E.Z. Melamed. 3 vols. Jerusalem: Magnes Press.

Fishbane, M.
1985 *Biblical Interpretation in Ancient Israel*. Oxford: Clarendon Press.

Fraade, S.D.
1991 *From Tradition to Commentary*. Albany: State University of New York Press.

Friedman, S.
1978 "אל דרך חקר הסוגיה: פרק האישה." In מחקרים ומקורות, ed. H. Dimitrovski. New York: Jewish Theological Seminary of America.
1990 תלמוד ערוך: השׂוכר את האומנין. הפירושים. Jewish Theological Seminary of America. Jerusalem: Yad Izak Ben-Zvi.

Frye R.N.
1966 *The Heritage of Persia*. Toronto: Mentor.

Gafni, I.M.
1990 יהודי בבל בתקופת התלמוד. Jerusalem: Zalman Shazar Center For History.

Geertz, C.
1966 "Religion as a Cultural System." In *Anthropological Approaches to the Study of Religion*, ed M. Banton. London: Tavistock.

Gereboff, J.
1985 "When to Speak, How to Speak, and When Not to Speak: Answers from Early Rabbinic Stories." *Semeia* 34.

Goldenberg, R.
1977 "The Deposition of Gamaliel." In *Persons and Institutions in Early Rabbinic Judaism*, ed. W.S. Green. vol. 1. Missoula, MT: Scholars Press.

Goodblatt, D.
1975 *Rabbinic Institutions in Sassanian Babylonia*. Leiden: E.J. Brill.

Goody, John (Jack) R.
1968 *Literacy in Traditional Societies*. London: Cambridge University Press.
1977 *The Domestication of the Savage Mind*. New York: Cambridge University Press.

1986 *The Logic of Writing and the Organization of Society*. New York: Cambridge University Press.

1987 *The Interface Between Written and Oral*. New York: Cambridge University Press.

Goody, J.R., and I. Watt

1985 "The Consequences of Literacy." *Comparative Studies in Society and History*. vol. 5, 1962-63, 304-45. Reprinted 1985 in *Language and Social Context*, ed. P.P. Giglioli, 311-57. Harmondsworth, Middlesex, Great Britain: Penguin.

Green, W.S.

1979 "What's in a Name? The Question of Rabbinic Biography." In *Approaches to the Study of Ancient Judaism*, ed. W.S. Green. vol. 1. Missoula: Scholars Press.

1983 "Reading the Writing of Rabbinism: Toward an Interpretation of Rabbinic Literature." *JAAR* 51.

Gumperz, J.

1985 "The Speech Community." In *International Encyclopaedia of the Social Sciences*, 381-86. New York: Macmillan. Reprinted 1985 in *Language and Social Context*, ed. P.P. Giglioli, 219-31. Harmondsworth, Middlesex, Great Britain: Penguin.

Harris, J.R.

1971 *The Legacy of Egypt*. 2nd ed. London: Oxford University Press.

Hauptman, J.

1988 *The Development of the Talmudic Sugya: Relationship between Tannaitic and Amoraic Sources*. New York: University Press of America.

Heilman, S.

1976 *Synagogue Life: A Study of Symbolic Interaction*. Chicago: University of Chicago Press.

Hyman, A.M.

1964 תולדות תנאים ואמוראים. 3 vols. Jerusalem: Hotza'at Kiriyah Ne'emanah.

Jacobs, L.

1984 *The Talmudic Argument*. Cambridge: Cambridge University Press.

1991 *Structure and Form in the Babylonian Talmud.* Cambridge: Cambridge University Press.

Jaffee, M.S.
1989 "The Babylonian Appropriation of the Talmud Yerushalmi: Redactional Studies in the Horayot Tractates." In *New Perspectives of Ancient Judaism.* vol. 4, *The Literature of Early Rabbinic Judaism: Issues in Talmudic Redaction and Interpretation*, ed. A.J. Avery-Peck. Lantham, MD: University Press of America.

Kalmin, R.
1989a *The Redaction of the Babylonian Talmud: Amoraic or Saboraic?* Cincinnati: Hebrew Union College Press.

1989b "The Stam and the Final Generation of the Amoraim: Assessing the Importance of their Relationship for the Study of the Redaction of the Talmud." In *New Perspectives of Ancient Judaism.* vol. 4, *The Literature of Early Rabbinic Judaism: Issues in Talmudic Redaction and Interpretation*, ed. A.J. Avery Peck. Lantham, MD: University Press of America.

Kraemer, D.
1989 "The Beginning of the Preservation of Argumentation in Amoraic Babylonia," In *New Perspectives of Ancient Judaism.* vol. 4, *The Literature of Early Rabbinic Judaism: Issues in Talmudic Redaction and Interpretation*, ed. A.J. Avery-Peck. Lantham, MD: University Press of America.

1990 *The Mind of the Talmud.* New York: Oxford University Press.

Levin, B.M
1971 איגרת רב שׁרירא גאון. Jerusalem: Makor.

Levine, L.I.
1985 מעמד החכמים בארץ ישׂראל בתקופת התלמוד. Jerusalem: Yad Izhak Ben Zvi.

Lightstone, J.
1977 "Sadoq the Yavnean." In *Persons and Institutions in Early Rabbinic Judaism*, ed. W.S. Green. vol. 1. Missoula, MT: Scholars Press.

1979 *Yose the Galilean: Traditions in Mishnah-Tosefta*. Leiden: E.J. Brill.

1983 "Form as Meaning in the Halakic Midrash." *Semeia* 27.

1984 *The Commerce of the Sacred: Mediation of the Divine among Jews in the Graeco-Roman Diaspora*. Chico, CA: Scholars Press.

1985 "When Speech is No Speech: The Problem of Early Rabbinic Rhetoric as Discourse." *Semeia* 34:54-55.

1988 *Society, the Sacred, and Scripture in Ancient Judaism*. Waterloo, ON: Wilfrid Laurier University Press.

1990 "Names Without Lives: Why No Lives of the Rabbis in Earliest Rabbinic Literature?" *Sciences religieuses/Studies in Religion* 19.

1991 "The Modern Study of Ancient Judaism: Scholarship and Contemporary North American Jewish Identity." In *Past and Future Directions in Religious Studies; University of Manitoba Studies in Religion I*, ed. L. Hurtado and K. Kloestermaier. Atlanta: Scholars Press.

1992 "The Social Scientific Study of Ancient Judaism." In *Essays in the Social Scientific Study of Judaism and Jewish Society*, ed. S. Schoenfeld et al. vol. 2. New York: Ktav Publishing.

1993 "The Institutionalization of the Rabbinic Academy in Late Sassanid Babylonia and the Redaction of the Babylonian Talmud." *Sciences religieuses/Studies in Religion* 22.

1994a "Ancient Judaism's Perceptions of History." In *Under History's Canopy*, ed. K. Parry and J. Penton.Toronto: University of Toronto Press. Forthcoming.

1994b "Sacred Text and Social Transformation: Part 1, The Institutionalization of Rabbinic Associations in Late Antiquity and the Redaction of the Mishnah," In *Essays in the Social Scientific Study of Judaism and Jewish Society*, ed. E. Taboury et al. vol. 3. Lewiston, NY and Queenston, ON: Edwin Mellen Press. Forthcoming.

1994c "Form, Formularies and Meaning in the Babylonian Talmud: The Case of Bekorot 2a-b." In *New Approaches to the Study of Ancient Judaism*, ed. J. Neusner. vol. 6. Atlanta: Scholars Press. Forthcoming.

Mack B.

1990 *Rhetoric and the New Testament*. Minneapolis: Fortress Press.

Malherbe, A.J.

1986 *Moral Exhortation, A Greco-Roman Sourcebook*. Philadelphia: Westminster Press.

Matheson, P.E., trans.

1940 *The Discourses of Epictetus*, In *The Stoic and Epicurean Philosophers*, ed. W.J. Oates, 282-383. New York: Random House.

Melamed, E.Z.

1988 מדרשי הלכה של התנאים בתלמוד בבלי. Jerusalem: Magnes Press.

Neusner, J.

1969-70 *A History of the Jews in Babylonia*. vols. 5 and 6. Leiden: E.J. Brill.

1970 *Development of a Legend*. Leiden: E.J. Brill.

1971 *The Rabbinic Traditions about the Pharisees before AD 70*. 3 vols. Leiden: E.J. Brill.

1973 *Eliezer ben Hyrcanus*. Leiden: E.J. Brill.

1977 *A History of the Mishnaic Law of Purities, Part 21, Formulation and Redaction*. Leiden: E.J. Brill.

1979 *A History of the Mishnaic Law of Holy Things, Part 3*. Leiden: E.J. Brill.

1981 *Judaism, the Evidence of the Mishnah*. Chicago: University of Chicago Press.

1983a *Midrash in Context*. Philadelphia: Fortress Press.

1983b "Judaism and Society." In *Take Judaism, for Example*, ed. J. Neusner. Chicago: University of Chicago Press.

1983c *Judaism in Society, the Evidence of the Yerushalmi*. Chicago: University of Chicago Press.

1985a *Torah: From Scroll to Symbol in Formative Judaism*. Philadelphia: Fortress Press.

1985b *The Peripatetic Saying: The Problem of the Thrice-told Tale in Talmudic Literature*. Chico, CA: Scholars Press.

1986a *The Oral Torah*. San Francisco: Harper & Row.

1986b *Judaism: The Classical Statement, the Evidence of the Bavli*. Chicago: University of Chicago Press.

1986c *Sifre to Numbers: An American Translation and Explanation*. vol. 1, *Sifre to Numbers 1-58*. vol. 2, *Sifre to Numbers 59-115*. Atlanta: Scholars Press.

1986d *Israel and Iran in Talmudic Times*. Lantham, MD and London: University Press of America.

1987a *The Making of the Mind of Judaism: The Formative Age*. Atlanta: Scholars Press.

1987b *Sifre to Deuteronomy: An Introduction to the Rhetorical, Logical and Topical Program*. Atlanta: Scholars Press.

1987c *Oral Tradition in Judaism: The Case of Mishnah*. New York and London: Garland Publishing.

1988a *The Philosophical Mishnah*. vol. 1, *The Initial Probe*. Atlanta: Scholars Press.

1988b *A Religion of Pots and Pans: Modes of Philosophical and Theological Discourse in Ancient Judaism. Essays and a Program*. Atlanta: Scholars Press.

1988c *The Systemic Analysis of Judaism*. Atlanta: Scholars Press.

1989a *Medium and Message in Judaism. First Series*. Atlanta: Scholars Press.

1989b *The Mishnah: An Introduction*. Northvale, NJ and London: Jason Aronson Press.

1990a *Making the Classics in Judaism: The Three Stages of Literary Formation*. Atlanta: Scholars Press.

1990b *The Economics of the Mishnah*. Chicago: University of Chicago Press.

1990c *Tradition as Selectivity: Scripture, Mishnah, Tosefta and Midrash in the Talmud of Babylonia*.

The Case of Tractate Arakhin. Atlanta: Scholars Press.

1991a *How the Bavli Shaped Rabbinic Discourse*. Atlanta: Scholars Press.

1991b *Rabbinic Political Theory: Religion and Politics in the Mishnah*. Chicago: University of Chicago Press.

1991c *The Bavli that Might Have Been: The Tosefta's Theory of Mishnah Commentary Compared with the Bavli's*. Atlanta: Scholars Press.

1991d *The Bavli's One Voice: Types and Forms of Analytical Discourse and their Fixed Order of Appearance*. Atlanta: Scholars Press.

1991e *The Rules of Composition of the Talmud of Babylonia*. Atlanta: Scholars Press.

1991f *The Talmud, A Close Encounter*. Minneapolis: Fortress Press.

1992 *The Bavli's Massive Miscellanies: The Problem of Agglutinative Discourse in the Talmud of Babylonia*. Atlanta: Scholars Press.

Parsons, T.

1954 *Essays in Sociological Theory*. Glencoe, IL: Free Press.

1977 *The Evolution of Societies*. Englewood Cliffs, NJ: Prentice-Hall.

Polzin, R.

1977 *Biblical Structuralism. Semeia Studies*. Missoula, MT: Scholars Press.

Porton, G

1979 *The Rabbinic Traditions about Rabbi Ishmael*. 2 vols. Leiden: E.J. Brill.

Radcliffe-Brown, A.R.

1952 *Structure and Function in Primitive Society*. London: Cohen and West Ltd.

Reisner, A.I.

1989 "The Character and Construction of a Contrived Sugya: Shevuot 3a-4a." In *New Perspectives of Ancient Judaism*. vol. 4, *The Literature of Early Rabbinic Judaism: Issues in Talmudic Redaction and Interpretation*, ed. A.J. Avery-Peck. New York: University Press of America.

Robbins, V.K.
1984 *Jesus the Teacher: A Socio-rhetorical Interpretation of Mark*. Philadelphia: Fortress Press.

Saldarini, A.J.
1982 *Scholastic Rabbinism*. Chico, CA: Scholars Press.

Safrai, S., ed
1987 *The Literature of the Sages. First Part: Oral Tora, Mishnah, Tosefta, Talmud, External Tractates. Compendia Rerum Iudaicarum ad Novum Testamentum*. Assen/Maastricht: Van Gorcum and Philadelphia: Fortress Press.

Sanders, James A.
1972 *Torah and Canon*. Philadelphia: Fortress Press.

Schuerer, E.
1973-87 *The History of the Jewish People in the Age of Jesus Christ*. Revised and edited by G. Vermes and F. Millar. 4 vols. Edinburgh: T & T Clark.

Smith, J.Z.
1978 "The Temple and the Magician." In *Map is not Territory*. Leiden: E.J. Brill.

Smith, M.
1978 *Jesus the Magician*. San Francisco: Harper & Row.

Stowers, S.K.
1988 "The Diatribe." In *Greco-Roman Literature and the New Testament*, ed. D.E. Aune. Atlanta: Scholars Press.

Sykes, P.
1969 *A History of Persia*. London: RKP. Reprint of 1930 edition.

Tenenblatt, M.A.
1972 התלמוד הבבלי: בהתהוותו ההיסטורית. Tel Aviv: Dvir.

Urbach, E.E.
1958 "הדרשה כיסוד ההלכה ובעיית הסופרים." תרביץ 27:166-182.
1984 ההלכה: מקורותיה והתפתחותה. Tel Aviv: Masada Press.

Urbach E.E., et al.
1983 מחקרים בספרות התלמודית. יום עיון לרגל מלאת

שמונים שנה לשאול ליברמן. Jerusalem: Israel Academy of Sciences and Humanities.

Weber, M.
1963 *The Sociology of Religion*. Boston: Beacon Press.
1968 *Economy and Society: An Outline of Interpretive Sociology*. New York: Bedminster Press.

Weiss, A.
1975 "דרכי הסוגיה ומטרתה." In מחקרים בתלמוד. Jerusalem.

Weiss-Halivni, D.
1986 *Midrash, Mishnah, and Gemara: The Jewish Predilection for Justified Law*. Cambridge: Harvard University Press.

West, E.W.
1965 *Pahlavi Texts*. Part 1. In *Sacred Books of the East*, ed. F.M. Mueller. vol. 5. Dehli, Varanasi and Patna: Banarsidass Press. Reprint of the 1880 edition by Oxford University Press.

Zahavy, T.
1977 *The Traditions of Eleazar ben Azariah*. Missoula, MT: Scholars Press.

Zeitlin, S.
1962 *The Rise and Fall of the Judean State*. 3 vols. Philadelphia: Jewish Publication Society.

Index

Compiled by Maria Mamfredis, Montreal, Quebec

SR SUPPLEMENTS

Note: Nos. 1 to 8, 10, 12, 13, 15, 18 and 20 in this series are out of print.

9. ***Developments in Buddhist Thought: Canadian Contributions to Buddhist Studies***
   Edited by Roy C. Amore
   1979 / iv + 196 pp.
11. ***Political Theology in the Canadian Context***
   Edited by Benjamin G. Smillie
   1982 / xii + 260 pp.
14. ***The Moral Mystic***
   James R. Horne
   1983 / x + 134 pp.
16. ***Studies in the Book of Job***
   Edited by Walter E. Aufrecht
   1985 / xii + 76 pp.
17. ***Christ and Modernity: Christian Self-Understanding in a Technological Age***
   David J. Hawkin
   1985 / x + 181 pp.
19. ***Modernity and Religion***
   Edited by William Nicholls
   1987 / vi + 191 pp.

STUDIES IN CHRISTIANITY AND JUDAISM / ÉTUDES SUR LE CHRISTIANISME ET LE JUDAÏSME

Note: No. 1 in this series is out of print.

2. ***Anti-Judaism in Early Christianity***
   Vol. 1, ***Paul and the Gospels***, edited by Peter Richardson with David Granskou
   1986 / x + 232 pp.
   Vol. 2, ***Separation and Polemic***
   Edited by Stephen G. Wilson
   1986 / xii + 185 pp.
3. ***Society, the Sacred, and Scripture in Ancient Judaism: A Sociology of Knowledge***
   Jack N. Lightstone
   1988 / xiv + 126 pp.
4. ***Law in Religious Communities in the Roman Period: The Debate Over* Torah *and* Nomos *in Post-Biblical Judaism and Early Christianity***
   Peter Richardson and Stephen Westerholm
   with A. I. Baumgarten, Michael Pettem and Cecilia Wassén
   1991 / x + 164 pp.
5. ***Dangerous Food: 1 Corinthians 8-10 in Its Context***
   Peter D. Gooch
   1993 / xviii + 178 pp.
6. ***The Rhetoric of the Babylonian Talmud, Its Social Meaning and Context***
   Jack N. Lightstone
   1994 / xiv + 317 pp.

THE STUDY OF RELIGION IN CANADA / SCIENCES RELIGIEUSES AU CANADA

1. ***Religious Studies in Alberta: A State-of-the-Art Review***
   Ronald W. Neufeldt
   1983 / xiv + 145 pp.
2. ***Les sciences religieuses au Québec depuis 1972***
   Louis Rousseau et Michel Despland
   1988 / 158 p.
3. ***Religious Studies in Ontario: A State-of-the-Art Review***
   Harold Remus, William Closson James and Daniel Fraikin
   1992 / xviii + 422 pp.
4. ***Religious Studies in Manitoba and Saskatchewan: A State-of-the-Art Review***
   John M. Badertscher, Gordon Harland and Roland E. Miller
   1993 / vi + 166 pp.

EDITIONS SR

Note: Nos. 1 to 3, 5, 6 and 9 in this series are out of print.

4. ***Le messianisme de Louis Riel***
   Gilles Martel
   1984 / xviii + 483 p.
7. ***L'étude des religions dans les écoles : l'expérience américaine, anglaise et canadienne***
   Fernand Ouellet
   1985 / xvi + 666 p.
8. ***Of God and Maxim Guns: Presbyterianism in Nigeria, 1846-1966***
   Geoffrey Johnston
   1988 / iv + 322 pp.
10. ***Prometheus Rebound: The Irony of Atheism***
    Joseph C. McLelland
    1988 / xvi + 366 pp.
11. ***Competition in Religious Life***
    Jay Newman
    1989 / viii + 237 pp.
12. ***The Huguenots and French Opinion, 1685-1787: The Enlightenment Debate on Toleration***
    Geoffrey Adams
    1991 / xiv + 335 pp.
13. ***Religion in History: The Word, the Idea, the Reality / La religion dans l'histoire : le mot, l'idée, la réalité***
    Edited by / Sous la direction de Michel Despland and/et Gérard Vallée
    1992 / x + 252 pp.
14. ***Sharing Without Reckoning: Imperfect Right and the Norms of Reciprocity***
    Millard Schumaker
    1992 / xiv + 112 pp.
15. ***Love and the Soul: Psychological Interpretations of the Eros and Psyche Myth***
    James Gollnick
    1992 / viii + 174 pp.

COMPARATIVE ETHICS SERIES / COLLECTION D'ÉTHIQUE COMPARÉE

Note: No. 1 in this series is out of print.

2. ***Methodist Education in Peru: Social Gospel, Politics, and American Ideological and Economic Penetration, 1888-1930***
   Rosa del Carmen Bruno-Jofré
   1988 / xiv + 223 pp.
3. ***Prophets, Pastors and Public Choices: Canadian Churches and the Mackenzie Valley Pipeline Debate***
   Roger Hutchinson
   1992 / xiv + 142 pp.

DISSERTATIONS SR

1. ***The Social Setting of the Ministry as Reflected in the Writings of Hermas, Clement and Ignatius***
   Harry O. Maier
   1991 / viii + 230 pp.
2. ***Literature as Pulpit: The Christian Social Activism of Nellie L. McClung***
   Randi R. Warne
   1993 / viii + 236 pp.

Available from / en vente chez :
Wilfrid Laurier University Press
Waterloo, Ontario, Canada N2L 3C5

Published by Wilfrid Laurier University Press for the Canadian Corporation for Studies in Religion/ Corporation Canadienne des Sciences Religieuses